METHODS OF COMMUNICATION

Methods of Communication

Dr Anil Kumar Dixit

B.Sc., L.L.M.

Presently working as

Asst. Prof. of Low in Bundelkhand University,

Jhansi (U.P.)

AMAN PUBLICATIONS

NEW DELHI

Published by
Rajiv Jain for Aman Publications
LG-4A, Ganpati Bhawan,
4675-B/21, Ansari Road,
Darya Ganj, Delhi - 110002
PH: 23255012, 23282127
E-mail: sshjbs@yahoo.com

First Published – 2010

ISBN-81-8204-062-0
ISBN-978-81-8204-062-5

SOLE DISTRIBUTOR
JINDAL BOOK SERVICES
LG-4A, Ganpati Bhawan,
4675-B/21, Ansari Road,
Darya Ganj, Delhi - 110002

Jacket Designed by :
S.M. Graphics

Printed by:
Balaji Offset, Delhi, India

Preface

Methods of communication can be important for facilitating learning, participation, dialogue and behavioural change, especially where information is being shared between different cultures and contexts. Development workers, when faced with different cultural contexts, often expect people to accept new ideas that may be radically different from those they have grown up with. This can lead to ideas being rejected simply because they are 'foreign' or because they are not appropriately communicated. External approaches which attempt to influence attitude, behaviour or practice may be ineffective unless workers adopt an approach which takes into account cultural norms, beliefs and knowledge.

Communication stands so deeply rooted in human behaviours and the structures of society that scholars have difficulty thinking of it while excluding social or behavioral events. Because communication theory remains a relatively young field of inquiry and integrates itself with other disciplines such as philosophy, psychology, and sociology, one probably cannot yet expect a consensus conceptualization of communication across disciplines. Currently, there is no paradigm from which communication scholars may work. One of the issues facing scholars is the possibility that establishing a communication meta theory will negate their research and stifle the broad body of knowledge in which communication functions.

—Author

Contents

1

Communication and Methods for Effective Communication

In today's world, EQ (Emotional Quotient) is more desirable than IQ (Intelligence Quotient). Emotional Quotient comprises of various traits, however, the most important of all is the ability to communicate effectively with others. Subscribers to the Harvard Business Review rated "the ability to communicate" as the most important factor in making an executive "promotable"-more important than ambition, education and the capacity for hard work.

One 20 year study that followed the progress of Stanford University MBAs' revealed that the most successful graduates shared personality traits that distinguish good communicators. "A desire to persuade, an interest in talking with other people and an outgoing ascendant personality."

What is Communication?

It is the sending and receiving of ideas, thoughts or feelings from one person to one or more persons in such a way that the person receiving it understands it in the same way that the sender wants him/her to understand. Hence it is a two-way process for which the binding force is the feedback loop. Unless the receiver gives feedback-verbal or non-verbal-to the speaker, the speaker will not be able to continue the information for too long.

Communication can be broken down into three major areas:

Verbal

1. Spoken.
2. Written.

Non Verbal

1. Body Language.

Listening

1. Active Listening.
2. Passive Listening.
3. Reflective Listening.

Tom Peter's, business consultant and co-author of the book, 'In Search of Excellence', emphasizes that one key to business success is careful listening. "Find out what the customers' really care about, and then act. Listening-that is the key." The most important type of listening is Active Listening. Active Listening goes beyond regular listening as the listener encourages both the share of information as well as feelings. Active Listening is the key to building relationships as it displays genuine interest.

Passive Listening is appropriate when there is a key note speaker who does most of the talking and the audience is in the training or education mode. Reflective Listening is appropriate when the person is worried, frustrated, confused or upset. It is about acknowledging the feeling more than the content. You reflect or echo what the person seems to be feeling by saying something like-"It seems as if these instructions are a little confusing and thus frustrating."

Here is an instance of poor listening:

A devout Hindu in USA ordered a snack at his local Taco Bell (a fast food place that sells Mexican food). Because eating beef is forbidden in his religion, he emphasized twice to the person at the counter that he wanted a burrito containing only beans and not meat. After taking a bite of the burrito, he discovered to his horror that the burrito contained beef and not beans. The customer later sued (and won) Taco Bell for millions of dollars claiming emotional distress as well as medical expenses and loss of wages.

By improving our listening we can make a dramatic impact on our communication skills thereby positively affecting all aspects of our life. "Communication is really all anyone ever gets paid for ultimately . . . and if you cannot effectively communicate . . . you will PAY . . . and not get paid." Doug Firebaugh.

As the article indicates, good communication skills are a must in business today. MMM Training Solutions conducts a one day seminar on Communication Skills that extensively trains you on improving your skills in this area.

Effective Communication

Can you imagine having a key that could unlock any lock or door? We hear of people, heroes or heroines, being awarded the 'key' to the city. This is simply a metaphor for the privileges extended to the honoree. What if you literally had a key that could unlock any door or lock? Now let's take that another step further, let's kick that up another notch. Suppose you had a key that could unlock every lock or door and also had the ability to break down any barrier that you encountered? Can you imagine the possibilities?

On Solomon's Key Ring, he had just such a key. You are about to learn one of the most powerful 'keys' that you will ever learn. This is the key to success in relationships, in family matters, in situations with your job or career or business. This key can open the minds of your employer or your employees, your business associates or customers, your relatives or your children, your friends and even your enemies.

This is Solomon's key to effective communication. Don't let the name fool you. Again preconception and social conditioning confront us. Some terms have been misused to the point that we have become desensitized to their actual meaning. I'm sure that when you complete this section of our study of Solomon's Keys to success you'll have a completely different interpretation of 'effective communication'.

There are several Proverbs that deal with effective communication and support a very important idea that relates the heart (the seat of emotion) and the mind (the seat of intelligence). These are only a few for brevity's sake.

Proverbs 15:7 (NIV) says:

"The lips of the wise spread knowledge; not so the hearts of fools."

Proverbs 15:28 (NLT) says:

"The heart of the godly thinks carefully before speaking; the mouth of the wicked overflows with evil words."

Proverbs 16:23 (NIV) says:

"A wise man's heart guides his mouth, and his lips promote instruction."

Proverbs 27:3 (Amplified Bible) says:

"For as he thinks in his heart, so is he."

There are many passages that speak of the tongue or of our methods of communication. The important thing for us to realize is that we can either speak life into a situation or person or we can speak death into a situation or a person.

Before we continue let's take a moment to look at what the Bible has to say about one of the most powerful members of the human body - the tongue.

James 3:4-6 says:

And a small rudder makes a huge ship turn wherever the pilot chooses to go, even though the winds are strong. 5 In the same way, the tongue is a small thing that makes grand speeches. But a tiny spark can set a great forest on fire. 6 And the tongue is a flame of fire.

James 3:2 says:

"Indeed, we all make many mistakes. For if we could control our tongues, we would be perfect and could also control ourselves in every other way."

1 Corinthians 14:9 (New Living Translation)

"It's the same for you. If you speak to people in words they don't understand, how will they know what you are saying? You might as well be talking into empty space."

James 1:19

"Understand this, my dear brothers and sisters: You must all be quick to listen, slow to speak, and slow to get angry.

1Peter 3:10 "For the Scriptures say,

"If you want to enjoy life and see many happy days, keep your tongue from speaking evil and your lips from telling lies.

1 Peter 4:11

Do you have the gift of speaking? Then speak as though God himself were speaking through you. Do you have the gift of helping others? Do it with all the strength and energy that God supplies. Then everything you do will bring glory to God through Jesus Christ. All glory and power to him forever and ever! Amen.

There are too many pages in the Holy Scripture that talk about 'effective communication' to list here with reproducing the entire *Holy Bible.* I brought these scriptures into play simply to give an idea of the absolute power that is wielded in our tongue or our speech.

For the purposes of this study we'll concentrate on the instructions and admonitions given us in The Proverbs. Before we begin with the methods of 'effective communication', let's take a look at the effects of non-effective communication. This situation is more prevalent and more easily identified.

There have been millions of ideas and innovations totally ignore for one reason. It may not have been that the idea way a bad on but the method of communicating the idea was defective. In your home and in your work there are probably a ton of instances where ineffective communication has resulted in misunderstanding or the rejection of a great idea. We have discovered through a survey of CEO's and corporate level managers that the greatest problem with industries today is ineffective communication. It can quickly determine the life or the death of a company. Bringing this to an even greater personal level, ineffective communications or better yet, the lack of effective communication skills has been the ruin of many relationships, personal and business. As you learn and master the methods that Solomon offers in effective communication, you will not only see a dramatic.

We can demonstrate the effects of ineffectual communication at home, a setting in which we all are involved. Most women are right brain dominant and most men are left brain dominant. This equates to an often uncomfortable problem. Women have a need to feel connected and because of their emotional disposition, they feel a need for meaningful communication. On average a woman will speak from 25 to 50 thousand words per day. Men on the other hand are less interested in emotional connection and usually speak only 15 to 25 thousand words per day. We see the effect of this in deteriorating relationship.

Often, at home, parents poorly communicate with their children, often destroying the emotional well being of their children. It is so often that parents denigrate their children for a childish act rather than encourage the child to act differently. Too often parents convince their children that they are 'stupid' or 'useless' rather than encouraging the child in a positive manner to do better.

Diligently study Solomon's Principles for Effective Communication in the Proverbs to help develop the effective communication skills that you need to propel you to an ever greater level of success in all areas of your life, especially those that will help you become a more successful communicator of God's message.

Effective Forms of Communication

Forms of communication can be important for facilitating learning, participation, dialogue and behavioural change, especially where information is being shared between different cultures and contexts. Development workers, when faced with different cultural contexts, often expect people to accept new ideas that may be radically different from those they have grown up with. This can lead to ideas being rejected simply because they are 'foreign' or because they are not appropriately communicated. External approaches which attempt to influence attitude, behaviour or practice may be ineffective unless workers adopt an approach which takes into account cultural norms, beliefs and knowledge.

By discovering a culture's traditional, creative forms of communication and expression, we can present new ideas in ways which are locally appropriate and relevant. Some examples of this traditional communication might be local folk artists, proverbs, storytellers and fables.

Making it Work

This involves understanding the insider's perspective, learning about the community's culture and using local language. Communications also become more effective in promoting change when they use vivid, personal images, when people have control of the communications process and when popular formats such as soap operas, oral tradition, theatre and television are used. But what happens when practitioners work with different cultures and environments, requiring different forms of communication? How does one effectively communicate with people who are in different parts of the world, or who have different realities? What is happening in this field?

Often the communication and dissemination of our work to beneficiaries seems to be something taken for *grant*ed, with little attention paid to this part of the process. However, the importance of how we communicate can make a big difference when we try to engage, empower and build capacities. In this way traditional and modern forms of communication can be integrated to increase the appeal of new ideas and the effectiveness of their exchange. This combination of approaches to communication can no longer be seen as 'expert' outside advice provided for 'recipient' organisations. We must consider it as the sharing of knowledge in a process of mutual exchange.

Communication-Effectiveness

There are several factors that will determine what the best or most appropriate method of communication:

- Content of the message (e.g. is it confidential or lengthy)
- Speed required
- Amount of feedback wanted
- Type of feedback required – e.g. is a decision required from the person to whom the communication is sent
- Cost.

The advancement of information technology has altered the way that many businesses communicate. For example, fax was a popular form of communication for businesses in the 1980's. Whilst it still has its uses, people now largely use e-mail instead. The internet is a key tool for many firms now to communicate with many different groups, such as advertising to customers and finding suppliers. Investing in the new technology is costly however and potentially it can become outdated within a few years. There is also the need to train many staff on how to use the technology effectively and even then some employees may be reluctant to change from their traditional methods.

Formal communication occurs when channels of communication are used which have been established by the firm. This may be when workers communicate with managers via works councils or trade union representatives. Informal communication is often known as communication through the grapevine and it can be useful for a manager as they can hear some useful and interesting information which they would not from official channels. This can often be akin to gossiping and it can transmit information quickly but not always accurately (just think how rumours and gossip spread through a school!). Businesses need to have in place appropriate structures or technology in order to aid communication (e.g. e-mail facilities for all employees) but on an every day level it is down to individual managers and employees to ensure that they communicate their messages or information effectively. Not all managers for instance will naturally have good communication skills and there is an obvious need for training in this case to ensure they are able to choose the most appropriate communication method to get their message across clearly.

To be effective the message must be clearly understood by the receivers and also the receivers should be able to supply some feedback. When feedback occurs it is known as two-way communication and is seen as the most effective form of communication. The best example of this is direct face-to-face communication as the sender can get an immediate reaction in terms of the oral reply and also importantly from the receivers body language. One-way communication occurs when there is no feedback given on a message, for example putting a notice on a notice board. This is suitable in some circumstances, if for instance someone is announcing a change of time for a meeting and little feedback is required, but generally employees should try to maximise methods that encourage two-way communication and feedback. Two-way feedback is becoming relevant in firms for two main reasons.

Many firms are introducing new techniques and initiatives, such as kaizen or total quality management, which rely on employee participation and feedback. In addition two-way communication is a pre-requisite for a democratic management style, which is becoming increasingly popular in businesses. For many firms one of their main objectives is to grow in size (gaining market share or entering new markets) as this is seen as the way to boost profits. As a firm expands one of the major problems they will face will be to continue to communicate effectively with their increasing workforce and so maintain motivation levels.

Effective Business Communication

Face-to-face meetings can result in awkward pauses and initial shyness for those who are not brimming with confidence. To help you over this hurdle, you can approach the meeting fully prepared and well armed if you have a look at the following factors.

In order to get your message across, think about what you are trying to achieve during the dialogue:

- What information do you wish to convey?
- What do you want the other person to do as a result?

Organise yourself beforehand. Jot down notes about your major points. Be positive and keep the message simple.

Clarity is Paramount for Effective Communication

What is communication? In short, it's signalling. The transmission, by speaking, writing or gestures, of information which evokes understanding. That's simple enough, isn't it? Straightforward in theory but in practice it's fraught with dangers-particularly if you have high expectations from these important business connections.

Communication is not just speaking, writing or gesticulating. It's more than the transmission of information. Something else has to occur for the communication to be complete. The other party in the communication process has to engage their brain and receive the message.

There are some points to remember when considering the various methods of communication and some hazards to be aware of when dealing with business relationships:

- Only 7% of the impact you make comes from the words you speak.
- The rest is visual-your appearance, the sound of your voice and your body language.
- You can break that 7% further down into sections:
- the type of words you use
- the sort of sentences you use
- how you phrase them.

Effective Communication: Turn this Weakness into a Strength

Corporate leaders are trained in economics, strategy and a variety of other business skills. Few are trained in communication, yet experts agree that communication is one of the most important skills leaders should have on their list of competencies. To ensure successful communications within your organization, it is best to start with the very basics: your knowledge of verbal and nonverbal communications. In the workplace, these types of communications are continually exchanged, oftentimes without much planning or even the thought that such communications are taking place.

The Importance of Nonverbal Communication

A famous study by Albert Mehrabian found that nonverbal language makes up 55 percent of how we communicate in face-to-face interactions. He also concluded that we communicate as much as 38 percent of our message through our voice (tone, pitch and so on), with as little as 7 percent through the words we actually say. Understanding and recognizing the signs and signals that make up this 55 percent can help you when you communicate with others. There are times when we send mixed messages – we say one thing yet our body language reveals something different. This nonverbal language affects how we act and react to others, how they react to us, and whether or not we gain and maintain credibility.

For instance, it's not always just what you say. It's also how you "say" it – taking into account your eyes, your posture, your overall body language, the voice in which you offer the exchange, and even your appearance at the time the communication is exchanged. In verbal communication, an active dialogue is engaged with the use of words. At the same time, however, nonverbal communication takes place, relying on nonverbal cues, such as gestures, eye contact, facial expressions, even clothing and personal space.

Nonverbal cues are very powerful, making it crucial that you pay attention to your actions, as well as the nonverbal cues of those around you. If, during your meeting, participants begin to doodle or chat among themselves, they are no longer paying attention to you. Your message has become boring or your delivery is no longer engaging. When I was a business program facilitator at the Disney Institute, I had a friend who used to say, "Watch the audience. If they're bored, you're boring them!"

While eye contact, facial expressions, posture, gestures, clothing and space are obvious nonverbal communication cues, others strongly influence interpretation of messages, including how the message is delivered. This means paying close attention to your tone of voice, even your voice's overall loudness and pitch. Be mindful of your own nonverbal cues, as well as the nonverbal cues of those around you. Keep your messages short and concise. This means preparing in advance whenever possible. And for the impromptu meeting, it means thinking before you speak.

Barriers to Effective Communication

Barriers can arise at any stage of the communication process. When communication is failing, it is of primary importance to identify where the causes for failure are within the communication process. Take a few minutes and think about the barriers to effective communication in your organization, division or department. Some of the most common barriers that I hear when working with leaders in organizations are:

- Lack of time to communicate effectively
- Staff is spread geographically
- Don't have the tools
- Language barriers
- Ethnic and cultural barriers
- Educational differences
- Differences in experience of the workforce.

In reality, all barriers to effective communication fall into three broad categories. These categories are related to:

1. External environment, e.g.,
   a. The space in which you are communicating
   b. The communication tools used (handouts, PowerPoint or no tools used)
   c. The method of communication (written, verbal, meetings, one-on-one)
   d. Communication as it relates to your corporate culture.
2. Speaker-related
   a. Language barrier between speaker and listener
   b. Lack of training for the speaker
   c. Lack of understanding of the audience
   d. Educational difference between the speaker and the audience.
3. Internal receiver-related
   a. Language barrier between the listener and the speaker
   b. Lack of experience of the listener
   c. Educational differences between the speaker and the listener
   d. Pre-conceived ideas or opinions of the listener.

It is always best to take the time to plan for any communication. The following simple process will help you to overcome these barriers and ensure precise, professional and effective communication in your organization. The communication process is comprised of four basic elements:

1. Sender.
2. Message.
3. Method and environment.
4. Receiver.

The Communication Process

Sender: The sender must establish credibility by displaying knowledge of the subject, the audience and the context of the delivery. The burden of responsibility lies with the sender to ensure that the message is understood and that expectations for deliverables are clearly defined.

Message: Consider the message being sent. Written, verbal and nonverbal communications are affected by the sender's tone, method of communication, and what is included or left out of the message. If you choose to send a written message, be sure that it is professional, precise, clear and written in simple language.

Always remember that written communications are open to interpretation.

Proof your written communication for typos, grammar, punctuation and sentence structure to reduce the chances of miscommunication and to ensure that you maintain professional credibility. Method and environment: Messages are conveyed through channels. These channels are affected by the method and environment with which you choose to communicate. Potential channels include verbal communication, face-to-face, telephone, video conference, written communication, meetings, etc.

It is wise to consider the method of communication prior to communicating your message. For example, an e-mail, letter or memo may not be the best way to communicate critical information. All written communication is one-way communication, meaning that there is little to no opportunity for people to ask questions, express concern or gain clarification in a timely manner. If the message that you are sending is informational in nature, sending it in written form, such as e-mail, is a very efficient way to communicate quickly with many people based in a wide geographic area.

If, however, the message conveys critical information – such as changes in policies, processes, procedures or organizational changes – the best method of communication is face-to-face. You will have to give some thought as to the right environment for the face-to-face communication – e.g., one-on-one individual communication or communicating the information to a group in a meeting.

Receiver: Messages are delivered to your audience, the receivers of the message. Your audience enters into the communication process with ideas and feelings that influence their understanding of your message and dictates their response.

Often, the receivers have pre-conceived ideas or opinions about the topic of your communication. For example, you may be communicating a new initiative and the audience is already tuning you out because this idea was tried two years ago and it did not work.

As the sender, you must also consider the barriers that may interfere with the receivers' ability to understand the message. These barriers include language, ethnic cultural beliefs, level of education and/or level of experience, to name a few. While creating your plan for effective communication, consider not only the communication process outlined above, but also the following four strategies:

Strategy No. 1: Communication methods must meet individual needs

- Know your employees as individuals, understand the receiver
  - Personality traits
  - Gender
  - Generation
  - Ethnicity/culture/language
  - Education.
- Utilize resources relevant to employee needs, select the right method. Resources may include:
  - Meetings (monthly, weekly, daily)

- One-on-one meetings with employees (face-to-face, telephone)
- Newsletters
- Bulletin boards
- Voicemails
- E-mails
- Pagers
- Video conferencing.

• Regularly assess the effectiveness of communication methods

• Evaluate the environmental factors and internal receiver factors

- Possible distractions
- Time
- Comfort of the room.

Strategy No. 2: Communication must be timely

• Avoid premature communication

• Communicate change as soon as possible

• Determine the appropriate method for the situation.

Strategy No. 3: Communication must be inclusive

• Ensure that communication flows intra-departmentally and inter-departmentally

• Consider the variables of the workforce.

Strategy No. 4: Understand the impact of nonverbal and written communication

• Be aware of how nonverbal communication (body language) affects the message

• Ensure that written communication sends a concise and

professional message

- Double-check spelling, grammar and punctuation
- Use a readable font
- Use humor sparingly or avoid altogether.
    * Because written communication is open to interpretation, we do not recommend the use of humour
    * If you insist on injecting humour into your written communication, be sure that it is appropriate for all audiences and cannot be misconstrued in any way.
- Follow this example format to assure that your written communication is clear, precise and actionable:

What is the key point or message?

Why is this important/ how is it relevant to goals?

Action: what you need them to do

Contact: For questions or concerns, provide contact information

In a recent survey of recruiters from companies with more than 50,000 employees, communication skills were cited as the single-most-important decisive factor in choosing managers. The survey, conducted by the University of Pittsburgh's Katz Business School, points out that communication skills, including written and oral presentations, as well as an ability to work with others, are the main factor contributing to job success.

In reality, no matter the size of your business, by successfully getting your message across, you convey your thoughts and ideas effectively. When not successful, the thoughts and ideas that you actually send do not necessarily reflect what you think, causing a communications breakdown and creating roadblocks that stand in the way of your goals – both personally and professionally.

2

Communication Theory

There is much discussion in the academic world of communication as to what actually constitutes communication. Currently, many definitions of communication are used in order to conceptualize the processes by which people navigate and assign meaning. We might say that communication consists of transmitting information from one person to another. In fact, many scholars of communication take this as a working definition, and use Lasswell's maxim, "who says what to whom in what channel with what effect," as a means of circumscribing the field of communication theory.

A simple communication model with a sender transferring a message containing information to a receiver. Other commentators suggest that a ritual process of communication exists, one not artificially divorceable from a particular historical and social context.

Communication stands so deeply rooted in human behaviours and the structures of society that scholars have difficulty thinking of it while excluding social or behavioral events. Because communication theory remains a relatively young field of inquiry and integrates itself with other disciplines such as philosophy, psychology, and sociology, one probably cannot yet expect a consensus conceptualization of communication across disciplines. Currently, there is no paradigm from which communication scholars may work. One of the issues facing scholars is the possibility that establishing a communication meta theory will negate their research and stifle the broad body of knowledge in which communication functions.

Definitions of Communication

Currently, many definitions of communication are used in order to conceptualize the processes by which people navigate and assign meaning. Communication is also understood as the exchanging of understanding. Additionally the biocommunication theory investigates communicative processes within and among non-humans such as bacteria, animals, fungi and plants. We might say that communication consists of transmitting information from one person to another. In fact, many scholars of communication take this as a working definition, and use Lasswell's maxim, "who says what to whom in what channel with what effect," as a means of circumscribing the field of communication theory.

Other commentators suggest that a ritual process of communication exists, one not artificially divorcible from a particular historical and social context.

There is an additional working definition of communication to consider. This is a progression from Lassell's attempt to define human communication through to this century and revolutionized into the constructionist model. Constructionists believe that the process of communication is in itself the only messages that exist. The packaging can not be separated from the social and historical context from which it arose, therefore the substance to look at in communication theory is style for Robert Lanham and the performance of self for Erving Goffman.

Scholars chose to view communication as the rival to the over encompassing use of CBS model (which pursued to further the transmission model). CBS model argues that charity, brevity, and sincerity are the only purpose to prose discourse, therefore communication. If words matter too, if the whole range of human motive is seen as animating prose discourse, than rhetoric analysis leads us to the essential questions about prose style. This is saying that rhetoric and style are fundamentally important; they are not errors to what we actually intend to transmit. The process which we construct and deconstruct meaning deserves analysis.

The performance of self as the most important frame to understand communication. "What does seem to be required of the individual is that he learn enough pieces of expression to be able to 'fill in' and manage, more or less, any part that he is likely to be given." The truth in both cases is the articulation of the message and the package as one. The construction of the message from social and historical context is the seed as is the pre-existing message is for the transmission model. Therefore any look into communication theory should include the possibilities drafted by such great scholars as Robert A. Lanham and Erving Goffman that style and performance is the whole process.

Communication stands so deeply rooted in human behaviours and the structures of society that scholars have difficulty thinking of it while excluding social or behavioural events. Because communication theory remains a relatively young field of inquiry and integrates itself with other disciplines such as philosophy, psychology, and sociology, one probably cannot yet expect a consensus conceptualization of communication across disciplines.

Currently, there is one paradigm from which communication scholars may work, a universal law, posited by S. F, Scudder (1900). "The Universal Law of Communication states that, "All living entities communicate.". All living entities communicate via movements, sounds, reactions, physical changes, gestures, languages, breath, etc. Communication is primarily used as a means of survival. Examples such as the cry of a hungry infant (communication that it is hungry), the browing a leaf (communication that it is dehydrated), the cry of an animal (communication that it is injured) falls under the Universal Law of Communication. Everything living must communicate, primarily as a means of survival."

History of Communication Theory

The Academic Study of Communication

Communication has existed since the beginning of human beings, but it was not until the 20th century that people began to study the process. As communication technologies developed, so did the serious study of communication. When World War I ended, the interest in studying communication intensified. The social-science study was fully recognized as a legitimate discipline after World War II.

Before becoming simply communication, or communication studies, the discipline was formed from three other major studies: sociology, psychology, and anthropology. Sociology is the study of human behaviour, psychology is the study of society and social process, and anthropology is the study of communication as a factor which develops, maintains, and changes culture. Communication studies focus on communication as central to the human experience, which involves understanding how people behave in creating, exchanging, and interpreting messages.

Communication Theory is based on one universal law. The Universal Communication Law states that, "All living entities communicate." All living entities communicate via movements, sounds, reactions, physical changes, gestures, languages, breath, etc. Communication is a means of survival. Examples such as the cry of a hungry infant (communication that it is hungry), the browing a leaf (communication that it is dehydrated), the cry of an animal (communicating that it is injured falls under this universal communication law. Everything living must communicate as a means of survival."

Communication Theory Framework

It is helpful to examine communication and communication theory through one of the following viewpoints:

- *Mechanistic*: This view considers communication as a perfect transaction of a message from the sender to the receiver.
- *Psychological*: This view considers communication as the act of sending a message to a receiver, and the feelings and thoughts of the receiver upon interpreting the message.
- *Social Constructionist* (Symbolic Interactionist): This view considers communication to be the product of the interactsnts sharing and creating meaning. The Constructionist View can also be defined as, how you say something determines what the message is. The

Constructionist View assumes that "truth" and "ideas" are constructed or invented through the social process of communication. The Constructionist View or the constitutive view as it's called in his article, as ". . . an ongoing process that symbolically forms and reforms our personal identities." The other view of communication, the Transmission Model, sees communication as robotic and computer-like. The Transmission Model sees communication as a way of sending or receiving messages and the perfection of that. But, the Constructionist View sees communications as, "...in human life, info does not behave as simply as bits in an electronic stream. In human life, information flow is far more like an electric current running from one landmine to another". The Constructionist View is a more realistic view of communication because it involves the interacting of human beings and the free sharing of thoughts and ideas. Daniel Chandler looks to prove that the Transmission Model is a lesser way of communicating by saying "The transmission model is not merely a gross over-simplification but a dangerously misleading representation of the nature of human communication". Humans do not communicate simply as computers or robots so that's why it's essential to truly understand the Constructionist View of Communication well. We do not simply send facts and data to one another, but we take facts and data and they acquire meaning through the process of communication, or through interaction with others.

- *Systemic*: This view considers communication to be the new messages created via "through-put", or what happens as the message is being interpreted and re-interpreted as it travels through people.

- *Critical*: This view considers communication as a source of power and oppression of individuals and social groups.

Inspection of a particular theory on this level will provide a framework on the nature of communication as seen within the confines of that theory.

Theories can also be studied and organized according to the ontological, epistemological, and axiological framework imposed by the theorist.

Ontology essentially poses the question of what, exactly, it is the theorist is examining. One must consider the very nature of reality. The answer usually falls in one of three realms depending on whether the theorist sees the phenomena through the lens of a realist, nominalist, or social constructionist. Realist perspective views the world objectively, believing that there is a world outside of our own experience and cognitions. Nominalists see the world subjectively, claiming that everything outside of one's cognitions is simply names and labels. Social constructionists straddle the fence between objective and subjective reality, claiming that reality is what we create together.

Epistemology is an examination of how the theorist studies the chosen phenomena. In studying epistemology, particularly from a positivist perspective, objective knowledge is said to be the result of a systematic look at the causal relationships of phenomena. This knowledge is usually attained through use of the scientific method. Scholars often think that empirical evidence collected in an objective manner is most likely to reflect truth in the findings. Theories of this ilk are usually created to predict a phenomenon. Subjective theory holds that understanding is based on situated knowledge, typically found using interpretative methodology such as ethnography and also interviews. Subjective theories are typically developed to explain or understand phenomena in the social world.

Axiology is concerned with what values drive a theorist to develop a theory. Theorists must be mindful of potential biases so that they will not influence or skew their findings (Miller, 21-23).

Mapping the Theoretical Landscape

A discipline gets defined in large part by its theoretical structure. Communication studies often borrow theories from other social sciences. This theoretical variation makes it difficult to come to terms with the field as a whole. That said, some common taxonomies exist that serve to divide up the range of communication research. Two common mappings involve contexts and assumptions.

Contexts

Many authors and researchers divide communication by what they sometimes called "contexts" or "levels", but which more often represent institutional histories. The study of communication in the US, while occurring within departments of psychology, sociology, linguistics, and anthropology (among others), generally developed from schools of rhetoric and from schools of journalism. While many of these have become "departments of communication", they often retain their historical roots, adhering largely to theories from speech communication in the former case, and from mass media in the latter. The great divide between speech communication and mass communication becomes complicated by a number of smaller sub-areas of communication research, including intercultural and international communication, small group communication, communication technology, policy and legal studies of communication, telecommunication, and work done under a variety of other labels. Some of these departments take a largely social-scientific perspective, others tend more heavily toward the humanities, and still others gear themselves more toward production and professional preparation.

These "levels" of communication provide some way of grouping communication theories, but inevitably, some theories and concepts leak from one area to another, or fail to find a home at all.

Assumptions

Another way of dividing up the communication field emphasizes the assumptions that undergird particular theories, models, and approaches. While this approach also tends to have as its basis institutional divisions, theories within each of the seven "traditions" of communication theory that Robert Craig suggests tend to reinforce one another, and retain the same ground epistemological and axiological assumptions. His traditions include:

- rhetorical-practical art of discourse
- semiotic – intersubjective mediation through signs in order to mediate between different perspectives
- phenomenological-experience of otherness, dialogue
- cybernetic-information processing and explains how all kinds of complex systems, whether living or nonliving, macro or micro, are able to function, and why they often malfunction
- sociopsychological-expression, interaction and influence
- critical-discursive reflection
- sociocultural-reproduction of social order.

Each of these clearly defined against the others, and remaining cohesive approaches to describing communicative behaviour. As a taxonomic aid, these labels help to organize theory by its assumptions, and help researchers to understand why some theories may seem incommensurable.

While communication theorists very commonly use these two approaches, theorists decentralize the place of language and machines as communicative technologies. The idea (as argued by Vygotsky) of communication as the primary tool of a species defined by its tools remains on the outskirts of communication theory.

It finds some representation in the Toronto School of communication theory (alternatively sometimes called medium theory). It seems that the ways in which individuals and groups use the technologies of communication — and in some cases are used by them — remain central to what communication researchers do. The ideas that surround this, and in particular the place of persuasion, remain constants across both the "traditions" and "levels" of communication theory.

Theory of Communication

Organisations can not operate without communication. Communication can take various forms but all forms involve the transfer of information from one party to the other. In order for the transfer of information to qualify as communication, the recipient must understand the meaning of the information transferred to them. If the recipient does not understand the meaning of the information conveyed to them, communication has not taken place.

Communication is the life source of organisations because organisations involve people. People cannot interact with each other without communication. In the absence of communication, everything would grind to a halt. For example;

The workers in an organisation would not know the organisation's objectives so they would not strive to achieve the organisation's objectives.

- The workers in an organisation would not know what their roles and responsibilities were, so they would not be able to carry out their daily tasks and duties.
- The managers would not be able to train their workers reports so the workers would not possess the skills they needed to carry out their jobs.
- The managers would not be able to inform workers of changes
- The organisation would not be aware of their competitors activities

And the list is endless...............

On the whole people are able to communicate with each other as this is a basic human function. However successful organisations strive not only for communication but effective communication.

Interpersonal Communication

This is defined as communication between two or more people and involves the transfer of information (or message) from one person to the other(s). The person transferring the information is called the sender or transmitter. The people receiving the message are known as receivers. The transmitter will need to send the information in a format that the receiver(s) will understand. Converting the information into a format that the receivers will understand is known as Encoding.

Messages can be encoded into a variety of formats oral, written or visual. After encoding the message is transferred via a medium called a channel, for example a letter, fax, phone call, or e-mail. After transference the information will need to be interpreted by the receiver. This process of interpretation is known as decoding. Finally the receiver will send a message back to the transmitter confirming whether the information sent has been understood. This back check is known as feedback.

The communication process involves seven key elements as illustrated in the diagram below.

Barriers to Effective Communication

At each stage in the process encoding, transference, and decoding there is the possibility of interference which may hinder the communication process. This interference is known as noise. Often a comparison is made between communication and a leaky bucket. If you use a leaky bucket to carry water, water will be lost at various points in your journey from the water tap to your destination. It is not possible to stop losing water because the bucket contains holes. The amount of water you will lose will be determined by the number of holes in the bucket, the size of the holes, the route you take to your final destination and length of time it takes you to get to your destination. There may also be other events that occur during your journey which increase the amount of water lost. Similarly when information is transferred from the transmitter to the receiver not all of the information may be received by the receiver because of holes called noise. Each of the noise may be affect the amount of information transferred. Just as in a leaky bucket, more holes decrease the amount of water, more noise decreases the amount of correct information received. Noise can take a variety of forms including

Language issues and Cultural Differences : The receiver(s) may not (fully) understand the language used by the transmitter. This may occur if the transmitter's language is foreign to the receiver. There may also be language problems (that the communication process) if the message contains technical information and the receiver's is not familiar with the technical terms used. Cultural differences created by an individual's background and experience affect their perception of the world. Such cultural differences may affect the interpretation (decoding) of the message sent.

Environmental issues: If the environment that the transmitter or receiver are in, is noisy and full of sound, the sounds may prevent the message being fully understood. Background noise is often created by colleagues or machinery.

Channel issues: If the channel used to transfer the information is poor it may prevent all or some of the information being transferred. Examples include a faulty fax machine, a crackling phone, handwriting that cannot be read or in the case of oral messages incorrect facial gestures.

Receivers Attitude and behaviour: If the receiver(s) is not interested in the message (or unable to give their full attention to decoding) this may reduce the amount of information received or the accuracy of the information transmitted to them. Similarly the receiver(s) may misinterpret the message by "jumping to conclusions" or reading the message in a manner that suits their own interests/ objectives and distort the true meaning of the message. Transmission journey, i.e. steps in the message, If the message is complicated or there are lots of steps taken to transfer the message it may affect the accuracy or interpretation. Comparing with the leaky bucket if the leaky bucket has to carry water over a longer distance more water will probably lost than if the journey was shorter.

Internal/Organisational Communication

This is communication that takes place within (or across) an organisation. In addition to the usual face to face, telephone, fax or mail; modern organisations may use technology to communicate internally. Technology may be used for e-mails or a linked internal communication system such as the intranet which is an internet system designed solely for use by those working for the organisation.

External Communications

Conversely external communication is communication between the organisation and those outside the organisation. Modern organisations may design technological systems so that they can communicate with customers and undertake e-Commerce. Alternatively they communicate with other businessess through the internet or similar systems and undertake e-Business.

Functions of Internal and External Communications

Technology has rapidly expanded the types of internal and external communication available to organisations. The diagram illustrates the vast array of internal and external communication available. Combined together internal and external types of communications allow various sectors of the local, national and international community to interact, liaise and conduct business.

Formal and Informal Communications

Formal communication is defined as communication which occurs through the official organisational channels or is undertaken by an employee to do their job.

For example official meetings, letters and a manager asking an employee to carry out a particular task. Conversely informal communication is that which occurs outside the recognised communication networks such as talking in the lunchroom or hallways between employees. Informal communication can be productive or negative. It has the potential to build teams, improve working relationships and generate ideas as employees are in a relaxed environment.

Upward and Downward Communications

Downward communication is communication created by directors and managers and passed down the hierarchy of workers in the organisation. In traditional organisations this is the preferred method of communication ie Managers decide what the systems, rules and procedures will be and then they pass these down to employees they manage and supervise. Downward Communication can increase efficiency by synchronising organisational procedures and can ensure that everybody is working towards the same overall aims and objectives. Types of downward communication include job descriptions, appraisals/evaluations, organisational policy, and organisational systems.

Although there are advantages to downward communication organisations have began to encourage upward communication. This is communication which originates at the lower level of the employment hierarchy and is then communicated up through the line. Organisations encouraging upward communication believe that everybody is capable of generating thoughts and ideas which may help the organisation to progress, particularly when they are working closely in the area that the idea applies to.

Upward communication may increase motivation and make employees feel valued and respected whilst enabling managers to understand how employees are feeling. Furthermore if problems occur at they are more likely to be identified earlier by those working closely in the area that they occur. Types of upward communications include suggestion schemes, feedback forums/ surveys, grievance procedures and employee-manager discussions.

Lateral Communication

This is communication that occurs between employees on the same level in the organisation. As this can involve decision making it can create efficiency as employees do not have to wait for managerial approval. On the other hand if the manager is not kept informed or if the manager fails to set boundaries there is potential for conflict.

Diagonal Communication

This occurs when communication occurs between workers in a different section of the organisation and where one of the workers involved is on a higher level in the organisation. For example in a bank diagonal communication will occur when a department manager in head office converses with a cashier in a branch of the bank based on the high street.

3

Principles of Effective Communication

Objective

To familiarize the participants with the elementary principles of successful oral communication of information and to heighten awareness of the factors that interfere with communication and reduce its effectiveness

Suggested Method of Instruction

- Lecture/discussion with maximum trainee participation through questioning and relating of personal experience

Aids

- Overhead transparencies
- Handouts

Time frame

- One hour lecture/discussion

Content

- Effective communication
- Interference
- Ways of avoiding interference

Presentation Suggestions

The foregoing module is easily adapted to discussion. The trainer should attempt to elicit from the trainees their experiences with transmission, interference and ways of avoiding interference, which are well within the purview of trainee experience. Trainees should be asked to tell the course participants about good communicators and poor communicators they have known, describing why they are memorable. The reasons they give should be related to the types of interference and ways in which interference was or could have been avoided.

Such a discussion invariably brings out other indirectly related aspects of spoken communication which provide points of reference when subjects in later modules are being dealt with.

Learning Outcome

Participants should be aware of effective communication principles.

Effective Communication

Communication specialists compare the way people communicate to the way a radio transmission takes place. That is to say:

Transmitter (Speaker/writer) ® Message ® Receiver (Listener/reader)

Three types of transmission are identified:

- Spoken
- Written
- Gesture/sometimes referred to as "body language"

Transmission is in code:

- Spoken language
- Written language
- Gestures

In spoken language the unit of code is the word, heavily supported by gestures. Some communication specialists believe that at least 40 percent of the full meaning of messages transmitted by speech is conveyed by body language (gestures). In written language the units of code are words and symbols (e.g. figures, punctuation). In the remainder of this module and the modules that follow reference to communication is to spoken communication only and assumes the transmitter can be seen by the receiver.

Interference

Frequently the message suffers from interference. That is, something interferes with the message between its transmission and reception and distorts it. The following are some types of interference.

Weak transmission

- Speaking too softly
- Speaking in a flat voice (monotone) without inflection
- Not speaking in a direct line with the receiver
- Insufficient volume of transmission to prevail over competing transmissions and localized noise (static)

Garbled transmission

The transmitter (speaker) often scrambles the contents of the message so that the facts it contains are not in logical order and often appear unrelated.

Wrong language

The transmitter may use words, terms and expressions unknown to the receiver.

Pitching message at the wrong level

The speaker may transmit information in a context beyond the experience of the receiver (this may involve the use of wrong language).

This is sometimes called "transmitting or talking over the receiver's head". Examples are teaching food control procedures or HACCP to people who have no experience in food safety or food processing, or transmitting detailed and profound scientific messages to a receiver without a scientific background.

Receiver not receiving

- Receiver turned off (gone to sleep!)
- Tuned into another transmitter
- Transmission too weak
- Strength of receiver diminished (lack of interest-boredom)
- Receiver distracted by a competing focus of interest (an attractive person walks by)
- Receiver fatigued

Competing transmissions

The receiver may be unable to select between transmissions (too many people talking at once).

Overloading the message

The receiver does not possess the capacity to retain all of the information contained in the message. This frequently leads to receiver confusion/fatigue and anxiety.

Ways of Avoiding Interference

- Speak up and out
- Speak slowly and deliberately
- Use language that the receiver understands
- Do not talk over the receiver's head
- Ensure you have the attention of the receiver
- Only transmit your message in suitable surroundings where there is no, or little, competition

- Make the message succinct (as few words as possible) and transmit it in the simplest terms
- Plan the message in logical order

Summary

To be a successful communicator:

- Use your voice effectively
- Know your subject
- Know what you want to say
- Prepare your message carefully
- Arrange your points logically
- Display interest and enthusiasm
- Sound convincing and sincere

Effective Oral Communication

Objective

To assist the trainee-trainers to identify and become acquainted with the essential elements of getting the message across and becoming an effective oral communicator

Suggested method of instruction

- Lecture/discussion with maximum trainee participation through questioning
- An exercise in impromptu speaking to an audience

Aids

- Overhead transparencies
- Handouts

Time frame

- One hour lecture/discussion

- One hour of approximately three-minute impromptu speeches (time depends on the number of participants)

Content

- The importance of being an effective oral communicator
- Essential elements in transmitting a message
- Communication hazards

Presentation suggestions

The trainer should put much effort into preparing for presentation of this module.

The presentation should commence with a discussion based on a series of questions carefully devised by the trainer, for example:

- What makes a good communicator? (This question is a link to Module 1 and offers the opportunity for a few minutes revision of the previous module).
- What are the essential characteristics of effective oral communication?

It is important that the trainees identify the characteristics and convert them to elements by themselves. As each is identified it could be discussed in detail.

The trainer can project transparencies showing the elements to reinforce them in the minds of trainees, but only after they have been identified by the trainees.

Exercise

Each trainee is required to give a three-to four-minute impromptu talk. The following are examples of possible subjects:

- My reasons for attending the course
- The aspect of my work I enjoy the most
- Why I think HACCP (or food control) is important

In giving this talk the trainee will be expected to take into account the essential elements in transmitting a message.

A handout sheet may be helpful to assist the trainees with their short presentations. The following is an example:

- Describe your work.
- Why is it important to you?
- Which aspect of your work do you enjoy the most?
- Which aspect do you dislike the most?
- What do you think you are best at?
- What aspect of your work would you like to know more about?
- If you had a choice, which aspect of "Quality control" would you like to specialize in and why?

Learning outcome

The participants should be familiar with the essential elements of effective oral communication.

The Importance of Being an Effective Oral Communicator

As a trainer much of your effectiveness is measured by your ability to speak with clarity and conviction in getting your messages across. Men and women in training positions are expected to be highly competent at presenting ideas, giving directions and explaining procedures. In fact, this quality of being an effective communicator is generally considered to be an essential element of the effective trainer's skills.

The information you communicate as a trainer is often critical to the people you train and to the workings of the organization as a whole. The way you explain procedures or give directions can make the difference between an employee being productive or frustrated. Sometimes clear information from you can make the difference between people doing a job safely or unsafely, working efficiently or inefficiently or doing things correctly or incorrectly.

How you present even an obviously brilliant idea can make the difference between whether or not anyone listens to you. The way in which you interpret and transmit information about agency policies, goals, values and procedures has significant influence on the way your staff or subordinates develop their perceptions and their commitments to the organization. Communicating clearly-"getting your message across"-is not an inherited ability; people are not born with it. It is a learned skill developed through planning and practice.

Essential Elements in Transmitting a Message

This encourages receivers (listeners) to focus on your information and be more receptive. They will not be distracted by trying to guess what your point is, but will be mentally prepared to follow along as you develop your discussion. Stating your main point right away captures your listeners' attention and helps them remember the most important part of your message.

Introductory phrases like the following help to make your purpose clear at the start.

- My purpose in speaking to you is...
- It is important that I discuss with you...
- The subject of what I have to say to you is...
- As a result of new policies adopted by the organization you should know...

After the main point has been made, it can be highlighted with expressions like:

- Now, what this means in effect is...
- Put in another way, this means...
- You can expect that what will happen next will be...
- My main concern about this proposal is...
- The point that I wish to emphasize is...

Strengthen your main point with supporting points

Your explanations, instructions or ideas are more compelling when supported by clear facts and observations. Your objective is to gain respect and belief from your listeners and for them to gain insight into the details of the message you are communicating. The following guidelines will make the transmission of your message effective.

- Use simple language. Avoid technical jargon unless you are sure that everyone understands it.
- Keep your explanation short so you do not risk boring people. Do not swamp them with unnecessary detail (which is called "overloading").
- Choose reasoning that is natural and familiar to your listeners and your topic.
- Make your explanations as colourful as possible, using examples to illustrate your point.
- List all your supporting points first; then return to each point and fill in the details.
- Use visual aids, where possible, to illustrate your points.

Check to see whether you got your message across

You must find out whether you got your message across. Checking this may also introduce you to views of your listeners that were not apparent to you, or reveal misunderstandings that need to be quickly corrected. In addition, checking often helps listeners feel involved: they are being consulted. Their responses might uncover some problems not earlier apparent to you. The best way of checking is by questions. For example:

- Would somebody like to restate the steps of the new procedure?
- What do you think about...?
- What effect do you think the new arrangement will have?

- Is there anyone who disagrees with what is being proposed?
- Which of the points I have made do you think is the most important?

Respond to reactions to what you have presented

It is important that your trainees see you as somebody who is honest with them. A good part of this quality of openness is reflected in the way you respond to people when they question your statements, instructions or opinions. Listeners question speakers because they have not received (not understood) the message, or because it is unclear, or because the details are vague. Generally, they are not challenging the speaker as a person; they are simply seeking clarification. In answering questions, make sure you understand the question. If you do not understand the question, ask the questioner to repeat it. If you still do not understand it, start questioning the questioner. For example:

- Do you mean...?
- I understand that you are asking me...
- I am not sure that I understand you, but I think you are saying...

Sometimes you may understand the question or statement but feel that other listeners are having trouble with it. In such cases put the question or statement into your own words and restate it, ensuring that your restatement is correct by asking for confirmation from the person who has proposed the question or statement. Never, never make fun of a questioner who has completely missed your message. Make light of the misunderstanding, and repeat the message to help him or her understand. You might introduce your statement as follows:

- I think there is a misunderstanding here. Let me repeat my main point again.
- This is a very complicated matter and difficult to understand fully. Let me repeat the main points.

Summarize your Main Point(s)

Your listeners will probably not be able to remember everything you have said, especially if you have presented several ideas. A short, simple restatement of the essential message(s) helps the listeners to remember and respond.

Communication Hazards

Nervousness, forgetfulness and losing track. At one time or another all trainers (transmitters) experience these problems. Two ways to prevent these difficulties are:

- Use notes
- Rehearse the presentation of your message

Speakers familiar with their message seldom, if ever, suffer from severe interference. Do not get defensive when a trainee asks a question or makes a statement that is or appears to be a criticism of or an attack on you. As a trainer and communicator you must retain your objectivity. To become defensive and subjective quickly signals to the listeners that you are not sure of yourself or your facts, and they may assume that what you are saying is unreliable. This can lead to loss of your credibility.

Criticism of your Presentation

Look upon critical statements or questions as a form of feedback. The information in them can tell you whether you are on the right track. However difficult it might be, handle yourself pleasantly and diplomatically, using responses such as:

- I'm glad you brought that up. It's an interesting question.
- Perhaps you could explain that a little more before we have a look at it.
- I can understand how you feel about the matter, but try and look at it this way.
- I understand your concerns. Let's try to come up with some alternatives.

- I can see that the matter is of great concern to you. Let's discuss it personally at the coffee break.

Why Train? The Trainer's Role and Responsibility

Objective

To introduce the participants to the basic principles of training in the simplest possible way and to establish fully the responsibility of the trainer

Suggested method of instruction

- Lecture/discussion
- An exercise in identifying the role of each of the senses in learning
- An exercise in planning a skill training session

Aids

- Overhead transparencies
- Handouts

Time frame

- One hour lecture/discussion

Content

- The process of learning
- Factors that hinder learning
- Obtaining and holding the learners' attention
- Facilitating understanding
- Steps in skill training.

Approach

This module is important because it is essentially the introduction to the training modules that follow. Discussion should play a major part in the presentation. Because of their life-experiences the trainees will be familiar with learning, even though they may never have analysed the process.

Therefore the major task of the trainer is to plan a sequence of questions that will lead the trainees to an identification of the elements and steps in the learning process and the factors that hamper learning.

Trainees should be encouraged to recall the good trainers and teachers they have known and to identify the skills that made their training and teaching memorablé. The material in the lecture and overhead transparencies is in point form and requires explanation by the trainer.

The Process of Learning

The successful trainer possesses insight into the process of learning. The learning process conforms to the following pattern: external sensations stimulate the sense organs-ears, eyes, body (touch), nose and tongue-and the nervous system conveys impressions to the relevant sections of the brain. The brain then transmits impulses to the muscles and organs of movement and speech, and the end result is a reaction.

Creating an impression

Receiving an impression is the first step in learning. Therefore, the trainer must ensure that the trainee receives strong impressions. The strength of the impression will depend on:

- The number of senses involved
- The vividness of the impression
- Whether the impression registers

Observing the learners

The only way the trainer can know if people have learned the material is by observing their behaviour:

- Their actions

- Their written impressions
- Their speech

Factors That Hinder Learning

- The learning plateau: at intervals the rate of learning flattens out as the brain rests
- Saturation: if the message is overloaded the receiver rejects the excess and learning stops
- Fatigue: a tired receiver is not as receptive as an alert one
- Inability to concentrate: the longer the message, the more concentration decreases from beginning to end

Obtaining and Holding the Learners' Attention

Before people can learn any material they must focus their voluntary attention on it. The desire to learn comes from within; it is spontaneous.

The good trainer tries to gain and maintain voluntary attention in every session he or she presents.

- Relate what you aim to teach to those subjects in which you know the trainees are interested.
- Introduce the session in such a way that the trainees will not only see and become interested in this relationship, but will want to learn more about it.
- Begin with a good story to which the trainees can relate. An effective trainer makes it his or her business to know the background of the trainees.
- Having done these things, maintain the trainees' attention by doing all that is possible to facilitate their understanding and absorption of the material.
- Ensure that the trainee's learning is an active process in which the trainer and trainees are equal partners in terms of participation.

Facilitating Understanding

To facilitate understanding, the trainer proceeds from:

- Known to unknown
- Simple to complex
- Whole to part and back to whole
- Concrete to abstract
- Particular to general
- Observations to reasoning
- Point to point in logical order

To facilitate absorption, remember that trainees learn only by impressions received through their senses.

Steps in Skill Training

Having learned a skill, trainees must reinforce its acquisition by using it.

Learning by doing is the basic principle underlying the acquisition of any skill.

When teaching skills, the trainer most often achieves the best results by keeping the talk short and by working through a set sequence of discrete steps, as follows:

- Show the trainees the actual skill they are to acquire.
- Demonstrate and explain, step by step, the operations involved (this requires an analysis of the total procedure by the trainer).
- Have trainees imitate the necessary actions.
- Have trainees practise performing the operations.
- Devote at least 50 percent of the session to trainee practice time.

Summary

The first rules of training are:

- Make the best use of the most effective channels to the brain-the senses: sight, hearing, touch, taste and smell.
- Use a combination of the senses. For knowledge, use the trainees' eyes and ears. For manual skills, use the trainees' hands, eyes and ears.
- Make presentations as vivid as possible.

These are the basic principles of instruction-the means by which the instructor reaches and makes an impression on the brains of the trainees.

4

The Power of Visual Communication

What we see has a profound effect on what we do, how we feel, and who we are. Through experience and experimentation, we continually increase our understanding of the visual world and how we are influenced by it. Psychologist Albert Mehrabian demonstrated that 93% of communication is nonverbal. Research at 3M Corporation concluded that we process visuals 60,000 times faster than text. Further studies find that the human brain deciphers image elements simultaneously, while language is decoded in a linear, sequential manner taking more time to process. Relatively speaking, in terms of communication, textual ubiquity is brand new. Thanks to millions of years of evolution, we are genetically wired to respond differently to visuals than text. For example, humans have an innate fondness for images of wide, open landscapes, which evoke an instant sense of well-being and contentment. Psychologists hypothesize that this almost universal response stems from the years our ancestors spent on the savannas in Africa.

People think using pictures. John Berger, media theorist, writes in his book *Ways of Seeing*, "Seeing comes before words. The child looks and recognizes before it can speak." Dr. Lynell Burmark, Ph.D. Associate at the Thornburg Centre for Professional Development and writer of several books and papers on visual literacy, said, "...unless our words, concepts, ideas are hooked onto an image, they will go in one ear, sail through the brain, and go out the other ear. Words are processed by our short-term memory where we can only retain about 7 bits of information (plus or minus 2). This is why, by the way, that we have 7-digit phone numbers. Images, on the other hand, go directly into long-term memory where they are indelibly etched." Therefore, it is not surprising that it is much easier to show a circle than describe it. When it comes to quick, clear communication, visuals trump text almost every time. Presented with the following textual and visual information, would you pet this dog?

The very same visual elements that we are indelibly drawn to and so quickly absorb not only communicate data more efficiently and effectively but also affect us emotionally. For instance, research shows that exposure to the colour red can heighten our pulse and breathing rates. What is your reaction to the following picture?

How do you feel when you look at this picture? How quickly did you feel that way? Can you see how this image could be used to quickly elicit a strong emotional response and influence the viewer? If I were to textually describe this picture, your emotional reaction would not be as strong and it would take more time to digest the information. J. Francis Davis, an adult educator and media education specialist, captured it well when he said, "...in our culture pictures have become tools used to elicit specific and planned emotional reactions in the people who see them." Visuals are not only excellent communicators but also quickly affect us psychologically and physiologically. Don Norman, author of *Emotional Design*, said in a *Discover* magazine article, "Beauty and the Beastly PC: The Graphics on Your Computer Screen Can Affect the Way You Feel—and Think," "I started out as an engineer, and I thought that what was really important was that something worked. Appearance—how could that matter? And yet for some reason, I would still buy attractive things, even if they didn't work as well as the less attractive ones. This puzzled me. In the last two years, I've finally come to understand that it's a result of the extremely tight coupling between emotion and cognition. Emotion is about judging the world, and cognition is about understanding. They can't be separated."

How many times have you heard, "I didn't believe it until I saw it." Studies show that the old saying "seeing is believing" is mostly true. Of course, we know that what we see can be manipulated but the point is that visuals are persuasive. The Stanford Persuasive Technology Lab asked 2,440 participants how they evaluated the credibility of Web sites they were shown. Almost half (46.1%) said that the Web site's design look was the number one criterion for discerning the credibility of the presented material. The following are some of the captured participant comments:

"This site is more credible. I find it to be much more professional looking."-M, 38, Washington

"More pleasing graphics, higher-quality look and feel..."-F, 52, Tennessee

"Just looks more credible."-M, 24, New Jersey

"I know this is superficial, but the first thing that struck me is the colour difference. The... site is a soothing green (sort of like money) while the [other] site is a jarring purple."-M, 56, Virginia

The ability of visual stimuli to communicate and influence is undeniable and inescapable. Through evolution, human beings are compelled to view and disseminate visuals. Recognizing the importance of visual communication is key to your success. Allen Ginsberg, poet and author, stated, "Whoever controls the media—the images—controls the culture." As early as the late nineteenth century, advertisers, based on their collective experience, were convinced that illustrations sold goods. World War II propaganda posters were very effective at manipulating popular opinion.

The Sunday *New York Times* published, "Good as a Gun: When Cameras Define a War," an article that effectively dealt with how the images photojournalists capture have influenced world affairs. Despite the best efforts of politicians, commanders, generals, and others involved with the war efforts, it was imagery that became the catalyst for some of the most pronounced changes. Reading or hearing about a situation is very different from seeing it. In 1986, a 3M-sponsored study at the University of Minnesota School of Management found that presenters who use visual aids are 43% more effective in persuading audience members to take a desired course of action than presenters who don't use visuals. The goal of the experiment was to persuade undergraduates to commit their time and money to attending time management seminars. Presenters of various skill levels participated. Researchers found that average presenters who used visual aids were as effective as more advanced presenters using no visuals. In addition, the study found that the audience expected the advanced presenters to include professional, quality visuals. What about you? Have you noticed the increase in visual aids during presentations? Do you prefer presentations with or without visuals?

Human communication has existed for about 30,000 years. In the beginning of recorded history, the vast majority of what we communicated was not text based. Textual communication has been with us in one form or another for only 3,700 years. With the invention of tools like Gutenberg's movable type printing press in 1450, text took centre stage. Graphics were too costly to include. As printing costs dropped graphics soon resurfaced and their frequency is rising.

In 1995, Charles Brumback, the chairman of the Newspaper Association of America, said, "as newspaper penetration falls... the culture itself moves from textual to visual literacy." Gunther Kress is a Professor of English and Education at the School of Education, University of London. His research confirms this change over. As an example, Kress compares science textbooks from 1936 and 1988 showing that textbooks have progressed from a majority of text to a majority of graphics.

The change isn't limited to textbooks and newspapers. Signs, maps, instructions, schematics, icons, symbols, and packaging sell products, warn of possible hazards, and give visual direction when words alone are not sufficient. Graphics are found on Web sites, TV shows, appliances, and computers; in vehicles and books; and at museums, malls, restaurants, and grocery stores. More and more professions that rely heavily on communication and persuasion are embracing graphics as a tool of choice.

In the *Boston Globe* article, "Courtroom Graphics Come of Cyber-Age," author Sacha Pfeiffer found that "... new technologies—and a new willingness in legal circles to embrace them—have taken the use of visual images in the courtroom to a level unimaginable even a decade ago... The result is a slow but significant shift in the way many trial lawyers, who historically have relied largely on their verbal skills to sway juries, try cases... More prosecutors see high-tech graphics not as a luxury, but as a necessity." Graphic communication is more ubiquitous than ever before. Why? Because graphics do what text alone cannot do. They quickly affect us both cognitively and emotionally:

1) *Cognitively*: Graphics expedite and increase our level of communication. They increase comprehension, recollection, and retention. Visual clues help us decode text and attract attention to information or direct attention increasing the likelihood that the audience will remember.
2) *Emotionally*: Pictures enhance or affect emotions and attitudes. Graphics engage our imagination and heighten our creative thinking by stimulating other areas of our brain (which in turn leads to a more profound and accurate understanding of the presented material). It is no secret that emotions influence decision-making:
"(Emotions) play an essential role in decision making, perception, learning, and more... they influence the very mechanisms of rational thinking."

Behavioural Psychologists agree that most of our decisions are based on intuitive judgment and emotions. Herbert A. Simon, Nobel Prize winning scholar at the Carnegie Mellon Institute in Pittsburgh, studied corporate decision-making and found that people often ignored formal decision-making models because of time constraints, incomplete information, the inability to calculate consequences, and other variables. Intuitive judgment was the process for most decisions. Neurologist Antonio Damasio studied research on patients with damaged ventromedial frontal cortices of the brain, which impaired their ability to feel but left their ability to think analytically intact. Damasio discovered that the patients were unable to make rational decisions even though their ability to reason was fully functional. He concluded that reasoning "depends, to a considerable extent, on a continual ability to experience feelings."

Psychologists Amos Twersky and Nobel Prize winner Daniel Kahnerman demonstrated that decision-making also depended on how the problems were framed or described, which results in predictable cognitive patterns and errors in judgment. Consider the following example:

> "A bat and a ball cost $1.10 in total. The bat costs $1 more than the ball. How much does the ball cost?"

The question is asked in a way that clouds the correct answer. If the question were worded as follows:

> A bat and a ball cost $1.10 in total. The bat cost $1.05. How much does the ball cost?

The answer would be obvious: 5 cents. Much as phraseology influences the response to a question, how and what you show influences the audience's response. So visuals are processed 60,000 times faster than text, graphics quickly affect our emotions, and our emotions greatly affect our decision-making. If most of our decisions are based on relatively quick intuitional judgment and emotions, then how many decisions are influenced by visually appealing, easily digested graphics? The answer is no secret to advertisers.

Billions of dollars are spent annually to find the right imagery to sell a product, service, or idea. The United States Military spent $598 million in 2003 on advertising to increase "brand identity" and meet their annual recruitment goals. Nike spent $269 million in 2001 on its image to sell their products. Anheuser-Busch spent $440 million to promote its products in 2001. Pepsi budgeted over $1 billion in 2001 on its image. Not to be out done, Coca-Cola budgeted $1.4 billion for its image in the same year. Graphics help create "brand identity." Visuals paint the picture of who the advertiser is, what they stand for, and how the audience may benefit. Graphics sell because of their ability to influence. How you use graphics greatly affect how you and your business are perceived.

Study after study, experiment after experiment has proven that graphics have immense influence over the audience's perception of the subject matter and, by association, the presenter (the person, place, or thing most associated with the graphic) because of these neurological and evolutionary factors. The audience's understanding of the presented material, opinion of the presented material and the presenter, and their emotional state are crucial factors in any decision they will make. Without a doubt, graphics greatly influence an audience's decisions. Whoever properly wields this intelligence has a powerful advantage over their competition.

Larry Tracy, who now trains corporate executives to make oral presentations for government contracts, headed the Pentagon's top briefing team and worked for years with the Department of State. He was aware that graphics were so influential in the government's decision to purchase goods and services that bad buying decisions were made based on the quality of the visuals in the presented materials. This has in turn led to the government, at times, putting constraints on presented graphics by requiring black and white submissions, or even requiring that no graphics be used in a presentation in order to reduce the likelihood of high-quality, polished graphics unfairly persuading evaluators.

I spent many years analyzing how the proposal industry works (an industry that focuses on the submission of written and oral presentations to secure work that will increase or maintain a company's revenue). I found that the priority of graphic development increases as award value rises. The industry understands the influence that graphics have on their audience. It is common knowledge to companies like Northrop Grumman, Raytheon, Boeing, and Lockheed Martin that graphics are an essential part of winning new government business. In fact, it is not uncommon, when exceptional graphics are used, for government evaluators to commend the presenter on their use of graphics.

Flags, eagles, and other symbols of patriotism are often included on proposal covers simply because of the positive emotional influence patriotic imagery has on government evaluators. Part of the cover's goal is to instantly establish that the presenter is a supportive, trustworthy, reliable patriot. As a result, the government evaluator is more likely to be in a positive, agreeable state of mind when reading the proposal. As stated earlier, emotions influence the very mechanisms of rational thinking, so if the evaluator's mood is elevated by the visuals, the more likely he or she is to agree with the presenter.

I am not saying that graphic communication is better than text. The combination of graphics and words has a communicative power that neither singularly possesses.

"Pictures interact with text to produce levels of comprehension and memory that can exceed what is produced by text alone."

Without graphics, an idea may be lost in a sea of words. Without words, a graphic may be lost to ambiguity. Robert E. Horn, an award-winning scholar at Stanford University's Centre for the Study of Language and Information, said, "When words and visual elements are closely entwined, we create something new and we augment our communal intelligence... visual language has the potential for increasing 'human bandwidth'—the capacity to take in, comprehend, and more efficiently synthesize large amounts of new information."

Virtual Telecommunications Access Method

Virtual Telecommunications Access Method (VTAM) is IBM's software package that provides communications via telecommunication devices for mainframe environments. It is the implementation of Systems Network Architecture (SNA) for mainframes. VTAM provides an API for communications applications, and controls communications equipment such as communications adapters and communications controllers. In modern terminology, VTAM provides a communications stack and device drivers.

VTAM supports several network protocols, including SDLC and Token Ring.

VTAM has been renamed to be the SNA Services feature of *Communications Server for OS/390*. This software package also provides TCP/IP functions.

In a VTAM environment, the actual network communication took place either by a communications adapter in the mainframe it self, or (for the larger mainframes), by a separate front-end processor, the IBM 3745/3746 Communications Processor, with its own operating system, the Network Control Program NCP. These machines, usually costing several hundred thousand dollars, are now obsolete and are no longer actively marketed by IBM, but support continues. IBM provides hardware maintenance and microcode updates for the estimated 20,000 installed 3745/3746 controllers. A robust third party industry of smaller 3745/3746 specialty companies provide such controllers, upgrades, features and related support services. VTAM and SNA are still in use by many enterprises. The VTAM subsystem is controlled via commands issued through the system console (or in exceptional cases through special control cards in the JES).

Initially, VTAM only allowed communication between mainframes and peripheral equipment, such as terminals, distributed processors and minicomputers. Later, "cross-domain" services were introduced (not to be confused with TCP/IP domains!) allowing SNA network with more than one mainframe. A subsequent development was SNA Network Interconnect, allowing networks of different organisational entities (firms) to be interconnected with a high degree of independence. Finally, Advanced Peer to Peer Networking functions were added to VTAM. In APPN the mainframe is no longer the heart of the network, but all nodes in the network are considered as peers. One of the reasons why APPN was introduced was to act as a DECnet-killer, but by the time APPN was actually shipped the popularity of DECnet had already declined. APPN was a very complicated way to introduce simplicity, and as such it did not survive the rise of TCP/IP and internet in the early 1990s.

The name "VTAM" can be explained as follows: VTAM is an access method, the name used in mainframe operating systems for software allowing application programs to read and write data to and from external devices, and it is called "virtual" because it was introduced at the time that IBM was introducing virtual storage, by upgrading the operating systems of the System/360 series to virtual storage versions. VTAM was supposed to be the successor for various older telecommunications access methods, notably BTAM and TCAM (that were maintained for compatibility reasons). As such, VTAM is comparable with VSAM, at the time a new and supposedly converged access method for disk storage.

When it was introduced, VTAM was provided free of charge, just as all systems software at the time. Later, VTAM became the first piece of systems software that was provided for a licence fee. Then it was renamed to ACF/VTAM (where ACF stands for Advanced Communication Function). Contrary to the popular belief, IBM did not stop providing free systems software because of antitrust reasons, but because non-IBM plug-compatible mainframe processors emerged at the time. Of course, there is no point for a commercial company in providing free software to be used for competitive equipment. In later years, ACF/VTAM licences became very expensive, in the $10000 bracket per month, but later the price was reduced again because mainframe cost of ownership became incompetitive due to software pricing.

The Various Forms of Communication

Forms of Communication

There are several forms of communication. These forms of communication fall under the umbrellas of communication that is symbolic, written, verbal, and of the body. In addition, there are digital and/or electronic forms of communication. Although these latter forms of communication are efficient, we must be mindful of the human element of face to face live communication that we require as human beings, and that a steady diet of digital and electronic communication can have a tendency to alienate us from one another.

Symbolic and Written Forms of Communication

Symbolic and written communication enabled humankind to communicate and record history that took place many years ago; in fact, it is believed that some of the symbols scribed on the inside of caves were made from early humans that dated as far back as one million years BC.

Some of the oldest forms of communication were symbolic in nature; for example, the Ancient Egyptians developed an alphabet with symbols that represented each letter in their alphabet, and they would put words together that formed sentences through clustering them vertically. Early native peoples did much the same thing through using physical symbols through the medium of smoke signals to warn their people of danger or to signal an attack to begin battle. As the human race has evolved globally, our form of written communication has become what it is today: more sophisticated with grammar and vocabulary.

Verbal Communication

Verbal communication is also one of the oldest forms of communication and it too dates back to the times of early humans where sounds such as grunts, groans, and other guttural sounds, at different volumes or inflections, indicated friendly communication or a threat or warning to stay away from food or belongings. As is the case with the development of writing, our verbal communication has progressed and has become as we know it today.

Body Language

Another form of communication that is neither verbal nor written is body language. Reading a persons body language can indicate if they are upset, nervous, stressed out, or angry. On the other hand, body language can also show if a person is relaxed, tired, happy or sad. Body language is a very effective form of communication that is used by children and adults, but it is also used by domestic or wild animals; for example, you can tell just as easily if a saber-toothed tiger is about to attack or when your pet cat wants a back rub, yet both of these forms of communication through body language are at opposite ends of the spectrum.

Digital or Electronic Forms of Communication

Our world has progressed quickly over the years with the inception of digital and electronic forms of communication. From that fateful day Alexander Graham Bell invented the telephone to the present, humankind has swiftly moved forward in its digital or electronic communication. Instruments and tools such as computers, e-mail, faxes, radio, satellite television, the telephone, and the cellular phone have aided humankind in its quest to communicate efficiently. Unfortunately, it has also increased the workload experienced by people around the world.

Conclusion

Communication is such an important and large part of our lives that encompasses each moment of our existence. The latest innovations in technological communication (digital and/or electronic) are wonderful tools and resources that can enhance our lives through the convenience of communication that is fast and efficient. Nonetheless, we need to be conscious of the fact that we are human beings with emotions, feelings and thoughts, unlike the digital electronic tools that enable us to communicate with anyone anywhere around the world within seconds. Thus, the best form of communication, due to our human nature, is face to face live verbal communication where we are able receive the person, come to know them in their entirety, and have the benefit of more accurate perceptions that can easily be misconstrued via e-mail or another of the many digital or electronic technologies. Indeed, technology is a wonderful tool, but it is not an end to our means. As mentioned previously in my Blog, I believe in using technology in a practical manner. When we communicate in any way other than face to face (live) we lose that part of the humanness that makes us unique and special to each other. We must never forget our roots of communication and not allow digital or electronic forms of communication to alienate us from each other. I realize that when we desire to communicate with someone that is up north, in another province, or half way around the world, the most practical means of communication is digitally or electronically. As I have mentioned before, the more practically we use technology, the better technology will serve us and our planet.

Visual Communication Across Cultures

The purpose of this paper.

By analysing the forms (*visual syntax*) that the advertisements take: the semiotic structure of the images, with less emphasis on their content (*visual lexis*), it is possible to find systematic differences that relate to the specific locations of the advertisements in a given social cultural context.

We hope that by doing this, it becomes clear how visual representations are dependent on a specific culture and that intercultural communication can be deeply conditioned by the degree of understanding of visual semiotics as a cultural code.

Theoretical framework and descriptive categories for the discussion of data

We will discuss my data with reference to Halliday's (1978, 1985) notion of three metafunctions in human communication, which are later applied by Kress and van Leeuwen (1990, 1996) for the analysis of visual images. They are (quote from Kress and van Leeuwen 1996):

1) The Ideational metafunction the ability of semiotic systems to represent objects and their relations in a world outside the representational system or in the semiotic system of culture (Ibid:45).
2) The Interpersonal metafunction the ability of semiotic system to project the relations between the producer of that sign or complex sign, and the receiver/reproducer of that sign, that is to project a particular social relation between the producer, the viewer and the object represented (Ibid:41).
3) The Textual metafunction the ability of the semiotic system to form texts, where complexes of signs cohere both internally and with the context in and for which they were produced and different Compositional arrangements which allow the realization of different textual meanings (Ibid:41).

Descriptive Categories: As one realisation of the Ideational metafunction, I will draw attention to the directionality that visual images create or embody within them: what I call *visual directionality*.

With respect to the Textual metafunction, I will examine the way in which visual space is used in terms of distribution of meaning. In other words, I will focus on what visual elements appear in what part of visual space with what kind of meaning.

In this paper, I will deal with one type of textual composition: Left/Right. This category will be used to explore value distribution in each spatial domain: which represented participant with what kind of meaning appears in which part of visual space in advertising texts. With its starting point in the framework by Kress and van Leeuwen (1996), which deals exclusively with Western visual representations, I will examine how far their framework can be applied and consider the cultural specificness of the distribution of values in spatial dimensions.

The textual composition of Left and Right will be considered, first of all, based on the proposition in Kress and van Leeuwen (1996), in relation to the structure of information value in English speech, 'Given' and 'New'. 'Given', in English speech, marks a point of departure of certain propositions, which is followed by 'New' information, which forms the nucleus part of the message. 'Given' is something already known and 'New' is something to be found out, something 'at issue'. Kress and van Leeuwen propose that, according to Western visual semiotic, the meaning of 'Given' and 'New' are distributed in the visual domain of Left and Right, respectively.

The system of Contact

It is possible for represented participants to involve the viewer in a certain (imaginary) *action:* This is termed as an "image act" (Kress and van Leeuwen 1996). An Image act can be realised by a certain action, with which a represented participant is depicted. For example, an image of a woman who is holding a glass of wine towards the viewer, smiling, can be said to engage in an image act, in that she is represented to be inviting the viewer to take part in the action: accepting the glass of wine. As one of the formal categories which provides the medium through which represented participants can interact with the viewer, there is eye contact between the two parties. This is *Contact.*

Contact has two kinds of realisations: *Demand* and *Offer*. The former interactive meaning is realised when a represented participant has eye contact with the viewer; such as a represented participant looking at or smiling at the viewer.

The latter type of interaction is realised when a represented participant has no direct eye contact with the viewer and the represented participant presents him/her/itself to be 'looked at' by the viewer, that is, "it 'offers' the represented participants to the viewer as items of information, objects of contemplation, impersonally, as though they were specimens in a display case".

The System of Social Distance

The 'distance' between represented participants and the viewer also indicates the relationship between them. This forms the system of *Social Distance*: *Intimate/Personal*, *Social* and *Impersonal*. Represented participants who/which are depicted with *Personal* distance can allow the viewer to be posirioned relatively closer to them, than the ones with *Social* distance. Hall (1964) calls them "Silent assumptions in social communication" in Disorders of communication 42:41-55:

Intimate distance	the head and face only
Close personal distance	the head and shoulders
Far personal distance	from the waist up
Close social distance	the whole figure
Far social distance	the whole figure with space around it
Public distance	the torso of at least four or five people

The manipulation of *Social Distance* is a realisation of the Interpersonal relationship between the represented participants and the 'world' they represent and the viewer. In this way, the distance of depicted participants from the viewer is one of the materialisations (material realisations) of social interaction in a given context.

The System of Attitude

Apart from *Contact* and *Social Distance*, represented participants can be coded with another type of interactive meaning: *Attitude* of represented participants towards the viewer, or that of the given advertisement itself towards the addressee of the advertisement. What I mean by *Attitude* of represented participants includes the degree of involvement (how far a given participant is depicted to have possible involvement with the viewer and what it implies), which is realised by a *horizontal angle* and the power relationship between the participants and the viewer realised by the use of a *vertical angle* participants in the sense that it can place represented participants either 'close' or 'away' from the viewer's standpoint. But here I use the word 'attitude' in a specific meaning that implies the degree of involvement and power relationship between represented participants and the viewer.

The degree of 'involvement' can be coded by angles from which represented participants are depicted. Represented participants can be photographed either with *Frontal* angle or *Oblique* angle. If a represented participant is depicted with the former type of perspective, the viewer is given a full dimension of the participant: this participants have an interactive meaning of *involvement. Oblique* angle, on the other hand, gives a sense of *detachment* in relation to the viewer position, in that oblique perspectives of represented participants restrict what can be seen by the viewer, in comparison to what the *Frontal* angle allows.

Power relationships between represented participants and the viewer can be manifested by the manipulation of another type of angle: vertical angles. For example, if a represented participant is photographed or represented from a high angle, this would allow the viewer of the text to 'look down on' them. If they are taken from a low angle, by contrast, the viewer is positioned where it looks as though represented participants are looking down on the viewer. To use Kress and van Leeuwen's terms, the former realises *Viewer power* and the latter manifests *Representation power*, between the two of which is *Equal power*.

'Visual directionality', 'Use of space' and 'Social interactions' thus work as descriptive categories that allows documentation of given texts from the perspectives of three metafunctions of communication. In this paper, more notably, these three aspects are going to be dealt with from a cross-cultural perspective. That is, to compare the way in which Japanese and British visual representations realise these metafunctions through formal categories of 'Visual directionality', 'Use of space' and 'Social interactions'.

Writing Systems

Language, when it is *written*, as opposed to when it is spoken, is realised as a physical and graphic substance in a given space. In this sense, language can be treated as a *visual entity*. Thus when one looks at an advertisement which consists of both visual images and verbal captions, both elements (regardless of the type of medium: visual or verbal) come into the viewer's eye as a visual entity, as a block of visual material and a block of language as text. The visual, whether as image or as a block of language has semantic impact at that initial level: the viewer goes on to read the visual and recognise the linguistic meaning of the verbal captions. At the next level of analysis, the visual and the verbal are each treated in terms of their own 'semantics', the semantics of the visual as image and semantics of the verbal as linguistic message.

The historical complexity of the Japanese system of writing makes it necessary to discuss it in relation to the Ideational, the Textual nd the Interpersonal metafunction. I focus on two aspects in relation to the Japanese system of writing: that of choices in *writing directions* and that of *writing units*.

First, the range of writing directions available in Japanese are these: whereas English has a single way of writing: in rows; and from left to right, horizontally, with the rows ordered from top to bottom, using the letters of the Roman alphabets. Japanese has two choices of writing direction : *horizontally* in rows and *vertically* in columns. I call the former type *horizontal writing* and the latter *vertical writing*.

The horizontal writing proceeds in rows and from left to right as English, which creates the visual directionality of left to right. Vertical writing is written from top to bottom and each column proceeds from right to left. Horizontal writing creates the visual directionality of left to right (as an individual row), which guides the viewer's reading direction from top to bottom as a sequence of rows. Vertical writing creates the visual directionality of top to bottom (as an individual column), and also produces the viewer's reading direction from right to left as a sequence of columns. In Japanese writing, horizontal and vertical writing forms can be juxtaposed within a single text. The use of multiple writing directions gives a text multiple visual directionality at the level of scriptorial directionality.

Vertical writing is the older form of writing in Japanese, and consequently, can embody a sense of 'traditionality'. It can be used therefore as a signifier to imply Japanese 'authenticity' or 'indigenity" as opposed to that suggested by the horizontal way of writing, which suggests a western influence in the modern history of Japan: a sense of 'Westerness' that is at the same time that of 'modernity'. This type of writing is preferred among post-war generations, who are more strongly influenced by western cultures than older generations (Haarmann:1986). The choice of writing direction serves three metafunctions: the Ideational, the Textual and the Interpersonal. For example, the writing direction may suggest a dynamic vectorial process, which is the Ideational metafunction. The choice between vertical and horizontal writing also realises a sense of 'traditionality' or 'modernity' and 'Westernisation', which is related to the Interpersonal metafunction. The particular choice of writing direction can guide a viewer's readings of the directionality of a page as a whole, or direct reading in certain ways: this serves the Textual metafunction.

Second, the Japanese system has a choice of several types of *writing units*: the Interpersonal metafunction. Japanese writing makes use of characters (*kanji*) and two kinds of syllabaries called *kana: hiragana* and *katakana*. Each of the *kana* consists of fifty-four letters. Two types of *kanas* serve distinctive purposes: *hiragana*, which makes use of round, curved lines in its shapes, serves grammatical purposes in sentences: it is used for items such as articles and auxiliaries. *Katakana*, on the other hand, is characterised by its angular shapes; it is often used to write foreign words. This characteristic of the Japanese writing system allows a number of choices for linguistic representation, in terms of 'channels of realisation'. For example, it is possible to write a sentence using either *hiragana* or *katakana* alone or as a combination of two of them (*hiragana* and *katakana*) together with *kanji* (Chinese characters), depending on the type of writing.

The relative proportion of *kanji* used within a piece of writing (either at the sentence level or passage level) is one of the factors that realises the degree of formality. Formal writing has a higher proportion of *kanji*. The use of *kanji* is therefore closely related to the genre of writing. Legal documents, for instance, have a higher proportion of *kanji* than other types of writing, such as personal letters and children's writing.

Children start learning to write using only *hiragana* and *katakana*, and the more advanced the level of writing, the greater proportion of *kanjis* he or she can mix with these *kanas*. In the usual writing of Japanese adults, both *kanji* and *kana* are mixed. If the writing consists only of *kana*, it gives the text a sense of 'unaccomplished' or 'childish' writing, in comparison with standard, 'accepted', or 'adult-like' writing style.

The physical appearance of these three writing systems has significant implications in terms of the Interpersonal metafunction of visual semiosis. Compared with *kana*, *kanji* has a higher density of visual elements on the page. Consequently, writing with a higher proportion of *kanji* is *visually* more dense than texts with a lower proportion of *kanji*. Given that the use of *kanji* is one marker of formality, the visual density created by the choice of writing systems is another semiotic feature contributing to the degree of formality. This, again leads to one aspect of realization of textual genre. Writing with a higher visual density means for users of the Japanese language, a high degree of formality, which serves the Interpersonal metafunction. Therefore, in Japanese, the degree of formality in writing can be manifested 'visually' by the choice and combination of these three writing methods.

Textual Analysis and Discussion

Visual directionality (The Ideational metafunction)

The isotype is a system established by the Viennese philosopher and social scientist Otto von Neurath (1937, 1948). It is a system where modified and simplified visual images are used to convey information to the general public. Von Neurath believed this system to be universally communicative, as opposed to the opacity of verbal language, which he viewed as "a disfiguring medium for knowledge" in that "its structure and vocabulary fail to be a consistent, logical model of objects and relations in the physical world".

In order to "provide a universal bridge between language and nature", the isotype has to be reduced to an abstract representation, while sustaining the 'vocabulary', which is done at the cost of weakening the relationship between the image and the actual object. Another aspect of the isotype that makes it "universally acceptable" is as Lupton states, its *consistency*. The isotype can visualise the same concept across cultures. For example, to realise the concept 'exit', it is possible to use similar visual images regardless of the context in which they are used. The question arises here: can isotype representation be completely culturally neutral?

The Japanese and British isotypes, which indicate the presence of an exit. Both of them realise the same meaning (*"exit this way"*), but they are realised with different visual directionality. If, as von Neurath suggested, the isotype provides universality in the manifestation of visual information, the question arises regarding this difference in visual directionality: how can this difference in visual directionality be explained?

It is this feature which makes the isotype a useful starting point. As a sign, it is meant to be universal, yet its spatial orientation differs in the two cultures. My hypothesis is that the lexical aspects (the lexical content) are independently variable in relation to spatial orientation, and that the latter realises deep cultural configurations of the visual semiotic. Spatial orientation, right to left, or left to right, creates, implicitly, an indication of directionality.

The human represented participants, in the middle band of the text, are depicted as though they were rushing towards the left. This creates the pictorial visual directionality of right to left. The possible implication of this directionality is that people (the human represented participants) are hurrying, running to something worthwhile, which is expected to be somewhere to the left. 'Something worthwhile' might be the opening of this department store, and this is why these people are in a hurry.

Keikyu Department Store advertisement

This is an advertisement from *Sumitomo Bank*, for its instant loan service. There is a cartoon image of a black bear, which is walking towards the left, creating the visual directionality of right to left. Next to the cartoon bear is a verbal caption, which says, "Sumitomo card is always on my side and that's definitely something that I can rely on".

The cartoon bear is represented to be doing the *right* ('sensible') action; now that the cartoon bear has this card, the message is that, he is heading in the 'right', 'forward', or 'positive' direction, in the sense that he can rely on this loan service, even in an emergency. It can be argued therefore that the visual directionality of right to left (which is realised by the image of cartoon character) manifests 'positive' values in the context of this Japanese advertisement.

Sumitomo Bank advertisement

They makes use of visual directionality with a 'negative' or 'backward' implication, in order to make the 'positive' and 'forward' direction stand out. In other words, these advertisements attempt to make a selling point from giving represented participants the visual directionality with 'negative' implications.

Evening Standard advertisement

This is a symbolic representation of a boss and his subordinate at work, where the latter is pushed around by the former; a work environment which is far from satisfactory on the part of the subordinate. The man, who is behind the boss, realises the visual directionality of right to left.

That this is a depiction of an unwanted situation, or that this is not how it ought to be, is being formally shown by this directionality of right to left (realised by 'the man in trouble') as something 'negative'. In other words, in the context of British advertisements, an unwanted and negative sense is realised by the visual directionality of right to left. This 'negative' visual directionality of right to left is based on the 'forward' and 'positive' directionality of left to right.

A similar message in terms of the implication of visual directionality is conveyed in the other example, Plate 6. This is an image of a boy on a skateboard, facing towards the left. In fact, the verbal copy reinforces this point: *"Are you going in the right direction?"*, making an explicit point that the boy is *not* going in the right direction. Here as with Plate 5, a sense of 'negativeness' is visually expressed by the use of the visual directionality of right to left.

In this way, the visual representation of visual directionality which is read as 'negative' in Plate 5 and 6 sheds light on what is 'forward' and 'positive' directionality in the context of British advertisements. The visual directionality of right to left, which implies a negative sense in the context of British advertisements, would have realised a different meaning in the context of Japanese advertisements: where the visual directionality of right to left manifests a sense of 'positiveness', in Japan both participants (a man trailing behind an elephant as his boss, a boy on the skateboard) are *already* in the *right* direction. Both Plate 5 and Plate 6 prove that visual directionality is not merely a formal property, which is given to represented participants, but realises the core meaning of the advertising message.

Visual mode Writing Visual mode Writing

Given that each culture has a specific underlying spatial semiotic system, it follows that the difference in visual directionality between Japanese and British examples is not merely a formal distinction. Formal structure, like visual directionality, can itself manifest cultural implications. The differences in visual directionality are culturally *motivated.* In other words, visual directionality embodies the cultural metaphor of direction.

Use of Space (The Textual metafunction)

First of all, We will focus on the way in which the Left/Right part of textual space realises meaning. We will begin with a set of Japanese and British advertisements. The main copy reads, *"Ours is just different. You can rely on Svenson even on holiday"*. There are two photographs above the lead copy, both of which show a family of three (who appear to be on holiday; there is a suitcase, on which a little girl is sitting and the man is carrying a travel bag on his shoulder). These two photographs indicate the difference in the man's hair: in the left photograph, the man is represented as having hair, while the other photograph on the right shows him bald.

Summary

In terms of information value of Given and New, the Japanese text realises Given in the right and New in the left, while the British text manifests Given in the left and New in the right. Given in both texts suggests a *status quo,* the situation that is 'already there' or the point of departure, which leads to the New, something that is newly gained, or something that is worth paying attention to. A framework (distribution of values in visual domain) proposed by Kress and van Leeuwen (1996) can be applied to the British example, but not to the Japanese one. My assumption here is that Japanese visual representations tend to allow the realization of Given in the right and New in the left, which is different from that of British visual representations.

Social Interactions (The Interpersonal metafunction)

This section will focus on the way in which visual representations manifest the relationship between represented participants and the viewer; 'social interactions' between them. The examples of Western visual representations from school textbooks, a poster and paintings as well as advertisements, to which they apply the system of *Contact, Social Distance* and *Attitude* and through which they consider the notion of *modality:* they are concerned with the way in which visual syntax (or formal structures) construct the relationship between represented participants and the viewer, and the 'world' of visual representations in relation to the viewer in everyday life.

Given that, the present section will compare Interpersonal meaning making between Japanese and British advertising texts. It can be assumed, from what has been discussed in section 4.2, that advertising texts from the two different cultures manifest Interpersonal functions in different ways. We will draw attention to how the systems of *Contact, Social Distance* and *Attitude* are realised in the sample given texts, and what the systematic differences, if any, can suggest or reveal about underlying Japanese and British semiotic systems.

I will use two sets of Japanese and British examples, which are campaigns for the same products, which cross the cultural boundaries of Japan and Britain. The first set of examples is an advertisement for hair care products, called *Organics* and the second set of examples is taken from a Japanese and British campaign for the *De Beers Diamond Ring*. On a general level, in both cases, there is a similarity in the style of advertisements, in the sense that both Japanese and British examples use the same type of represented participants and in a similar layout. However, I would like to explore whether there is any cultural specificness in the way these represented participants are engaged in meaning making in the Interpersonal dimension. We will start with the analysis of human represented participants in the texts; and follow this with a discussion around the representation of non-human represented participants.

The system of Contact

This Japanese model therefore interacts with the viewer with a formal marker of *Offer,* which is accompanied by the lexis 'smiling'. On the other hand, is represented with *Demand Contact* in that she has direct eye contact with the viewer; more precisely, the interactive meaning is created which consists of a formal realisation of *Demand Contact* and a lexical feature 'smiling'. Although both are smiling, the degree of the smile is different between the two examples: the Japanese model is more 'subtly' smiling than the British model, who presents an 'explicit' or 'wide' smile.

The use of *Offer* in the Japanese examples might be read as a manifestation of what Japanese women are 'expected to be like' in Japanese society, that is, they are something that is passive and to be 'looked at', or 'visually appreciated'. In other words, the interactive meaning *Offer Contact* can realise a culturally accepted image of women. With respect to the British examples, the *Demand Contact* in the female participants represents them as more *actively interactive* in relation to the viewer, compared to their Japanese counterparts. It might follow, therefore, that the *Demand* type of *Contact* is realising a 'culturally favoured' image of women in British society.

The system of Social Distance

We now focus on interactive meanings realised by the system of *Social Distance*. The Japanese model is photographed with a longer shot than the British model.

The former shows her body 'from upper waist up' (a mid shot), which creates *Far personal distance* and the latter is photographed in the manner that reveals the head and shoulders (a close up), which realises *Close personal distance.* In other words, the formal representation of 'a close up' functions as a signifier of 'closer' distance between the represented participant and the viewer than that of 'a mid shot'. The Japanese model in Plate 9 has a greater *Social Distance* from the viewer than the British one in Plate 10. The type of *Social Distance* the British model is engaged in locates the viewer in a closer position in relation to her, while the Japanese models are shown at a greater distance from the viewer.

The Japanese and the British participants are shown at the same distance from the viewer: only their head and shoulders are shown, which is categorised as *Close personal distance.*

This might imply therefore, these participants (both Japanese and British models) are represented as someone who is 'close to' the viewer, in other words, a sense of personal relation between the participants and the viewer is created. The representation of the participants in a relatively close proximity to the viewer can convey the message 'it could happen to you [the viewer]' or it could be you'.

Just as the choice of *Contact* can represent the cultural value systems of Japan and Britain, it may be argued that the system of *Social Distance* also encodes cultural specificness in value systems. Here we will particularly note the difference in the realisation of the type of *Social Distance* between the two texts, on the grounds that the difference in the choice of *Social Distance* each human participant is represented with might be interpreted in relation to accepted social distance in each culture. The Japanese participant represented with greater distance from the viewer can be a representation of the accepted social distance in Japanese culture, where people tend to maintain greater social distance to each other in public, in comparison to that in British culture.

The System of Attitude

Regarding the system of *Attitude*, the Japanese female model is photographed from a lower angle, which realises *Representation power*. The British model is photographed with *Equal power*. The former angle from which the represented participant is depicted makes them slightly 'looking down on' the viewer, in other words, the *Representation power* angle positions the viewer so as to 'look up to' the represented participants. The latter type of angle: *Equal power* locates the viewer at the same level with that of the viewer.

We would like to note, first of all, the choice of *Frontal* and *Oblique angles* from which the Japanese and the British models are photographed. The British model in Plate 12 is depicted as facing the viewer with full involvement, being 'straight on', which is created by the use of the *Frontal angle* in use. The *Oblique angle* from which the Japanese model is taken makes her appear as if she was facing the viewer at a slight angle, which can imply partial involvement, as opposed to full involvement.

We now focus on what can be derived from the choice of the system of *Attitude.* The significance of the difference between *Representation power* in the Japanese example and the choice of *Equal power* in the British example. The latter type of angle creates a sense of a closer interaction between the represented participants and the viewer, compared to the case of the Japanese example, because the representation of the British model is at equal eye level it gives a sense of greater proximity to the viewer than from the Japanese represented participants, taken from a lower angle.

Representation power in the Japanese model, by contrast, gives rise to a sense of 'remoteness' and 'aloofness' from the viewer. Also *Representation power* in this Japanese participant allows stronger control (power) as an ideal: literally someone to look up to.

The *Oblique angle* from which the Japanese model is photographed creates a sense of detachment from the viewer, in comparison to its British counterpart, where the *Frontal angle* enables the participant to be represented as a more closely interactive figure in relation to the viewer.

The difference in the formal realisation of *Attitudinal meanings* between the Japanese and the British examples may have cultural implications, which are specific to each culture. As is the case with the system of *Contact* and *Social Distance*, discussed earlier, the fact that the Japanese and the British model are represented with different meanings of *Attitude* in relation to the viewer might also represent a particular aspect of Japanese and British cultural value systems.

The fact that the Japanese models are given *Representation power* while the British models are in *Equal power* relation to the viewer suggests that the individual viewer for the Japanese examples is given less power over the represented participants compared to that of the British examples. This might imply one aspect of Japanese cultural value system where a figure of 'authority' (such as a person in an advertisement or the institution they represent) is put before individuals.

The *Oblique angle* from which the Japanese model is taken represents these participants as 'distanced' from the viewer. In other words, the formal feature (the use of *Oblique angle*) therefore serves as a signifier of the 'remoteness' of the represented participant from the viewer.

This type of interactive meaning of *Attitude* might be serving as a formal manifestation of the Japanese cultural value system, with respect to women's position in society, where women are supposed to be less forward and more subservient. With respect to the representation of the British cultural value system, a sense of closer interaction created by the choice of the *Frontal angle* with the meaning of *Involvement* can be a reflection of different values, which is related to its representation of the image of women as much more forward and closely interactive figures, in comparison to Japanese women's 'passiveness' and 'remoteness'.

Summary

In this section, We have examined two sets of advertisements in order to see how similarly and differently the Japanese and British examples manifest the Interpersonal function: the manifestation of interactive meanings between represented participants and the viewer. Both sets of advertisements are campaigns for the same product: advertisements that cross the cultural boundaries of Japan and Britain.

Across the two sets of examples, the Japanese and the British advertisements consist of similar lexical items, in terms of the type of represented participants in use.

Both the Japanese and the British texts show the image of a female participant in a similar background, together with images of the products. The Japanese and the British campaign for the *De Beers Diamond Ring* have a similar organisation of what is represented in that each has an image of a female model, who is wearing a diamond ring, placed against a plain background.

It is the level of formal or syntactical realisation that differentiates the Japanese examples and the British examples, in terms of interactive meaning making between the represented participants and the viewer. Most notably, as far as the examples I have dealt with in this section are concerned, the Japanese model and the British model are represented in a different system of interactive markers, which gives rise to different interactive meanings between them.

In the case of both, it can be pointed out that the Japanese models tend to be depicted with a sense of 'passiveness', looking away from the viewer, and the British models are, by contrast, represented as more 'active' and 'forward' figures. The choice of one interactive marker instead of another realises this tendency.

For example, the Japanese models in the *Offer Contact*, without direct eye contact with the viewer, while their British counterparts are shown with *Demand Contact*, which allows the viewer direct contact with the participant. The different choice of horizontal and vertical angles from which each participant is shot can also be attributed to different realisations of interactive meanings: the *Oblique angle* from which the photograph of the Japanese model is taken makes her appear less involved with the viewer, in comparison to its British counterpart, who is photographed with a *Frontal angle*, which suggests a fuller involvement with the viewer. While the Japanese participant is represented with *Representation power* in relation to the viewer, the British model is photographed from the eye level of the viewer (*Equal power*).

Overall, due to the choice of the interactive markers in the system of *Attitude*, the Japanese models are less interactive with the viewer than the British ones: there is a greater distance from the viewer to the Japanese participants than to the British ones.

We would now like to consider what can be drawn from these differences in the formal realisation between the Japanese and the British advertisements, when the same type of lexical items are used. It can be argued that the different choice of forms: interactive meaning markers, itself has significance in terms of the cultural values of Japan and Britain which they realise.

It may be safe to say that the representation of the Japanese and the British models suggests one aspect of what is socially and culturally accepted in terms of women's position in each society. Japan is a society where women are expected to be rather 'passive', 'subservient' and 'controlled by social frameworks', compared to the accepted values for British women, which allow them to be more 'active', 'forward' and 'individualistic'.

Conclusion

Throughout the years, humans have used many different means in order to communicate with others. Face to face speaking, letter writing, telegram, and telephone are just several examples of these different media. The latest method that has emerged, though, is computer mediated communication, or CMC. This could be carried out through e-mail, listserves, usenet groups, chat rooms, MUDs, or MOOs.

Because of all of these different modes of communication by way of computers, Steve Jobs labels them "interpersonal computers" rather than "personal computers". Clearly, there are many factors of CMC that cause it to be different from face to face (FtF) communication, and it has been debated whether or not these differences render the communication more or less personal. Some of these aspects of CMC are the absence of context cues, the recordability of conversation, the rate of exchange, the level of formality, and the anonymity of the users. The main controversy surrounding CMC is whether these differences can help to improve communication and make it more personal, or whether they serve to diminish the level of intimacy that can be achieved.

The absence of social context cues, called the Cues Filtered Out Approach, is a major distinction that separates CMC from face to face communication. Because participants cannot see others' facial expressions, gestures, voice intonations, appearance, or physical adornments; it is harder to interpret statements and responses they might make. Joseph Walther of Northwestern University explains this phenomenon by the Social Presence Theory, which contends that the personal nature of a relationship is determined by the salience of the participants. Because CMC has this lack of nonverbal elements or feedback cues, participants are less able to get to know the person with whom they are conversing, thus leading to a less personal conversation. Also, according to this theory, people pay less attention to the other participants because their interest can be absorbed elsewhere without the presence of the other person to restrain them. Even when participants do become absorbed in the conversation, they are more likely to "flame" or insult other users, to focus more on themselves, and to equalize each other's status because of the lack of cues to show them what is appropriate. This can produce a relationship in which intimacy is impeded and a basis of trust is more difficult to form, directing participants to the kind of impersonal communication that is expected of CMC. However, according to many studies, these effects of the Cues Filtered Out Approach are restricted to only the beginning period of a CMC relationship. When studies are extended to examine longer amounts of time, it has been observed that many of these impersonal aspects disappear as participants exchange a greater number of messages. It seems that CMC groups can and do develop in relationally positive directions, as long as they are allotted sufficient time to mature.

One of these elements that takes time to ripen is the receptivity and trust felt among participants, which is expressed through the vulnerability of people's revelations and their self-disclosing opinions on different issues. When people feel more trust in another person, they are more likely to reveal personal details about themselves. Another aspect of communication is the composure or relaxation of the conversant. In other words, what is the intensity of the message?

How many misspellings does he or she allow to pass by, and what is the nature of his or her punctuation and capitalization? Obviously, when the participants feel more comfortable communicating with each other, they will not be as worried about catching mistakes. This also carries over into the formality of the messages. The form of address a writer chooses, as well as the figures of speech he or she employs, are evidence of the amount of formality he or she is aiming for. Next, the dominance displayed in a message can be revealed by the proportion of communication each participant exhibits, and the depth of a conversation can be measured by the private symbols writers include or the verbal shortcuts they utilize. All of these factors can be used to determine the personal nature of communication.

When applying these guidelines, though, it is important to take into consideration the rate of information exchange that is taking place in CMC. Obviously, when more messages are sent, the personal relation will increase as participants grow more comfortable with each other and interesting topics of conversation are brought up.

In the same way, at the beginning stages of any relationship, whether it be CMC or FtF, the communication will be more formal and less personal. The theory that describes this phenomenon is called the Social Penetration Theory because as the communication spans a greater amount of time, more of a personal nature is able to penetrate to the other person. In light of the fact that CMC can become more personal over time, it is interesting to note that this type of communication might start out even more personal than face to face interaction. People are less concerned about the impression they are making because of the inherent anonymity of the medium, and they are not as worried about proper turn taking or other formalities. Therefore, in its initial stages, CMC can be more intimate that FtF communication. Computer mediated communication may even initiate relationships that might never have begun if they required a face to face meeting. For instance, it is more likely that a student would approach a professor with a question over e-mail or some other form of CMC than to call him or her on the phone or arrange an appointment.

Another reason that CMC can foster more positive communication than FtF might support is that CMC allows for selective presentation of certain features of a participant's identity. Also, depending on the form of CMC used, a writer is allowed more time to plan a response that shows off his or her better side. The anonymity encouraged by CMC can eliminate a person's anxiety over how he or she will be judged based on his or her opinions, and it leads to a medium in which people feel more free to express themselves and to stand up for their rights.

Because there are networks in many businesses over which employees can converse with one another, CMC can help to develop lateral communication among these fellow workers, also leading to a more personal type of communication. Lateral communication refers to that which takes place between employees of the same rank, rather than between boss and employee. Some studies have shown that employees are more likely to discuss different good or bad aspects of their jobs using these types of networks than they would in face to face settings because of fear that they will get caught.

However, CMC can also be portrayed as a medium which discourages this type of lateral communication. One author describes CMC as the utilitarian "panopticon." A panopticon is a device proposed by Michel Foucault for prisons in which the prisoners are unable to see or communicate with one another. In a panopticon, a super ordinate presides over the building at all times, watching to make sure that the prisoners do not find some way to communicate. With this absence of lateral support, the prisoners are helpless to ignite a revolt or uprising. This can be compared to CMC because some say that there is a super ordinate like this that can preside over computer mediated communication. The boss or manager of a company that is networked might oversee the messages that are sent among employees, thus leading to less personal exchanges. Overall, CMC can have many different effects on business related communication. One of these influences is the fact that CMC will, at first, have more of a task orientation than FtF meetings would have. Because it requires much more effort and time to socialize over CMC, participants will usually go straight to the issue. However, despite this increased task focus, group consensus on a topic is less likely to occur because there are no social cues to adhere to and strong leaders cannot take charge of the discussion quite as easily as they could with a face to face meeting. Also, since the anonymity reduces the feelings of dominance or subordinance that ordinarily govern group meetings, more people will strive to make their opinions known. The decisions that are made, then, could be more extreme and less compromising.

Since there can be so many differing interpretations of the personal nature of CMC, it seems reasonable to assume that it can be more or less personal depending on the nature of the conversation, the participant, and the length of time involved. Laid back, informal communication, such as what occurs in chat rooms, is more likely to be of a personal nature, while business oriented discussions will probably be more technical.

In the case of the characteristics of the participant, it is important to realize that each person possesses a range of different characteristics, and any one of these might become prominent, depending on the situation. For example, in face to face interaction, a shy person might become loud and flamboyant around good friends, but he or she might seem reclusive in an unfamiliar situation. In the same way, participants on different forms of CMC can exhibit a number of different characteristics at different times. This theory is known as the Self Categorization Theory because each person decides which of his or her categorizations he or she will make salient at a certain time. Because of this fact, CMC can become more or less personal depending on how the participant expresses himself or herself.

The amount of time involved in a series of CMC messages, though important, is less significant than the number and length of these messages. The rate of information exchange for computer mediated communication is inherently slower because of the need to think about and type a response. It is much easier to simply speak a message instead of typing it out, so it requires more time and messages in CMC to give and take information than it would for face to face. In conclusion, because of the various opinions on whether CMC is more or less personal than FtF communication, one must recognize that the personal or impersonal qualities of CMC are not inherent to the medium. The personality and circumstances of the users must be taken into account when discussing this issue. Also, if a person's communication styles are built into him or her, then the mode of communication can do little to change how he or she interacts. Each different form of communication has its own features, so we will explore chat rooms, email, listserves, MOOs, MUDs, and Usenet groups in order to determine: how real is communication in the virtual world of cyberspace?

5

Information and Communication Technologies for Development

Information and Communication Technologies for Development (ICT4D) is a general term referring to the application of Information and Communication Technologies (ICTs) within the field of socioeconomic development or international development. ICT4D concerns itself with directly applying information technology approaches to poverty reduction.

ICTs can be applied either in the direct sense, wherein their use directly benefits the disadvantaged population, or in an indirect sense, wherein the ICTs assist aid organisations or non-governmental organizations or governments or businesses in order to improve general socioeconomic conditions. In many impoverished regions of the world, legislative and political measures are required to facilitate or enable application of ICTs, especially with respect to monopolistic communications structures and censorship laws.

The concept of ICT4D can be interpreted as dealing with disadvantaged populations anywhere in the world, but is more typically associated with applications in developing countries. The field is becoming recognized as an interdisciplinary research area as can be noted by the growing number of conferences, workshops and publications. Such research have been spurred on in part by the need for scientifically validated benchmarks and results, which can be used to measure the efficacy of current projects. Many international development agencies recognize the importance of ICT4D. For example the World Bank's GICT section has a dedicated team of some 200 staff working on these issues.

A good example of the impact of ICTs on development are African farmers getting better market price information and thus not being impoverished by unfair corps buy-out people. Another example includes mobile telecommunications and radio broadcasting fighting political corruption in Burundi. The dominant terminology used in this field is "ICT4D". Alternatives include ICTD and development informatics.

History

The history of ICT4D can, roughly, be divided into three periods:

- ICT4D 0.0: mid-1950s to late-1990s. During this period (before the creation of the term "ICT4D"), the focus was on computing / data processing for back office applications in large government and private sector organisations in developing countries.
- ICT4D 1.0: late-1990s to late-2000s. The combined advent of the Millennium Development Goals and mainstream usage of the Internet in industrialised countries led to a rapid rise in investment in ICT infrastructure and ICT programmes / projects in developing countries. The most typical application was the telecentre, used to bring information on development issues such as health, education, and agricultural extension into poor communities. More latterly, telecentres might also deliver online or partly-online government services.
- ICT4D 2.0: late-2000s onwards. There is no clear boundary between phase 1.0 and 2.0 but suggestions of moving to a new phase include the change from the telecentre to the mobile phone as the archetypal application; less concern with e-readiness and more interest in the impact of ICTs on development; and more focus on the poor as producers and innovators with ICTs (as opposed to just consumers of ICT-based information).

Projects

Anatomy

ICT4D initiatives and projects may be designed and implemented by international institutions, private companies (e.g. Intel's Classmate), governments (e.g. e-Mexico initiative), non-governmental organizations (e.g. International Institute for Communication and Development), or virtual organizations (e.g. One Laptop per Child).

ICT4D projects address one or more of the following issues:

- Access and *Infrastructure*: providing suitable computer hardware, operating systems, software, and connectivity to the internet. These would include the affordability of software and hardware, the ability to share software (as echoed in the Free Software movement), and the ability to sustainably connect to the internet.
- *Capacity building and training in ICT:* installing, maintaining, and developing hardware and software, digital literacy (technological literacy and informational literacy) and e-Awareness.
- *Digital content and services:* e-services (e-learning, e-health, e-business/e-commerce, e-Governance/e-Government), including concerns related to local-language solutions in computing, and the Open Access agenda.
- *Regulation of the ICT Sector and digital rights:* Universal Access vs. monopolistic structures, Intellectual Property Rights, privacy, security, and digital identity.
- *Ethics and Social Contexts*
- Environment and Agriculture
- Free and Open Source Software
- Gender and ICT
- Health and Medicine
- Policy and Social Analyses

- Technical Innovation for Development.

Problems

Projects which deploy technologies in underdeveloped areas face well-known problems concerning crime, problems of adjustment to the social context, and also possibly infrastructural problems. Literacy issue is one of the factor why projects fail in rural areas, proper education and training to make the user at least understand how to manipulate the application to get the proper information they needed. Constant follow up with the community to monitor if the project is being used or implemented.

Projects in marginalised rural areas face the most significant hurdles. Since people in marginalised rural areas are at the very bottom of the pyramid, development efforts should make the most difference in this sector. ICTs have the potential to multiply development effects and are thus also meaningful in the rural arena. However introducing ICTs in these areas is also most costly, as the following barriers exist:

- Lack of Infrastructure: no power, no running water, bad roads
- Lack of Health Services: diseases like HIV, TB, malaria are more common.
- Lack of Employment: there are practically no jobs in marginalised rural areas.
- Hunger: hungry users have problems concentrating.
- Illiteracy: Text user interfaces do not work very well, innovative Human Computer Interfaces are required.
- Lack of means to maintain the project: some projects may be left to deteriorate in time because if a component gets broken they are costly to repair and maintain.
- Lack of support from the local government
- Social Contexts: the potential users living in rural marginalised areas often cannot easily see the point of

ICTs, because of social context and also because of the impediments of hunger, disease and illiteracy.

- Corruption is one of the factors why it hampers the implementation of the ICT project in rural areas.
- Trainings and seminars must be conducted according the suitable time of the farmers, to make sure that their daily routine for livelihood must be done first.
- Proper applications are not user friendly.

The World Bank runs Information for Development Program (infoDev), whose Rural ICT Toolkit analyses the costs and possible profits involved in such a venture and shows that there is more potential in developing areas than many might assume. The potential for profit arsises from two sources-resource sharing across large numbers of users (specifically, the publication talks about line sharing, but the principle is the same for, e.g. telecentres at which computing / Internet are shared) and remittances (specifically the publication talks about carriers making money from incoming calls, i.e. from urban to rural areas). Remittances are estimated to have a volume of upward of 250 billion USD and websites have been established to take advantage of this fact (e.g. Aryty, Philippines; Mukuru.com, Zimbabwe.

Lessons Learned

What's crucial in making any ICT4D effort successful is effective partnership between four key stakeholders:

- Public sector (governments-from developed nations, developing nations, international bodies, and local governments)
- Private sector (companies belonging to members of the target audience, multi-national organizations wishing to expand their markets to the 4 billion people under US$2/ day, pro-poor or social companies)
- Informal sector (NGOs, advocacy groups, think tanks)
- Representation from the target audience

InfoDev have published 6 lessons from an analysis of 17 their pilot programmes. These lessons are backed by a variety of examples as well as a list of recommendations, which should be read by everyone starting an ICT4D project.

- Lesson 1: Involve target groups in project design and monitoring.
- Lesson 2: When choosing the technology for a poverty intervention project, pay particular attention to infrastructure requirements, local availability, training requirements, and technical challenges. Simpler technology often produces better results.
- Lesson 3: Existing technologies—particularly the telephone, radio, and television—can often convey information less expensively, in local languages, and to larger numbers of people than can newer technologies. In some cases, the former can enhance the capacity of the latter.
- Lesson 4: ICT projects that reach out to rural areas might contribute more to the MDGs than projects based in urban areas.
- Lesson 5: Financial sustainability is a challenge for ICT-for-development initiatives.
- Lesson 6: Projects that focus on ICT training should include a job placement component.

Sustainability and Scalability

A growing perspective in the field is also the need to build projects that are sustainable and scalable, rather than focusing on those which must be propped up by huge amounts of external funding and cannot survive for long without it. Sustaining the project's scalability is a huge challenge of ICT for development on how the target user will continue using the platform. Development on ICT is not one shot implementation but rather it is a complex process to undertake continuously and the progress of each project evolves around the pervasive education for adaptability of the technology

Also, many so-called "developing" countries, such as India (or other South Asian countries like Sri Lanka, Pakistan, and Bangladesh, as also nations like Malaysia, China, Indonesia, Brazil, South Africa and many others) have proved their skills in IT (information technology). In this context, unless these skills are tapped adequately to build on ICT4D projects, not only will a lot of potential be wasted, but a key indigenous partner in the growth of this sector would be lost. Also there would be unnecessary negative impact on the balance of payments due to imports in both hardware and software. Currently, the main two perspectives coming out of this sector either emphasize the need for external aid to build infrastructure before projects can touch viability, or the need to develop and build on local talent. Both approaches are, of course, not mutually exclusive.

Critics

As it has grown in popularity, especially in the international development sector, ICT4D has also increasingly come under criticism. For instance, questions have been raised about whether projects that have been implemented at enormous cost are actually designed to be scalable, or whether these projects make enough of an impact to produce noticeable change.

In Sri Lankan journalist Nalaka Gunawardene argues that thousands of pilot projects have been seeded without regard to generalisability, scalability, and sustainability, implying that these projects will always require external funding to continue running and that their impact is limited. This sentiment echoes a 2003 report by the World Bank.

Further criticism on ICT4D concerns the impact of ICTs on traditional cultures and the so-called cultural imperialism which may be spread with ICTs. For example, young males are tempted to spend their recreational time playing violent computer games. It is emphasised that local language content and software seem to be good ways to help soften the impact of ICTs in developing areas. Anriette Esterhuysen, an advocate for ICT4D and human rights in South Africa, pointed out that some ICT4D projects often gives more impetus to how ICT can help its beneficiaries economically rather than helping them gain a society where social justice and equal rights prevails. She Believes that sustainable development can only be achieved if there is human rights and people can speak freely.

Another point of criticism against ICT4D is that its projects are seldom environmentally friendly. Beneficiary communities are often given the responsibility to dispose of the toxic electronic scrap when an equipment breaks down beyond repair. Since transporting the equipment to a recycling facility is costly; the equipment is often disposed of improperly, thus contributing to the pollution of the environment.

Technology

ICT4D projects typically try to employ low-cost, low-powered technology that can be sustainable in developing environment. Desktop virtualization and multiseat configurations are probably the most simple and common way to affordable computing as of 2009. ICT4D projects needs to be properly monitored and implemented; the system's design and user interface should be suitable to the target users. ICT4D projects installed without proper coordination with its beneficiary community has a tendency to fall short of its main objectives. For example, the usage of ICT4D projects in farming sector in third world countries, where a majority of the population are considered to be technologically illiterate, projects lay idle and sometimes get damaged or become obsolete.

Furthermore, there should be a line of communication between the project coordinator and the user for immediate response to the query or the difficulty encountered by the user. Addressing properly to the problem will help encourage the user for the interactivity and participation.

Organizations

- APC Association for Progressive Communications
- Computer Aid International Computer Aid International
- Dialog Telekom Dialog Telekom PLC Sri Lanka

- LinkNet Zambia LinkNet Zambia
- PhilRice Philippine Rice Research Institute.

Notable Events

World Summit on the Information Society (WSIS)

A major event for ICT4D was the twin WSIS (WSIS)-lead organisation was the International Telecommunications Union (ITU). The first part of WSIS took place in Geneva, Switzerland in December 2003 (with a large ICT4D exhibition and an ICT4D symposium co-ordinated by infoDev). The second part of WSIS took place in Tunis, Tunisia, in November 2005. One of its chief aims of the WSIS process was to seek solutions to help bridge the so-called "digital divide" separating rich countries from poor countries by spreading access to the Internet in the developing world.

Perspectives on the WSIS are available elsewhere on Wikipedia, and this covers links to civil society, Tunis 2005, US priorities at WSIS, media responses, Tunis conference developments, roles for business and government, digital divide issues, the digital divide and the digital dilemma, common ground, a civil society study on WSIS, and external links.

Information and Communication Technologies for Environmental Sustainability

Information and Communication Technologies for Environmental Sustainability (ICT Ensure) is a general term referring to the application of Information and Communication Technologies (ICTs) within the field of environmental sustainability.

With the usage of new technologies the global community, can be supported in their collaboration to preserve the environment in the long term. New technologies provide utilities for Knowledge acquisition and awareness, early evaluation of new knowledge, reaching agreements and communication of progress in the interest of the human welfare.

This includes ethical aspects of protecting human life as well as aspects of consumer safety and the preservation of our natural environment.

Application Areas

More and more application areas are becoming relevant to sustainable development in industry, health care, agriculture and the information society. And they have an impact on the perspectives of ICT, the environment, policy and science. More and more interest has been emerged as well to risk and disaster management, adaptation to climate change and resource use.

- ICT for Energy Consumption/Efficiency
- ICT in Climate Change
- ICT in Natural Resource Management
- Eco-industrial Applications and ICT for Industrial Ecology
- ICT in Agriculture
- ICT for Biodiversity
- ICT for Landscape Ecology
- Personalized Information Systems and ICT for Quality of Life
- ICT for Sustainable Urban Development
- ICT in Health Care
- ICT for Environmental Risk Management.

Information and Communication Technologies

Information and communication technologies, or ICT, allows users to participate in a rapidly changing world in which work and other activities are increasingly transformed by access to varied and developing technologies.

By this definition, you could almost say ICT is technology's version of economic growth, to satisfy the needs and wants of the community over time. ICT is also a very age friendly mechagnmisom ICT tools can be used to find, explore, analyse, exchange and present information responsibly and without discrimination. ICT can be employed to give users quick access to ideas and experiences from a wide range of people, communities and cultures.

Economic Impacts

In recent decades widespread incorporation of ICTs into many tiers of business, political processes and eructuring of the global economy.

ICTs have increased international interconnectedness and sped up the process of globalization. They have been instrumental in the information revolution, facilitating the transition from industrial economies, driven by the manufacturing sector, to knowledge economies.

ICTs, in conjunction with globalization and the information revolution, have reshaped the workforce. By increasing the speed of international communication ICTs have enabled corporations to outsource jobs, both in the manufacturing as well as white collar sectors.

While this lowers production costs and as a result the cost of goods, it has also had fundamental and often detrimental impacts on labour conditions.

Outsourcing causes geographic fragmentation of commodity chains, in which production of goods occurs in specialized plants in different locations, often traversing international boundaries. Locations with no or minimal restrictions on wages, compensation and entitlements for workers therefor become economically attractive as sites of production. This can lead to the exploitation of workers in developing countries and undermine the bargaining power of organized labour in developed countries outsourcing causes geographic fragmentation of in which production of goods ocure in speciallixes pants in different occasion often traversoi international boundaries despite the international spread of ict the economic impacts have been gerographically uneven.

They have exacerbated prexistion desparities between developed coutries, which can aford to produce and consume the lates.

Despite the international spread of ICTs the economic impacts have been geographically uneven. They have exacerbated pre-existing disparities between developed countries, which can afford to produce and consume the latest technologies and developing countries, which cannot. This gap is known as the digital divide.

Social Impacts

ICTs have impacted societies on many levels. They have extended the reach of public administration, leading to a centralization of regional management into urban centres. They have led to new forms of employment in innovation and production of ICTs and a demand for highly skilled specialists. However ICTs have also enabled professionals in certain industries to be replaced by unskilled workers, or even made entirely redundant. Proponents of ICTs portray this as a 're-skilling' of the workforce, while to detractors it is a 'de-skilling' process.

The diffusion of ICTs within societies is varied, with some institutions and sections of society having greater access to ICTs then others. These divisions are reflected in the content of ICTs. For example the English language, which is understood by only 10% of the worlds population accounts for approximately 80% of internet content.

Despite these imbalance in power relations, many social justice movements believe ICTs can be used to promote equality and empower marginalized groups. These groups advocate ICTs as a means of providing accessible and affordable information and as a platform for voices that might otherwise go unheard.

Economic development

ICTs have been identified by many international development institutions as a crucial element in developing the worlds poorest countries, by integrating them into the global economy and by making global markets more accessible. The World Bank has collaborated with the International Finance Corporation to promote access to ICTs, an initiative which it describes as one of its most successful information and communication is most important to each and every organation with out IC can not growth org. In 2006 the United Nations launched an initiative called the Global Alliance for Information and Communication Technologies and Development.

6

The Internet and a Theory of Meaning-Making

What is communication meaning about? What is the individual actually experiencing during communication? What is going on between communicators? People typically think that to convey meaning effectively, one should simply define, explain, and exemplify ideas in detail. That approach helps, but is insufficient. Scholars know that no matter what words and nonverbals a person uses to convey meaning, the receiver will individualistically interpret those words in whatever way makes sense. In this article, the meaning of communication is explored as a way to achieve harmony. Defining meaning as a path to harmony is problematic. No matter what symbols are used to define meaning and harmony, readers will attach their own personal significance to the concepts. Depending on whom they are and what comes to mind, individuals might define *meaning* from one of many roles, which could be as a linguist, a spiritual leader, an existential philosopher, a physicist, a scholar of communication studies, or someone who never gave *meaning* much thought.

Beyond one's role, a person's understanding of meaning is affected by personal experience and cultural perspectives. In short, meaning-making is tied to various frameworks that communicators apply to events.

Western scholars have continued to analyse meaning-making in communication. This article proposes the idea that harmony can be achieved through meaning-making. Although meaning may not in itself be synonymous with harmony, meaning can lead to harmony. If one thinks of harmony as a balance of acceptance, this kind of accord is possible through understanding and nonjudgmental open-mindedness of the messages of another individual. Harmony does not necessarily mean agreement, but a type of synchronization of tolerance, belief, feelings, or values. How do Western scholars of communication on the Internet come to believe in meaning as a path to harmony? And beyond that, how do Western scholars of communication come to believe that the Internet can contribute to communication understanding that leads to harmony? The diversification of ideas caused by international scholars traveling to the United States and by United States (US) scholars living abroad has long been a method of opening up thinking in academia. Stories told via US faculty who worked outside the United States, for example, have helped scholars to better understand ideas and experiences of the people in those countries.

Although anecdotal, the professor becomes a type of ethnographer doing fieldwork. Autoethnography of people who have experience between cultural contexts can add understanding to intercultural communication. Communication between people of different cultures is complicated, but can provide examples for understanding how meaning might be used to reach harmony through communication. As we worked with colleagues and students of other cultures in foreign lands and via the Internet, we began to merge our ideas about meaning into cultural contexts. As authors, when we suggest that *harmony is achieved through meaning*, we know that something comes to the reader's mind. That *something* is elusive, unique, and changing. The reader's perceptions cannot be identical to the perceptions of the authors, nor are the perceptions of the authors necessarily in agreement with each other. The authors cannot expect the reader's understanding to be the same today as it was yesterday. The authors do, however, want to entice the reader to explore the idea of achieving harmony through meaning-making. As US Americans, the authors believe in the individual nature of communication and anticipate that readers can find their own conceptualization of harmony as achieved through meaning-making. Thus, this article will be an examination of ideas that may lead to theory-building. The purpose is to analyse a theory of meaning-making for harmony, which is accomplished through communication.

Empathy

If a communicator is focused on self-expression, harmony seems unlikely. If a communicator is focused on the self as a being in balance with others, harmony seems more likely. If a communicator is focused on the other person's expression and the communication context, harmony may be even more likely. In a face-to-face situation, for example, if an adaptive communicator is concerned about empathic listening, the person seeks to truly identify with the other person. That understanding of meaning may lead to harmony. On the Internet, the communicator who carefully frames an email—selecting words and tone with a mix of politeness and brief informality—may increase the chances for a harmonious connection.

Sense-making may be the closest synonym for the concept of meaning as used in this article. There are many synonyms—with a wide range of connotations— that reflect characteristics of *meaning*:

1. analysis
2. circulation
3. connection
4. consequence
5. flow
6. inference
7. influence
8. interpretation
9. osmosis
10. perception

11. reading
12. relationship
13. sense-making
14. significance
15. similarity
16. symbiosis
17. transference
18. transmission
19. understanding.

Harmony seems a close synonym for connective communication. How can a person think or communicate in harmony? We can offer many synonyms for *harmony*.

1. accord
2. agreement
3. balance
4. concord
5. empathy
6. equilibrium
7. openness
8. peace
9. spiritual connection
10. synchronization
11. tolerance
12. understanding.

From the perspective of meaning-making, harmony has important denotations and connotations. When two people communicate to achieve the same meaning, they may achieve harmony. That sense of understanding, acceptance, or adaptation suggests a state of temporary equilibrium between two people. Further, one could say that harmony and communication are synonymous. If by communication, one means that two people attach the same meaning to the communication event, then one can say that the two people have achieved a kind of symmetry in the communication process. In contrast, two people could have a negative communication experience—an argument, for example—in which the pair fails to achieve harmony. In such a case, are the two people attaching the same meanings? Is the communication simpatico?

Probably not. If the communication conjures up comparable information, feelings, and cognitions, then the two may achieve harmony through meaning-making. If there is no sense of harmony, does communication take place? In the United States, where individual success is considered important, communication is something that implies interaction and results. In the People's Republic of China (PRC), there seems to be more emphasis on the process and a result of harmony.

Individuals may intuitively know what is *meant* by the words *meaning* and *harmony* simultaneously, or attach different meanings at different times, or perceive different meanings from other people. The problematic nature of *meaning* is precisely why individuals have difficulty understanding what the elusive word represents. If we think in terms of languages, religious perspectives, ethnicity, and cultural influences, the concepts of *meaning and harmony* become even more complex. While teaching in the People's Republic of China, one professor from the US made a request of a Chinese college administrator. The professor used logic to substantiate the request, but the administrator used tradition to substantiate the denial. The professor thought that logic should not be denied. The administrator thought that tradition should not be questioned. How do these two individuals reach harmony in attaching meaning when they come from different cultural frameworks? *What is going on in the communication event?* Perhaps the answer is in cognitive science, quantum physics, or an area of biological science. Science tells us that when a person perceives a stimulus, the individual instantly attaches meanings. Intuition tells us that when two individuals perceive a stimulus, the individuals instantly attach *different* meanings. In this case, the US professor and the PRC administrator may have held different meanings for the communication event because of their culturally learned cognitive patterns.

In contrast, everyone has experienced times when meanings were close enough to generate a sense of harmony through communication. Through the sensory biological connections and cognitive processing—or some connections people do not yet understand—the stimulus instantly evokes a common sense-making response. Whether the meaning attached to the communication event is correct makes no difference: Each person must attach an individual meaning. If the person attends, then the individual cannot ignore the communication event and subsequently will automatically attach meaning.

Language

Language is a logical discussion point about meaning-making. Communication has been summed up in the old and well worn statements: "The meaning is not in the words," or "The map is not the territory." Nor is the meaning simply in the gesture or the behaviour. By examining the communication that *goes on* in an everyday conversation, one may see that people can seldom explain the meaning of talk simply by reference to the dictionary definitions of the words. Even the syntax of language is insufficient. Tannen (1990) took this position on meaning in talk: "Much—even most—meaning in conversation does not reside in the words spoken at all, but is filled in by the person listening". Tannen and other scholars of conversation would say that the listener engages in drawing inferences. What is spoken, or on the surface is interpreted to mean something beneath the surface, unobserved.

The words of a language influence the way people perceive the world. Further, the dynamic characteristic of language suggests that language is constantly evolving and changing. Although English has many words—500,000 to one million—making language choice precise, its words are highly limited. Mandarin is also a complex language. Mandarin is the most common language in the PRC, and it is the language of the government. Mandarin may be spoken by more people than any other language in the world. Cantonese and Xiâng are spoken in Sichuan province. Even to an untrained ear, the pronunciation of words varies drastically between locations just 50-100 miles apart. There appears to be social and class distinctions based on accent, which suggests a large number of possible underlying messages based on language and accent. Likewise, different meanings are attached in the United States when comparing a Massachusetts accent to a Mississippi accent. Such communication differences may be analyzed as *surface versus underlying meaning*. Sometimes the literal meaning is everything needed to understand basically what is meant, but usually people need to see through to the nonliteral meaning. Interestingly, when people are asked to define *communication*, they might say something like the following: "Communication is the transfer of information from one thing to another." The vague word *thing* keeps open the possibility of information transferring between computers and other electronic devices, as well as people or even animals. This definition conceives of communication as something that is transferred between points. As such, the definition emphasizes the surface aspects of meaning. In fact, the word *thing* meaning all forms of senders and receivers suggests a lack of concern about interpreting the message.

A distinction between the literal meanings expressed in discourse and the relational meanings could do much to help organize the large number of meanings generated with every communication interaction. Many theorists have referred to this distinction as content versus interactional meaning. Tracy (2002) described content as "the conventional meaning of words or phrases that were said. It is the literal or dictionary-level meaning that exists apart from any particular context". Interactional meaning, according to Tracy, is an utterance's meaning "for the participants in the situation in which the utterance (or more usually, a sequence of utterances) occurred." Tracy also said: "Interactional meaning arises from and depends on the context, and may be given or given off". When the communicators take into account what the other does or does not know, there is interactional meaning. In other words, interactional meaning answers the question: What are the people involved experiencing? The meaning of utterances in context that is *what is going on*. So, one can think of utterances as being assigned meaning according to the dictionary definitions of the words and according to their meaning in context.

Whether using English or a Chinese language, think for a moment about a cultural experience that made you feel extremely happy. Does the word "harmony" cover everything about the situation and feelings? Probably one word, even many words, facial expressions, tone of voice, and body movements fail to adequately describe everything attached to that moment. The actual words, vocal inflection, and accent suggest differences in interpretation of communication. The surface stimuli help people arrive at the underlying meaning. In an intercultural encounter using English, Americans may focus on language, while Chinese focus on implications. Americans tend to use language directly, emphasizing surface meaning. A businessperson from the US may become annoyed and call a Chinese businessperson "two-faced" because the American fails to understand the cultural context. The Chinese businessperson may allow the American to save face, while concentrating on the relational process.

The American businessperson may be impatient to finish the negotiations, find out who will do what, and get the project done. As frustrations mount, the American may ask "What is going on?" While the American wants the meaning explained, the Chinese wants the meaning expressed. As people talk about *what is going on*, individuals use language which expresses relational meaning and personal meaning, but the *way* they communicate is equally significant.

The Internet

Shedletsky and Aitken (2004) have conducted research on the Internet and are particularly interested in how people of different cultures communicate through the Internet. They suggested that in the United States, the Internet has created an array of paradoxes. The Internet makes communication easier in some ways and more difficult in others. The Internet brings some people together and simultaneously isolates other people. The digital divide suggests the inequity between people based on education and class is growing. The Internet may make communication more rapid, but also more shallow. In China, Internet communication seems to contain paradoxes as well. Tuinstra (2006), for example, contended that the Internet has strengthened the power of the central PRC government—not undermined it as originally anticipated—because for the first time in China's history, the central government is popular and people are able to know more about what is going on around the country. In fact, the Internet offers a way to regulate citizens and is considered similar to other media in that the Internet is an extension of the government. Kluver and Yang (2005) conducted an analysis of research on the Internet in China, through which they observed the following expectations.

1. The Internet has been a democratizing force in China.
2. The Internet may contribute to dismantling communism in China.
3. International business communication sees potential in the Chinese market.

Although the paradoxes between cultures may be different in some ways, the Internet affects the ability of people to communicate and the speed, frequency, accessibility, and nature of that communication. In many ways, communication via the Internet is empowering. While teaching communication through the Internet to hundreds of college students in Sichuan Province, for example, a professor from the United States found that students were extremely excited to come to their class held in a lab with 50 computers. These college juniors would cluster at the door waiting for class to begin. When the students were allowed in the room, they would run to the computers, laughing and yelling, and immediately begin communicating on the Internet. One of their tasks was to engage in a discussion board with US students in an intercultural communication course. Clearly, the students were excited to freely access the world through the Internet. What is happening in Internet communication? Walther, Loh, and Granka (2005) suggested that Internet communication has many similarities to interpersonal, face-to-face communication. Through the Internet, individuals have a sense of speed, immediacy, and informality.

How do people feel about the messages they receive through email, blogging, wikis, YouTube, webpages, news, and other Internet media? What is their understanding of the discourse on the Internet? Do people know what is meant by the communication they receive? One could attempt to answer the question of *what is going on?* by describing what the individual sees, hears, and senses about *the other* via the Internet. In analyzing Internet communication, one could just recount the words. One could add the photographs, tone of communication, and method of communication. One could analyse an exchange on YouTube. But these approaches will not account for what the individuals understand to be *going on*—what meaning they assign to the event. One might think that if one knew what the words referred to, then the person would know their meaning. Knowing what the words reference may help, but one still could not answer the question: *What is going on in this context? What appears to be going on* is that the experience of learning is organized against a backdrop of an historical narrative, a framework.

Referencing

Referencing affects communication. Referencing is the process of indicating, suggesting, or noting something. In what appears to be a simple act of pointing to an object, for instance, one cannot say what is meant and what is understood simply by recounting that an index finger is aimed at an object. Even in pointing, we need to take into account the framework in which the pointing occurs (Goodwin, 2003). Modifying a Goodwin example, consider the nature of communication during the horrors of the 2008 earthquake in Sichuan province. In fact, the framework of communication during that catastrophe became the subject of much discussion. Journalists referenced how open the Chinese government appeared, and how important Internet news became during the tragedy (Jacobs, 2008). One of the first videos to reach the world was a student video shot during the earthquake, which appeared on YouTube. Perhaps the external access to Internet news updates available through blogs and websites represented a new accessibility for the Internet. Once the openness is pointed out, does it become more pervasive?

Meaning and intention are never self-evident. Wu (2005) discussed the keen interest in media research about China today because of the Internet infrastructure and service explosion there. In addition, the world recognizes China's paramount position in politics and economics in the world scene. Wu suggested that in China, the online media are primarily news media. In the US, the key Internet function seems to emphasize person-to-person communication. One might suggest that although the Internet was primarily an information source in the US some years ago, Internet use has evolved into networking for personal, business, and educational purposes. Perhaps Chinese use of the Internet will evolve in a similar way or perhaps cultural values will take the Internet in different directions according to fundamental elements in the Chinese society. Is Internet use a social product of the cultural context? The way people act toward other people and things is based on meanings attached to those people and things (Blumer, 1969), which is consistent with Mead's concept of symbolic interaction. Although symbolic interactionism seems valid here, the theory fails to adequately explain how meaning is attached to people and things. Clark (2003) wrote: "Suppose Kay and I are walking in the woods when I suddenly and silently point in a particular direction. 'What is it?' she asks. 'A squirrel, that oak tree, the curious branch on that oak tree, a hidden nuthatch, or what?' Even if I point with care, she still needs to ask, 'Do you mean the bark of the tree, its colour, the mold, or what?' To complete my indication, she and I must arrive at a joint construal of the object, so I might reply, 'the oak tree.' And she might nod in acknowledgment. Only then will I have completed my indication" (p. 250). So too, referencing in any individual email, webpage, blog, wiki, social networking interaction and the cultural context of that message is equally confusing. The meaning of what people say to others is never self-evident.

How do people communicate ideas that they never explicitly conveyed? At first glance, one may think people are simply skilled at using metaphors or contextual cues. If a person uses indirect communication via the Internet, however, the traditional context used to interpret meaning is not there.

Apparently, the method of communication remains the same on the Internet. In Internet advertising, for example, An (2007) suggested that Eastern advertising uses more symbolic visuals, while Western advertising uses more literal visuals. One can find this sort of literal and nonliteral meaning communicated between people of different cultures. Perhaps the communication event of face-to-face interaction seems much clearer than the communication event of the Internet because of the lack of practice about the new and constantly changing Internet. Yet, Walther and others suggested that the Internet is comparable to face-to-face communication. Referencing may include a wide range of phenomena. Some of these related phenomena are levels of communication, knowledge, directness versus indirectness, face management, conflict, identity, interpersonal competence, and alignment. Perhaps these distinctions set up a false dichotomy, however, by using the word *versus*. In fact, significant communication comes from surface *with* underlying meaning, and directness *with* indirect meaning. If people could better understand how surface and underlying meaning are interrelated, they would be a long way toward understanding how meaning works toward achieving harmony. How is it that people *can talk about something* and yet understand that they are discussing something else, far removed? As soon as one raises this sort of question, dimensions of meaning come to mind, such as the following:

1. Concrete versus abstract meaning
2. Direct versus indirect meaning
3. Implied versus inferred meaning or innuendo
4. Information versus interpretation
5. Literal versus metaphorical
6. Literal versus symbolic
7. Literal versus ulterior
8. Literal versus figurative meaning
9. Message versus metamessage

10. Social action versus information
11. Surface versus underlying meaning
12. Tacit knowledge versus explicit knowledge.

Multiple levels of meaning and understanding are the rule, not the exception. Further, there are differences between family members, co-workers, friends, and strangers in everyday discourse within and between people of different cultures. The words one utters or writes influence meaning. First, the words can be a product of culture and personal perceptions of the world. In the People's Republic of China, for example, the word *listening* is a combination of symbols for ear and heart, suggesting complex underlying meanings about the process of listening. Language influences our ability to describe people, feelings, events, and actions. When people communicate, they go beyond the surface meaning of the words. The *way* people communicate also influences meaning. Individuals create their identities as they talk to other people. People also create their identities when communicating with people of different cultures because the experience of being outside one's culture teaches much about that culture.

Narratives

Although one may think of stories as being more significant in Eastern cultures, they are crucial to meaning and harmony in Western cultures too. When using narratives, the communicators (characters) seem to be "in a story." The listener fills in the missing parts of the story in order to fully understand *what is going on* in each case. Communication scholars know the importance of storytelling in creating meaning. Other theorists have tried to explain the concept of meaning by describing how others' expectations shape the people in their community (Pearce & Cronin). Bruner (1990) suggested that communication takes place within culturally defined contexts and explained that "people do not deal with the world event by event or with text sentence by sentence. They frame events and sentences in larger structures". For now, one can envision the larger structure as a story in which communication occurs. The story's structure becomes a type of context.

Two women who had never met, joined each other for a visit to Wolong, China, home of the world's most famous panda preserve. Their common bond was that they both knew a scientist who studied panda reproduction. After a fascinating visit to the panda preserve, the two women walked to a shop by their hotel that evening and came upon some beautiful bracelets. With the help of a Chinese scientist who accompanied them, the women negotiated a price for the bracelets. The shopkeeper seemed proud of his sale. The scientist seemed proud of the gift of a jade bracelet. The women seemed proud of their inexpensive treasures.

Their communication was about more than purchasing products. For the women, their pride came from obtaining a token to remind them of touching a culture deep in Sichuan. The people involved seemed to achieve harmony through a price negotiation process that left everyone in accord. Was there really harmony in this encounter, or did the two Chinese men behave in ways to accommodate the Americans? After the visit to China, the women maintained their distant relationship through email. Exactly one year later, a 7.9 earthquake in Wolong prompted a flurry of emails that gave different meaning to their communication. The enchanting hotel and shop with the bracelets was flattened. The Chinese scientist emailed them about missing and injured pandas. News of the deaths of townspeople and farmers conjured up vivid images of their every encounter. As the women talked by email, they described details of the people they met, the meals they ate, and the places where they stopped. While the joy of seeing the pandas had been the focus of their memories, it was the joy of their human encounters that became paramount after the horrible earthquake devastation. One woman said: "At least once a week I wear my wonderful antique silver bracelet with the dragon I snagged at a great bargain in one of the shops at Wolong. The tragic events make all the bargaining to get the bracelets now seem so selfish and humiliating." Their original communication was transformed into a completely opposite meaning. While trying to make sense of the tragic news reports from China, they gained new perceptions of the underlying meanings of their communication. A story of pride about how they negotiated for the bracelets turned into a story of humility and gratitude about their encounter.

Cultural stories create reality, just as each person's story reflects that individual's concept of the truth. The validity of a story is not as important as the underlying meaning of a story. These fantasy themes that use cultural values may be expressed in the form of metaphors, jokes, and narratives in group communication. Narrative fantasies offer a reality for people to share with each other. That shared reality creates a kind of balance or harmony among the people in a group or culture. The cultural context creates a climate that influences how people communicate. The Chinese may not realize that in the US, sometimes the word "story" is used to mean "lie."

Levels

The visualization of levels helps people talk about communication, which is called "metacommunication." Communicators can use levels to refer to the categories of communication, for example:

Intrapersonal communication, interpersonal communication, group communication, public, and mass communication. US college departments of communication typically are structured around these levels. As such, faculty teach courses in intrapersonal communication, interpersonal communication, small group, organizational communication, and mass communication. Professors are identified as belonging to one of these areas. US professional associations are similarly compartmentalized. There are divisions of intrapersonal, interpersonal, public, and mass communication as if each level exists on some kind of continuum. A person's use of levels, though, goes beyond how one sees the field of communication. Leveling is a conception that non-scholars apply to their descriptions of communication. One may refer to the *depth* of analysis, *the intellectual level, elevating in the communication,* or talking *in depth.* A US American may speak of *raising the bar* to suggest higher expectations or *getting down and dirty* to suggest a more base type of communication. There is the idea of colloquial and formal forms of language, as *low* and *high* (Salzmann, 1998).

Each person sees the world through his or her personal perspective. When people communicate, they are influenced by their perceptions, experiences, language, cognitive styles, and culture. Perception is the view, insight, or understanding people have of themselves, others, and the world. Each person has a slightly—sometimes extremely—different slant on the world from every other individual's perception. This perception affects how people attach meaning to communication messages. In addition, perception determines a person's view of harmony and his or her motivation to achieve harmony. Our perceptions influence everything.

Gender may be one of the many elements that affects perception. Some scholars suggest that most women of the United States are in positions of inequality to men. Gender-based comments about Hillary Clinton as a political candidate, for example, suggest that although many US Americans believe in equal opportunity and treatment, women are held to different standards than men are. One might argue, however, that in the United States, women have different opportunities than the women of China have. Qing scholars believed that Confucianism values gender inequality, which includes subservience of women to husbands and fathers, and these traditional values are maintained today. One cannot help but wonder if the free exchange of ideas through the Internet will affect perceptions about gender. Among Chinese youth, television exposure did not affect gendered perceptions of the ideal spouse. They explained that Confucian traditions advocated restraint and parental involvement in the selection of a spouse, and an obedience to family remained dominant. How might these values affect the way people communicate and the way cultural influences affect perceptions of the meanings between people?

Early research in the United States suggested major computer use differences based on gender, which seem to have disappeared today. Although Western studies about Internet technology use suggest that the original gender differences have diminished; the gender gap may still be significant in Singapore. Females seem to show preferences for certain types of Internet communication, such as texting and social networking. Although the gender gap seems to be narrowing regarding media use, in some cultures women have less access to computers, the Internet, email, and a more negative attitude towards media than men have.

Research suggests that there are different perceptions between Americans and Chinese regarding content and use of the Internet. Although the diversity of the Chinese people make generalizations difficult, one study examining Internet advertising suggested that people in Hong Kong found gambling and online chat services to be offensive. Advertisements with nudity or sexism also were offensive to consumers. They were more sensitive to these types of advertisements on the Internet than in other media. Although Western advertising research suggests that irritating advertising has some effectiveness, the research in Hong Kong suggests that edgy advertising should be avoided with people who are Chinese.

Virtuality on the Internet becomes interactive since it is engendered not just by Internet users' passive consumption of media images but also mostly by their very involvement in the interaction itself. The term "virtuality" to show a blurring of boundaries between cultures through Internet technology. When analyzing meaning, one can think of each communication event as situated within a definable cultural context. Our communication lives this way: "It is culture, not biology, that shapes human life and the human mind, that gives meaning to action by situating its underlying intentional states in an interpretive system". The ways in which language, beliefs about how things work, stories, myths, and folk psychology enter into ordinary transactions. As people communicate with others, they engage this backdrop of knowledge. The shared knowledge as critical to communication. In explaining *what is going on* in communication, one can speak of many levels of meaning that are simultaneously operating, which include meanings of the words, the nonverbals, social actions— such as implying or hinting—attitudes, social hierarchy, culture, context, gender, social class, and values.

Harmony Through Meaning Cognition

Perception, Personality, Information Processing, Open-Mindedness, Learning Styles, Multiple Intelligences, Cultural Values

Balance

Denotations, Connotations, Metaphors, Nonverbals, Content, Conflict, Explicit Meaning, Implicit Meaning, Interactional Meaning, Knowledge, Directness versus Indirectness, Face Management, Identity, Interpersonal Competence, Contextual Sensitivity, Alignment

Acceptance

Culture, Context, Purpose, Relational Meaning, Purification, Processing, Metacommunication

Levels, Cognition, and Purposes

After the evolution of research in the field of communication studies, US Americans have come to understand more about how people communicate. As the field has expanded to include intercultural communication in a global perspective, some scholars have come to suggest that communication is the advancement of culture. This idea suggests that in a global context, communication from a person in one culture needs to be focused on the person of the other culture. When considering the many different levels or dimensions of meaning operating when people communicate, one realizes that much is going on at high speed, even when people are simply looking at each other in silence.

One concern about communication is how people attach meaning according to cultural context. The idea is that the high-context culture of Asia relies on communication differently from the low-context culture of the United States (Hall, 2000). In a high-context culture, the communication emphasizes collectivist, relational, and un-spoken meanings. In a low-context culture, the communication emphasizes the individual, linear, and action-oriented approaches. The high-context culture is inherently more focused on strategies of harmony, which requires people from a low-context culture to learn new approaches to communication. Are Eastern communicators more aware of contextual cues, and thus able to interpret meanings more effectively? Perhaps a concern about collectivist and relational communication facilitates achieving harmony through communication.

Many theories of how we take in information—from theories about persuasion to theories about language processing—rely upon the idea that people are capable of high speed processing. For instance, according to Sherif's Social Judgment Theory, when a person hears someone speak about the world, the person "automatically" determines where the ideas lie with regard to attitude zones of (a) acceptance, (b) rejection, and (c) non-commitment. In terms of levels of meaning, one could say that the receiver spontaneously places ideas into one of these three categories immediately upon receiving the ideas. Does processing happen in the same way during communication in Chinese culture as US American culture? In the low-context approach of the United States, one expects the receiver to make a high speed decision on whether or not they believe the idea is true, and whether or not they agree with it. Further, the theory suggests that one of a cluster of ideas will function as an anchor point with regard to the others. Although perhaps a simplistic description, the meanings of the ideas received probably are organized in reference to one's most cherished ideas—the anchor marks our ego involvement. Other theories suggest that Americans process incoming messages with more or less attention to the details of argument. According to the Elaboration Likelihood Model, the central route is used where Americans are motivated and able to think about the specific evidence offered; the peripheral route is used to process messages more superficially. Both routes are set in motion without explicit or conscious choice. According to the Elaboration Likelihood Model, the level of attention varies between the central and peripheral routes. The individual operates to think about the world in a manner that is efficient while protecting the interests of the receiver. US Americans have purposes behind their direct communication. It would be interesting to know if research on Chinese communication reached the same conclusions.

According to Baxter and Montgomery (1996), relational dialectics are the push and pull of forces on close relationships. As people interact, they produce and determine the meanings of messages along three dimensions: (a) connectedness-separateness; (b) certainty and uncertainty; and (c) openness and closedness. People are pulled in two opposing directions at once. Contradiction is what Relational Dialectics sees as ongoing in close relationships. Certain of these elements seem more high-context: Connectedness, uncertainty, and openness.

In contrast, low-context communication seems more separate, certain, and closed in nature. Baxter and Montgomery also talked about the *messiness* of relationships. There is no ultimate resolution to communication, which seems consistent with a low-context approach. Much of communication work is accomplished without effortful thinking. Instead, communication is performed "intuitively" and at high speed. People also know that close attention in the communication process can be exhausting. The individual juggles dialectical tensions through the cognitive system, by producing and assigning meanings of various kinds and functioning to cope within the relationship. The individual must maintain the relationship. Meaning is in the untidy, complex, combination of the observed and the unobserved, the literal and the inferred. Every individual has known the experience inferring meaning that is contrary to the intended meaning.

Other theories of communication suggest that levels of meaning, cognition, and purpose are integral to the communication process and subsequent high or low contexts. Expectancy Violation Theory, for example, suggests that when individuals engage in communication, if what they expect fails to happen, the individuals become distracted and involved in interpreting the meaning of the violations (Burgoon, 1978). Perhaps in this case, people find themselves operating totally beneath the surface level. In addition, levels of meaning, cognition, and purpose work together as a system. At the level of intrapersonal communication, where people take in stimuli and assign meaning—whether language or nonverbals—cognitive systems decode and encode at various levels of meaning. The intrapersonal communication process regards purpose as significant: to make sense out of the world, to coordinate with others, to protect interests, and to persuade (Shedletsky, 1989). At the Internet level— where people are free to analyse meaning from a distant source, are individuals more influenced by cultural values? In other words, do people assign meaning based more on cultural expectations than individual experience?

The synthesis between observed behaviour, observed signs (surface), and inferred behaviour (underlying) explains *what is going on* in communication. People must look beyond the observable surface to determine the meaning of the communication event at the underlying realm of the mental or psychological domain. Perhaps the cognitive domain is more complicated in collectivist cultures than in individualist cultures. For the US communicator, creating meaning is quintessentially a cognitive feat. For the Chinese communicator operates through the collectivist culture. Meaning requires complex, underlying processing in all cultures. Even the simple act of pointing, which human infants begin to do within months of being born, is closely tied to *understanding* the deeper—not directly observed—domain of the mind.

Framework

The meaning of discourse is determined by what Foucault has called the "frameworks of interpretation" (1982). We speak differently to old friends than we do to new acquaintances, to young children than we do to peers, to those with authority over us and vice versa. We can think of these different kinds of meanings as operating at different levels. The "world hypotheses," our fundamental beliefs about the world, says that ordinary statements people make contain three constituents: (1) a content, what the statement literally talks about (e.g., "I will see Mr. Li tomorrow."); (2) an attitude, some degree of certainty or belief in what is said "Mr. Li is extremely helpful," (3) grounds for belief, such as an email about his plans for tomorrow, previous positive experiences, feelings of having achieved harmony on more than one occasion.

Theorists have described framework as a narrative, schema, script, scenario, folk psychology, culture, attitudes and beliefs, myths, and symbolic system. With framing comes the memories where framing resides. Through memory, an individual's analysis of current communication is kept for future reference. The affect—the feeling or emotional attitude—co-exists with the memory and analysis. An individual is likely to recall that during or after the communication, the individual felt tension, connection, happiness, guilt, harmony, or some other emotion. The person may recall the affect before remembering the reason that caused the feeling. Some theorists have speculated that framing functions not only to aid the individual to make sense out of experience, but also to allow for communicating experiences with others (Shotter, 1990). Zhou and Moy (2007) discussed how the Internet has come to frame many elements of China today. Although only 10% of the population of China uses the Internet, the information and influences enter into other media and subsequently reach people who do not have Internet access. Wu (2005) suggested that the Internet's pervasive influence in China—like in the United States--has become unstoppable. One could argue that the Internet's influence is framing some types of communication.

Conclusions

This article suggests that symbols fail to fully answer the question: *What is going on* in communication? Instead, the answer to the question is tied closely to the framework or context in which the interaction occurs (Shotter, 1990). When people anchor communication (Bransford & Stein, 1993), people understand meaning through context. The notion of framework may shed some light on the idea of surface and underlying meaning. To some extent, *underlying* is another way of referring to framework or the body of knowledge that frames the surface elements to be understood and remembered. Underlying may be another way of saying "the body of shared meaning beneath, supporting, or behind" the surface communication. Underlying meaning includes the relevant history, context, mutual knowledge, cultural perspective, rules. Also important are the communicators' attitudes toward one another or toward other things in the world, their roles, beliefs, and knowledge. In our musing about using meaning in communication to achieve harmony, this article sought to examine processes, including ones relevant to Eastern or Western communicators. To answer the question— *What is going on in the communication event?*—one must analyze levels (or types) of meaning:

1. content
2. cultural values

3. explicit
4. harmonious connection
5. implicit
6. interactional
7. literal
8. metaphorical
9. relational.

The idea of framing is introduced to discuss the kinds of information that take part in understanding contextual cues. In connection with framing, related notions include narrative, beliefs, attitudes, affect, and memory, which are essential in creating meaning. We do not want to suggest that these theories imply either-or relationships, contracts, and contradictions, but the theories do indicate integrated dimensions. One can consider, for example, Social Penetration Theory's (Altman & Taylor, 1973), a metaphor of a person's personality being like an onion and that one must peel away layers to reach the core of a person. Although the idea of layers makes sense, creating meaning in a communication context is something more because there is far more under the surface than one might guess. So too meaning is grounded in what came *before* the communication event. Further, the communicator who effectively focuses on *the other* improves the chances of achieving harmony through the communication. People communicate on multiple levels because they build upon their knowledge of each other. Their communicative interaction creates the foundation for their connection. This connection of frames influences their meaning-making. Amazingly, interpersonal-style Internet communication may seek the same kinds of connections as face-to-face communication. There is nothing objective about achieving harmony through communication because each individual's view depends on where the person stands. When the communicators empathize from the perspective of the other, however, there may be a harmonious result. In describing the communication process, one cannot think in terms of cause and effect relationships. It is difficult to predict exactly which level or which items in a particular level will lead to harmonious interpretation. The communicators may not know when or why a specific underlying level is sought. Individuals can be other-centered. While understanding frameworks located in the other—no matter how difficult that might be—people can achieve balance, acceptance, and openness. Communication meaning can move people along a path to harmony. Perhaps, these ideas can serve as a foundation for pursuing more effective intercultural communication, which goes beyond the surface and into underlying meanings.

7

Motivating Through Meaning Making Communication

Maybe the place to begin is to say what motivation isn't. Many people incorrectly view motivation as a personal trait – that is, some have it and others don't. Motivation is an important factor which encourages persons to give their best performance and help in reaching the enterprise goals. A strong positive motivation will enable the increased output of employees but a negative motivation will reduce the same performance. Motivation originally came from the Latin root word *'Movere'*, which means *"to move"*. It is derived from the word Motive. It may be defined as an inner state of our mind that activates and directs our behaviour. It can't be seen, but all that can be seen in behaviour. Some people work harder or exert more efforts than others. In other words, individuals with lesser ability can, and do, out perform their counter parts. In fact this is because of motivation. Motivation is some thing that moves a person to action, and continues him in the course of action already initiated. It is the case of management which shows that every human being earnestly seeks a secure, friendly and supportive relationship which gives him a sense of worth in face to face groups which are most important to him.

The role of Motivation is to develop and intensify the desire in every member of the organization to work effectively and efficiently in his position. We can say that motivated employees are in a state of tension and to relieve this tension, they exert efforts.

The greater the tension, the higher the effort level. If this effort successfully leads to the satisfaction of the need, tension is reduced. But since, in the organizations, we are interested in the work behaviour, this tension reduction effort must also be directed towards organizational goals. Therefore what we require is the individual needs to compatible and consistent with the organizations goals.

Motivation when viewed from the perspective of one versed in the organisational communication, focuses on effective transfer of information, which in turn reduces uncertainty. This information/ message content that reduces uncertainty is crucial in the motivational process. If employee's knowledge of specific and difficult goals is defined clearly, then they tend to do better, compared to moving without direction with nil or vague information. Apparently, workers seek meaning making information to reduce uncertainty and they perform better if the information held by their superiors is shared effectively and truly.

Depending on the situation and the subordinate, a leader and a manager may involve their subordinates in decision making process participatively. For this, they may have to share information and values with their subordinates to learn their needs and then mutually decide how they can attain their aims through their organisational goals. The information sharing process and effective multi-dimensional organisational communication play a vital role in organisational goals. For this, the personality, anxiety dimensions of the individuals concerned and their satisfaction of their present, potential needs and aspirations have to be kept in focus as much as attainment of their organisational goals.

The manager should inform the employees about the goals required to be attained by specific target dates and job description and behaviour pattern expected out of them clearly for an ideal fit to attain the organisational goals and point out how the worker can establish balance and consistency between his role and organisational roles. Research findings reveal that creativity flourishes when the message is communicated well, it's effectiveness measured and reviewed/ benchmarked, as is the case with the Raymond Corporation's(HQ New York) and its quarterly meetings and info-sharing processes therein. During the scheduled date and time of the meet, all available information are shared in good faith and trust to create and maintain subtle boundaries to power, status, role, occupational empowerment and specialisation, thus making up the fabric of the work culture of the Raymond Corporation.

Manager may inform the employees of the organisational goals and other relevant data to make sense to them, that facilitate the accomplishment of their allotted tasks and provide necessary feedback as to whether they are on the right tracks regarding attitude, behaviour and performance of duties. He may also provide information on the incentives, rewards, recognition, benefits and punishment related to such desired pattern. However, that alone is not enough. The manager should try to understand the subordinates empathetically. For this, he has to develop personal and informal inter personal relationship, learn as many relevant facts informally about the upbringing, culture, values, knowledge, skill and attitude, strength and weaknesses and try to match these to their roles. An employee having a general notion of his job responsibilities is normally eager to establish specific goals as perceived by him to increase his understanding of what is expected of him. Employees want to find out how their needs and expectations can be fulfilled through the organisation and how they can uphold their values while carrying out their respective roles. Employers on the other hand are normally unwilling to share success. Generally the Indian employees are uncertain about how to satisfy their needs and aspirations and restore balance while accomplishing their allotted organisational goals. In contrast, Prime Mover, a material handling manufacturer in Iowa, USA recognizes goal directed but 'unsuccessful teamwork' also `besides 'rewarding successful teams ' suitably. Genuine effort in good faith is the criteria with them.

Work-a-holic superiors may, to their benefit allow their subordinates to learn and practice ' meaning making language' while developing their own acumen at it. Video communication aided by cable TV and use of computer can be effective communication tools. Irrespective of the tools used, they should understand that even tea/ coffee club gossip may be meaning making as much as the informal small talk while traveling to office and back together, Rum punches or stray thoughts / revelations emerging from get-togethers or hobby clubs have remained an effective management technique foe meaning making communication since 500 BC as propounded by Chinese philosopher, Sun Tzu.

Steers and Porte (1975) asserted that work is meaningful to workers:

* For obtaining extrinsic and intrinsic rewards,
* For social interaction and integration,
* As a mechanism for symbolically identifying status or rank and
* *For establishing an identity in terms of their roles, value commitments and for societal purpose.*

For supervisors, the major function of meaning making language is to facilitate the construction of schema and scripts in subordinates which guide work behaviour in ways that are useful to the organisation. Rarely do supervisors consciously direct their communication along these lines. Instead, they normally play their roles as their organisational boss has directed them to adopt or as upholders of the norms embodied in the organisational culture. Job satisfaction plays a dominant role in receiving-'meaning making language ' as it is meant. Job satisfaction is the result of the positive feelings and beliefs regarding job characteristics and job related experiences held by the employees (Locke, 1976). It is developed by challenging work, recognition, good working conditions, high and equitable rewards, good opportunities for promotion, and advancement etc. It reduces absenteeism and turnover, although it does not necessarily increase performance (Landy and Trumbe, 1976; Locke, 1976). Rewards and recognition contingent on performance may increase job satisfaction although, the simple presence of reward may by itself be enough (Gupta,1980).

In meaning making communication, the employees and the management interact openly as a matter of routine through informal role playing. In this process, the manager normally develops his role as a representative of the organisation's beliefs, values and goals over a period of time after gaining the trust of the employees. For example a manager may say to his subordinate,." I am just so happy to tell you that your chances of promotion will be good if you do well on this project". These words reduce the worker's uncertainty about the correlation between his actions and goal attainment, which in turn may trigger his optimum efforts for goal accomplishment. Japanese managers have been successfully motivating their employees by using different kinds of language appealing to their 'head and heart' alike.

They spend a lot of time to know their employees personally and to have an insight in to their background, strengths and weaknesses through informal communication with them. They are deeply involved and committed in this process and are sincerely interested in them as 'human beings'. A manager who excels in 'meaning making communication' with their employees is normally considerate and empathetic towards them. This in turn results in the employees a high degree of self esteem, mutual trust, and emotional bond with the manager, based or shared values. Work motivation in such cases will be a natural fall out of these shared values and beliefs.

According to the goal setting theory, the goals are the most important factors in an employee's intent to work hard and long. When employees encounter utility and meaning in their work, they are motivated to work hard. (Erez and Sidon, 1984) found that ' goal acceptance' mediates between goal difficulty and performance.

The supervisor with his 'meaning making' communications can make significant contribution towards' goal acceptance', on the part of his subordinates. Meaningful communication also generates commitment among employees. Committed employees remain wedded to the organisational role and fulfil their role requirements effectively (Commings, 1983).

Meaning making indicators of the supervisor increasing the employees' information on goals and policies, help them to develop their perceptions that their supervisor's words and their work have a sense and meaning. The successful managers supply the information and the feedback needed by workers. Besides, they also exhibit a keen interest in communicating with employees as people with 'head and heart'. Their 'non-purposeful' communication in the downtime also makes a significant contribution to their motivation specially if channeled properly in tune with the work culture. Thus, motivating through meaningful language is a continuous phenomenon working on the minds consciously or subconsciously.

To conclude, successful managers have to learn three things:

a) What employees need to know

b) The importance of role playing and informal meaning making communication and

c) The importance of compassion and empathy.

In short, they must practice to know and develop their employees as human beings rather than as 'Cogs in the Wheel'. They have to understand that effective and consistent meaning making communication has been and will always be a challenge and one that should be on the topmost hit list 'to do' by each strata of management, everyday.

Telecommunication

Telecommunication is the transmission of signals over a distance for the purpose of communication. In earlier times, this may have involved the use of smoke signals, drums, semaphore, flags or heliograph. In modern times, telecommunication typically involves the use of electronic devices such as telephones, television, radio or computers. Early inventors in the field of telecommunication include Alexander Graham Bell, Guglielmo Marconi and John Logie Baird. Telecommunication is an important part of the world economy and the telecommunication industry's revenue was estimated to be $1.2 trillion in 2006.

History

For more details on this topic, see History of telecommunication.

Early Telecommunications

In the Middle Ages, chains of beacons were commonly used on hilltops as a means of relaying a signal. Beacon chains suffered the drawback that they could only pass a single bit of information, so the meaning of the message such as "the enemy has been sighted" had to be agreed upon in advance. One notable instance of their use was during the Spanish Armada, when a beacon chain relayed a signal from Plymouth to London signalling the arrival of Spanish ships.

In 1792, Claude Chappe, a French engineer, built the first fixed visual telegraphy system (or semaphore line) between Lille and Paris. However semaphore suffered from the need for skilled operators and expensive towers at intervals of ten to thirty kilometres (six to nineteen miles). As a result of competition from the electrical telegraph, the last commercial line was abandoned in 1880. Telegraph and Telephone

The first commercial electrical telegraph was constructed by Sir Charles Wheatstone and Sir William Fothergill Cooke and opened on 9 April 1839. Both Wheatstone and Cooke viewed their device as "an improvement to the [existing] electromagnetic telegraph" not as a new device.

Samuel Morse independently developed a version of the electrical telegraph that he unsuccessfully demonstrated on 2 September 1837. His code was an important advance over Wheatstone's signalling method. The first transatlantic telegraph cable was successfully completed on 27 July 1866, allowing transatlantic telecommunication for the first time.

The conventional telephone was invented independently by Alexander Bell and Elisha Gray in 1876. Antonio Meucci invented the first device that allowed the electrical transmission of voice over a line in 1849. However Meucci's device was of little practical value because it relied upon the electrophonic effect and thus required users to place the receiver in their mouth to "hear" what was being said. The first commercial telephone services were set up in 1878 and 1879 on both sides of the Atlantic in the cities of New Haven and London.

Radio and Television

In 1832, James Lindsay gave a classroom demonstration of wireless telegraphy to his students. By 1854, he was able to demonstrate a transmission across the Firth of Tay from Dundee, Scotland to Woodhaven, a distance of two miles (3 km), using water as the transmission medium. In December 1901, Guglielmo Marconi established wireless communication between St. John's, Newfoundland (Canada) and Poldhu, Cornwall (England), earning him the 1909 Nobel Prize in physics (which he shared with Karl Braun). However small-scale radio communication had already been demonstrated in 1893 by Nikola Tesla in a presentation to the National Electric Light Association. On 25 March 1925, John Logie Baird was able to demonstrate the transmission of moving pictures at the London department store Selfridges. Baird's device relied upon the Nipkow disk and thus became known as the mechanical television. It formed the basis of experimental broadcasts done by the British Broadcasting Corporation beginning 30 September 1929. However, for most of the twentieth century televisions depended upon the cathode ray tube invented by Karl Braun. The first version of such a television to show promise was produced by Philo Farnsworth and demonstrated to his family on 7 September 1927.

Computer Networks and the Internet

On 11 September 1940, George Stibitz was able to transmit problems using teletype to his Complex Number Calculator in New York and receive the computed results back at Dartmouth College in New Hampshire. This configuration of a centralized computer or mainframe with remote dumb terminals remained popular throughout the 1950s. However, it was not until the 1960s that researchers started to investigate packet switching — a technology that would allow chunks of data to be sent to different computers without first passing through a centralized mainframe. A four-node network emerged on 5 December 1969; this network would become ARPANET, which by 1981 would consist of 213 nodes.

ARPANET's development centred around the Request for Comment process and on 7 April 1969, RFC 1 was published. This process is important because ARPANET would eventually merge with other networks to form the Internet and many of the protocols the Internet relies upon today were specified through the Request for Comment process. In September 1981, RFC 791 introduced the Internet Protocol v4 (IPv4) and RFC 793 introduced the Transmission Control Protocol (TCP) — thus creating the TCP/IP protocol that much of the Internet relies upon today.

However, not all important developments were made through the Request for Comment process. Two popular link protocols for local area networks (LANs) also appeared in the 1970s. A patent for the token ring protocol was filed by Olof Soderblom on 29 October 1974 and a paper on the Ethernet protocol was published by Robert Metcalfe and David Boggs in the July 1976 issue of *Communications of the ACM*.

Key Concepts

A number of key concepts reoccur throughout the literature on modern telecommunication systems. Some of these concepts are discussed below.

Basic Elements

A basic telecommunication system consists of three elements:

- a transmitter that takes information and converts it to a signal;
- a transmission medium that carries the signal; and,
- a receiver that receives the signal and converts it back into usable information.

For example, in a radio broadcast the broadcast tower is the transmitter, free space is the transmission medium and the radio is the receiver. Often telecommunication systems are two-way with a single device acting as both a transmitter and receiver or *transceiver*. For example, a mobile phone is a transceiver.

Telecommunication over a telephone line is called point-to-point communication because it is between one transmitter and one receiver. Telecommunication through radio broadcasts is called broadcast communication because it is between one powerful transmitter and numerous receivers.

Analogue or Digital

Signals can be either analogue or digital. In an analogue signal, the signal is varied continuously with respect to the information. In a digital signal, the information is encoded as a set of discrete values (for example ones and zeros).

During transmission the information contained in analogue signals will be degraded by noise. Conversely, unless the noise exceeds a certain threshold, the information contained in digital signals will remain intact. Noise resistance represents a key advantage of digital signals over analogue signals.

Networks

A network is a collection of transmitters, receivers and transceivers that communicate with each other. Digital networks consist of one or more routers that work together to transmit information to the correct user. An analogue network consists of one or more switches that establish a connection between two or more users. For both types of network, repeaters on a base station may be necessary to amplify or recreate the signal when it is being transmitted over long distances. This is to combat attenuation that can render the signal indistinguishable from noise.

Channels

A channel is a division in a transmission medium so that it can be used to send multiple streams of information. For example, a radio station may broadcast at 96.1 MHz while another radio station may broadcast at 94.5 MHz. In this case, the medium has been divided by frequency and each channel has received a separate frequency to broadcast on. Alternatively, one could allocate each channel a recurring segment of time over which to broadcast—this is known as time-division multiplexing and is sometimes used in digital communication.

Modulation

The shaping of a signal to convey information is known as modulation. Modulation can be used to represent a digital message as an analogue waveform. This is known as keying and several keying techniques exist (these include phase-shift keying, frequency-shift keying and amplitude-shift keying). Bluetooth, for example, uses phase-shift keying to exchange information between devices.

Modulation can also be used to transmit the information of analogue signals at higher frequencies. This is helpful because low-frequency analogue signals cannot be effectively transmitted over free space. Hence the information from a low-frequency analogue signal must be superimposed on a higher-frequency signal (known as the carrier wave) before transmission. There are several different modulation schemes available to achieve this (two of the most basic being amplitude modulation and frequency modulation). An example of this process is a DJ's voice being superimposed on a 96 MHz carrier wave using frequency modulation (the voice would then be received on a radio as the channel "96 FM").

Society and Telecommunication

Telecommunication has a significant social, cultural and economic impact on modern society. In 2006, estimates placed the telecommunication industry's revenue at $1.2 trillion (USD) or just under 3% of the gross world product (official exchange rate).

Economic Impact

Microeconomics

On the macroeconomic scale, Lars-Hendrik Röller and Leonard Waverman suggested a causal link between good telecommunication infrastructure and economic growth. Few dispute the existence of a correlation although some argue it is wrong to view the relationship as causal. Because of the economic benefits of good telecommunication infrastructure, there is increasing worry about the inequitable access to telecommunication services amongst various countries of the world—this is known as the digital divide. A 2003 survey by the International Telecommunication Union (ITU) revealed that roughly one-third of countries have less than 1 mobile subscription for every 20 people and one-third of countries have less than 1 fixed line subscription for every 20 people. In terms of Internet access, roughly half of all countries have less than 1 in 20 people with Internet access. From this information, as well as educational data, the ITU was able to compile an index that measures the overall ability of citizens to access and use information and communication technologies. Using this measure, Sweden, Denmark and Iceland received the highest ranking while the African countries Niger, Burkina Faso and Mali received the lowest.

Social Impact

Telecommunication has played a significant role in social relationships, although forms of communication like the telephone were originally viewed from a non-social perspective. Because the telephone industry descended from the telegraph industry, telephone messages stressed practicality over all else. This can be seen in national advertisements for telephones in the early 20th century, which targeted businessmen and households and emphasized the device's usefulness in contacting customers and providers of home services. The ability to send invitations to social gatherings was occasionally advertised by the telephone companies, but themes of sociability in these advertisements were rare.

In fact, not only was sociability not mentioned in the early advertisements of AT&T and other independent phone companies; rather, using the telephone for social purposes was actually frowned upon and disapproved of in those times. For decades, the telephone industry discouraged sociability, referring to social phone conversations as "frivolous" and "unnecesary". Some phone companies even placed time limits on calls to limit this behaviour. It was not until the late 1920s and 1930s that sociability began its path to becoming a prominent theme in telephone advertisements. New promotions started appealing to consumers' emotions, stressing the importance of having conversations with and staying connected to family and friends.

The role which telecommunication is playing in social relations is also becoming increasingly important. In recent years, the popularity of social networking sites has increased dramatically. These sites allow users to communicate with each other as well as post photographs, events and profiles for others to see. The profiles can list a person's age, interests, sexuality and relationship status. In this way, these sites can play important role in everything from organising social engagements to courtship.

Prior to social networking sites, technologies like SMS and the telephone also had a significant impact on social interactions. In 2000, market research group Ipsos MORI reported that 81% of 15 to 24 year-old SMS users in the United Kingdom had used the service to coordinate social arrangements and 42% to flirt.

Telecommunication and Government

Many countries have enacted legislation which conform to the *International Telecommunication Regulations* establish by the International Telecommunication Union (ITU), which is the "leading United Nations agency for information and communication technology issues." In 1947, at the Atlantic City Conference, the ITU decided to "afford international protection to all frequencies registered in a new international frequency list and used in conformity with the Radio Regulation." According to the ITU's *Radio Regulations* adopted in Atlantic City, all frequencies referenced in the *International Frequency Registration Board*, examined by the board and registered on the *International Frequency List* "shall have the right to international protection from harmful interference."

From a global perspective, there have been political debates and legislation regarding the management of telecommunication and broadcasting. The history of broadcasting discusses some of debates in relation to balancing conventional communication such as printing and telecommunication such as radio broadcasting. The onset of World War II brought on the first explosion of international broadcasting propaganda. Countries, their governments, insurgents, terrorists, and militiamen have all used telecommunication and broadcasting techniques to promote propaganda. Patriotic propaganda for political movements and colonization started the mid 1930s. In 1936 the BBC would broadcast propaganda to the Arab World to partly counteract similar broadcasts from Italy, which also had colonial interests in the region.

Modern insurgents, such as those in the latest Iraq war, often use intimidating telephone calls, SMSs and the distribution of sophisticated videos of an attack on coalition troops within hours of the operation. "The Sunni insurgents even have their own television station, Al-Zawraa, which while banned by the Iraqi government, still broadcasts from Erbil, Iraqi Kurdistan, even as coalition pressure has forced it to switch satellite hosts several times."

Modern Operation

Telephone

In an analogue telephone network, the caller is connected to the person he wants to talk to by switches at various telephone exchanges. The switches form an electrical connection between the two users and the setting of these switches is determined electronically when the caller dials the number. Once the connection is made, the caller's voice is transformed to an electrical signal using a small microphone in the caller's handset. This electrical signal is then sent through the network to the user at the other end where it is transformed back into sound by a small speaker in that person's handset. There is a separate electrical connection that works in reverse, allowing the users to converse.

The fixed-line telephones in most residential homes are analogue — that is, the speaker's voice directly determines the signal's voltage. Although short-distance calls may be handled from end-to-end as analogue signals, increasingly telephone service providers are transparently converting the signals to digital for transmission before converting them back to analogue for reception. The advantage of this is that digitized voice data can travel side-by-side with data from the Internet and can be perfectly reproduced in long distance communication (as opposed to analogue signals that are inevitably impacted by noise).

Mobile phones have had a significant impact on telephone networks. Mobile phone subscriptions now outnumber fixed-line subscriptions in many markets. Sales of mobile phones in 2005 totalled 816.6 million with that figure being almost equally shared amongst the markets of Asia/Pacific (204 m), Western Europe (164 m), CEMEA (Central Europe, the Middle East and Africa) (153.5 m), North America (148 m) and Latin America (102 m). In terms of new subscriptions over the five years from 1999, Africa has outpaced other markets with 58.2% growth. Increasingly these phones are being serviced by systems where the voice content is transmitted digitally such as GSM or W-CDMA with many markets choosing to depreciate analogue systems such as AMPS.

There have also been dramatic changes in telephone communication behind the scenes. Starting with the operation of TAT-8 in 1988, the 1990s saw the widespread adoption of systems based on optic fibres. The benefit of communicating with optic fibres is that they offer a drastic increase in data capacity. TAT-8 itself was able to carry 10 times as many telephone calls as the last copper cable laid at that time and today's optic fibre cables are able to carry 25 times as many telephone calls as TAT-8. This increase in data capacity is due to several factors: First, optic fibres are physically much smaller than competing technologies. Second, they do not suffer from crosstalk which means several hundred of them can be easily bundled together in a single cable. Lastly, improvements in multiplexing have led to an exponential growth in the data capacity of a single fibre.

Assisting communication across many modern optic fibre networks is a protocol known as Asynchronous Transfer Mode (ATM). The ATM protocol allows for the side-by-side data transmission mentioned in the second paragraph. It is suitable for public telephone networks because it establishes a pathway for data through the network and associates a traffic contract with that pathway. The traffic contract is essentially an agreement between the client and the network about how the network is to handle the data; if the network cannot meet the conditions of the traffic contract it does not accept the connection. This is important because telephone calls can negotiate a contract so as to guarantee themselves a constant bit rate, something that will ensure a caller's voice is not delayed in parts or cut-off completely. There are competitors to ATM, such as Multiprotocol Label Switching (MPLS), that perform a similar task and are expected to supplant ATM in the future.

Radio and Television

In a broadcast system, the central high-powered broadcast tower transmits a high-frequency electromagnetic wave to numerous low-powered receivers. The high-frequency wave sent by the tower is modulated with a signal containing visual or audio information. The receiver is then tuned so as to pick up the high-frequency wave and a demodulator is used to retrieve the signal containing the visual or audio information. The broadcast signal can be either analogue (signal is varied continuously with respect to the information) or digital (information is encoded as a set of discrete values).

The broadcast media industry is at a critical turning point in its development, with many countries moving from analogue to digital broadcasts. This move is made possible by the production of cheaper, faster and more capable integrated circuits. The chief advantage of digital broadcasts is that they prevent a number of complaints with traditional analogue broadcasts. For television, this includes the elimination of problems such as snowy pictures, ghosting and other distortion.

These occur because of the nature of analogue transmission, which means that perturbations due to noise will be evident in the final output. Digital transmission overcomes this problem because digital signals are reduced to discrete values upon reception and hence small perturbations do not affect the final output.

In a simplified example, if a binary message 1011 was transmitted with signal amplitudes [1.0 0.0 1.0 1.0] and received with signal ampiitudes [0.9 0.2 1.1 0.9] it would still decode to the binary message 1011 — a perfect reproduction of what was sent. From this example, a problem with digital transmissions can also be seen in that if the noise is great enough it can significantly alter the decoded message. Using forward error correction a receiver can correct a handful of bit errors in the resulting message but too much noise will lead to incomprehensible output and hence a breakdown of the transmission.

In digital television broadcasting, there are three competing standards that are likely to be adopted worldwide. These are the ATSC, DVB and ISDB standards; the adoption of these standards thus far is presented in the captioned map. All three standards use MPEG-2 for video compression. ATSC uses Dolby Digital AC-3 for audio compression, ISDB uses Advanced Audio Coding (MPEG-2 Part 7) and DVB has no standard for audio compression but typically uses MPEG-1 Part 3 Layer 2. The choice of modulation also varies between the schemes. In digital audio broadcasting, standards are much more unified with practically all countries choosing to adopt the Digital Audio Broadcasting standard (also known as the Eureka 147 standard).

The exception being the United States which has chosen to adopt HD Radio. HD Radio, unlike Eureka 147, is based upon a transmission method known as in-band on-channel transmission that allows digital information to "piggyback" on normal AM or FM analogue transmissions. However, despite the pending switch to digital, analogue television remains transmitted in most countries. An exception is the United States that ended analogue television transmission on the 12th of June 2009 after twice delaying the switch over deadline. For analogue television, there are three standards in use. These are known as PAL, NTSC and SECAM. For analogue radio, the switch to digital is made more difficult by the fact that analogue receivers are a fraction of the cost of digital receivers. The choice of modulation for analogue radio is typically between amplitude modulation (AM) or frequency modulation (FM). To achieve stereo playback, an amplitude modulated subcarrier is used for stereo FM.

The Internet

The Internet is a worldwide network of computers and computer networks that can communicate with each other using the Internet Protocol. Any computer on the Internet has a unique IP address that can be used by other computers to route information to it. Hence, any computer on the Internet can send a message to any other computer using its IP address. These messages carry with them the originating computer's IP address allowing for two-way communication. The Internet is thus an exchange of messages between computers. As of 2008, an estimated 21.9% of the world population has access to the Internet with the highest access rates (measured as a percentage of the population) in North America (73.6%), Oceania/Australia (59.5%) and Europe (48.1%). In terms of broadband access, Iceland (26.7%), South Korea (25.4%) and the Netherlands (25.3%) led the world.

The Internet works in part because of protocols that govern how the computers and routers communicate with each other. The nature of computer network communication lends itself to a layered approach where individual protocols in the protocol stack run more-or-less independently of other protocols. This allows lower-level protocols to be customized for the network situation while not changing the way higher-level protocols operate. A practical example of why this is important is because it allows an Internet browser to run the same code regardless of whether the computer it is running on is connected to the Internet through an Ethernet or Wi-Fi connection. Protocols are often talked about in terms of their place in the OSI reference model (pictured on the right), which emerged in 1983 as the first step in an unsuccessful attempt to build a universally adopted networking protocol suite.

For the Internet, the physical medium and data link protocol can vary several times as packets traverse the globe. This is because the Internet places no constraints on what physical medium or data link protocol is used. This leads to the adoption of media and protocols that best suit the local network situation. In practice, most intercontinental communication will use the Asynchronous Transfer Mode (ATM) protocol (or a modern equivalent) on top of optic fibre. This is because for most intercontinental communication the Internet shares the same infrastructure as the public switched telephone network. At the network layer, things become standardized with the Internet Protocol (IP) being adopted for logical addressing. For the World Wide Web, these "IP addresses" are derived from the human readable form using the Domain Name System (e.g. 72.14.207.99 is derived from www.google.com). At the moment, the most widely used version of the Internet Protocol is version four but a move to version six is imminent.

At the transport layer, most communication adopts either the Transmission Control Protocol (TCP) or the User Datagram Protocol (UDP). TCP is used when it is essential every message sent is received by the other computer where as UDP is used when it is merely desirable. With TCP, packets are retransmitted if they are lost and placed in order before they are presented to higher layers. With UDP, packets are not ordered or retransmitted if lost. Both TCP and UDP packets carry port numbers with them to specify what application or process the packet should be handled by. Because certain application-level protocols use certain ports, network administrators can manipulate traffic to suit particular requirements. Examples are to restrict Internet access by blocking the traffic destined for a particular port or to affect the performance of certain applications by assigning priority.

Above the transport layer, there are certain protocols that are sometimes used and loosely fit in the session and presentation layers, most notably the Secure Sockets Layer (SSL) and Transport Layer Security (TLS) protocols. These protocols ensure that the data transferred between two parties remains completely confidential and one or the other is in use when a padlock appears in the address bar of your web browser. Finally, at the application layer, are many of the protocols Internet users would be familiar with such as HTTP (web browsing), POP3 (e-mail), FTP (file transfer), IRC (Internet chat), BitTorrent (file sharing) and OSCAR (instant messaging).

Local Area Networks

Despite the growth of the Internet, the characteristics of local area networks (computer networks that run at most a few kilometres) remain distinct. This is because networks on this scale do not require all the features associated with larger networks and are often more cost-effective and efficient without them.

In the mid-1980s, several protocol suites emerged to fill the gap between the data link and applications layer of the OSI reference model. These were Appletalk, IPX and NetBIOS with the dominant protocol suite during the early 1990s being IPX due to its popularity with MS-DOS users. TCP/IP existed at this point but was typically only used by large government and research facilities. As the Internet grew in popularity and a larger percentage of traffic became Internet-related, local area networks gradually moved towards TCP/IP and today networks mostly dedicated to TCP/IP traffic are common. The move to TCP/IP was helped by technologies such as DHCP that allowed TCP/IP clients to discover their own network address — a functionality that came standard with the AppleTalk/IPX/NetBIOS protocol suites.

It is at the data link layer though that most modern local area networks diverge from the Internet. Whereas Asynchronous Transfer Mode (ATM) or Multiprotocol Label Switching (MPLS) are typical data link protocols for larger networks, Ethernet and Token Ring are typical data link protocols for local area networks. These protocols differ from the former protocols in that they are simpler (e.g. they omit features such as Quality of Service guarantees) and offer collision prevention. Both of these differences allow for more economic set-ups.

Despite the modest popularity of Token Ring in the 80's and 90's, virtually all local area networks now use wired or wireless Ethernet. At the physical layer, most wired Ethernet implementations use copper twisted-pair cables (including the common 10BASE-T networks). However, some early implementations used coaxial cables and some recent implementations (especially high-speed ones) use optic fibres. Where optic fibre is used, the distinction must be made between multi-mode fibre and single-mode fibre. Multi-mode fibre can be thought of as thicker optical fibre that is cheaper to manufacture devices for but that suffers from less usable bandwidth and greater attenuation (i.e. poor long-distance performance).

8

Computer-Mediated Communication and the Online Classroom

Introduction: From Marks in the Sand to Computer Conferencing Via Fiber Optics

Throughout the history of human communication, advances in technology have powered paradigmatic shifts in education. Technology changes both what we can do and what we decide is best to do; big shifts in culture cannot occur until the tools are available. The printing press is an example. Before its invention there were people who could read and write; yet not much reading and writing took place because, for one thing, books were costly and scarce. The press enabled widespread literacy, with books accessible and more affordable for all. The spread of literacy in turn changed both the educational system and the class structure, with consequences that still shape our attitudes today. When people began to accumulate knowledge through the technology of writing and reading, they found a way to preserve it through succeeding generations without relying on memory—greatly changing the way education was conducted. The impact of the printing press on students of the time has been analyzed and reanalyzed. No longer did students have to write or remember everything the teacher delivered; students could use books. But they did not completely give up the oral/aural connection; witness the popularity of lecture classes even now. As new technology enables shifts at the level of delivery, old technologies are augmented, not totally replaced. Even though many of us have computers at our disposal, we still use books, speech, and pen or pencil writing in education.

More recently, the general availability of electricity has fostered an almost universal use of such inventions as radio, television, and, increasingly, computers. For decades, educational technologists have likened the impact of television and other electronic ways of presenting information to the impact of the printing press on learning. Although to date television has not had nearly the impact on school learning that books have had, we have yet to determine whether its impact on education as a whole will be as great and long lasting. Schooling is only a part of education. Much of education takes place outside of schooling, both as planned activities and unplanned learning. We may not understand the instructional goals of the Music Television (MTV) channel broadcasts, and those goals may differ from those of educators, but that does not mean MTV viewers do not learn anything. Ultimately we must consider what kind of world we as educators want to build. If we envision the merger of computers and telecommunications as a new tool for teaching and learning, now is the time to clearly articulate and promulgate our goals in order to shape future uses of instructional technology.

Educational Systems

For communications to take place, at a bare minimum, there must be a sender, a receiver, and a message. If this message is intended as instruction, then besides student, teacher, and content, we must also consider the environment in which this educational communication occurs — an environment that benefits the educational system in some ways and constrains it in others. Part of this learning environment can include various technologies and media. If "the medium is the message," that is, if technology changes what we can do and how we think about it, then the various media enabled by instructional technology also change both what we can do in education and how we conceive of it.

For many years, educators have been exploring ways to combine theories of differing learning styles and student-constructed knowledge with the theory of practice-centered learning. Instead of being passive recipients of knowledge, we now consider students capable of constructing their own knowledge with guidance from the teacher. We can offer part of this tutorial guidance by setting up an environment that will provide students with the resources necessary for independent exploration. In using emerging computer-based technology as a resource, students are encouraged to explore their own interests and to become active educational workers, with opportunities to solve some authentic problems.

As an agent for socialization and collaboration, the networked computer has an even greater potential in education than does the stand-alone, knowledge-server type of computer. The active environment of social learning provided by a computer with access to local, national, and international networks increases interaction and communication among students, their teachers, peers, parents, and other members of the world community. Although there are some differences between distance education and classroom education, the significant issues concerning the use of computer networking and other emerging technologies to promote learning in both are similar.

Distance Learning

In addition to being entertained, viewers seem to learn from the Music Television (MTV) channel's eclectic mix of music videos, news, instruction, and information on the world of popular music and performers. Broadcast at a distance, MTV's educational content appears largely unplanned in the sense that educators are not directly involved. However, the distance education now originating from universities and colleges attempts to plan educational content and activities for students removed in place and time from their instructors. Historically, we have not done a very good job of implementing the concept of learner-centered education in distance education. It is difficult, at best, to instill a mindset of lifelong learning in others if we do not understand it and demonstrate it ourselves. One of the reasons that we have failed in this area has been that the tools were not available to do much besides deliver education (as opposed to enable learning) at a distance. Now, computers and telecommunications have opened the way to formats other than pen-and-paper correspondence courses and allow for a more interactive, integrated learning environment.

The type of change enabled by computer-mediated communication (CMC) does not just involve adding new technology to old ways of organizing teaching and learning. Although the perennial problem is still one of instructional content and design, we must not pave over old cow paths. The paradigm shift is from a teaching environment to a learning environment.

Another notion current in educational circles is that we need to develop motivated, skilful, lifelong learners. As knowledge in many fields increases exponentially, we cannot hope to fill up students as if they were passive, empty vessels. During formal schooling, aspiring professionals can only begin to take in the amount of information that they will need during their career life times. The knowledge base of certain fields may have appeared static for decades, but we can no longer accept that view. Therefore, we must teach students to become lifelong learners by helping them locate the resources to continue learning.

Distance educators are now beginning to focus on a related set of notions: (a) there are different learning styles, (b) students create their own meaning when learning new things, and (c) what makes a difference in content retention and transfer is not so much what is done by teachers, but what students as learners can be encouraged to do themselves.

Much has been written about the importance of accommodating the learning styles of different kinds of students. Suffice it to say here that too often students have little choice in what to learn, how to learn it, or when to learn it. The body of literature on constructivism which has emerged over the past few decades has also contributed to our understanding of learning styles. When content is meaningless to the students' world view, when they are taught as if they were passive recipients of knowledge, or when they have little engagement in the instructional tasks, students have no incentive to construct their own knowledge and little motivation to retain information or transfer its use to novel situations.

The notion of practice-centered learning (PCL) is also important to distance learning. As we learn more about how learning occurs, it becomes increasingly clear that the educational process takes place in a complex internal and external environment. One of the teacher's roles is to become the creator of an effective external learning environment that stimulates the environment within. How do teachers and developers of instruction create environments that are conducive to and enhance student learning?

The technology that can help provide these new environments for education is emerging. This technology allows us to utilize such methods as cooperative learning, to recognize such concepts as interdisciplinary needs in education, and to provide an environment in which collaborative efforts are rewarded. These methods foster a view of knowledge in which expertise is distributed and created among the different participants. Now there is no shortage of technology, only a shortage of the educational vision necessary to use the technology to create new educational environments.

Computers and Telecommunications

What we have been discussing is a reengineering of education, not only in the sense of rethinking the organization of site-based schools, but also in the sense of finding ways to unite computers and telecommunications and bring down the schoolhouse walls; to deliver instructional content when and where it is needed-whether in the home, the workplace, or the school. Computer-mediated communication (CMC) promotes a type of interaction that is often lacking in the traditional teacher-based classroom. It allows learners the freedom to explore alternative pathways-to find and develop their own style of learning. What if content could be delivered in the form of graphics, text, and/or full-motion video, whenever and wherever in the world it is requested? How do we, as teachers and educators, responsibly participate in and make use of the inevitable technological changes at hand?

Computers are not a threat to the teacher (although the role of the teacher must change when using them), but computers may threaten the chalkboard. Computer technologies allow professionals to share with students tools that we use daily. Further, as educators, we can provide guidance to help students develop meaningful ways to construct their own knowledge, much as we ourselves do.

Technology enables us to implement these new visions in distance learning. [T]echnology makes it possible that these investigations are not limited to students from one classroom, school, grade, or country necessarily-nor to exclude experts in the field of inquiry from the collaboration. Effective learning hinges on active engagement by the student and the construction of knowledge on their own leads to understanding (Sheingold, 1991). This learning is not a solitary process. Rather, it occurs in a larger world of people and technology.

CMC and networking in general can promote long-distance collaboration among students and content specialists in many different areas. The integrated use of technology offers many educational opportunities and possibilities when driven by sound visions of learning. The students' ability to create knowledge can be enhanced when their instructors use varied instructional delivery formats to provide a richer environment than is used in most distance education practiced today. However, as Sheingold (1991) points out, these ambitious new goals for student learning, along with radical changes in the students' roles those goals bring about, must be met with radical, ambitious changes in the educational process. Indeed, information technology offers options for reorganizing and refining distance education. But our new visions of distance learning must drive our decisions about our use of technology, not vice versa.

Although major cultural shifts do not occur without the tools that make them possible, once those tools are at hand, the shifts are inevitable. Emerging technologies, such as interactive television and the "superhighway" for information exchange, may look different depending on who builds them (e.g., telephone companies, cable television companies, federal governments), but we may be assured that they will be built by someone. How we as educators will participate in this enterprise is a issue that deserves our closest attention. More than merely a shift within education, our participation in this movement will bring about major shifts in society and culture. As the number of students outside the ages of 18 to 25 increases, and the number of persons requiring off-campus classes rises, the very existence and future of a university or college may hinge on serving this newly defined and diverse population. In this book, we hope to show how CMC can help serve that population.

In combination with other media, computers can utilize an instructional design that teaches to the multiple intelligences that Gardner (1983) speaks of in *Frames of Mind* (linguistic, logico-mathematical, intrapersonal, spatial, musical, bodily kinesthetic, and interpersonal). The idea behind this instructional design is to use as many methods and formats for instruction (e.g., small group discussion, graphics, lecture, hands-on labs, writing/reflection, sound, CMC, and conferencing) as possible, provided that instructional goals and design dictate their use.

CMC in Distance Learning

The authors in this book use technological advances that enable them to start implementing some of the educational ideas we have been discussing with their students. Instead of unwittingly supporting isolated efforts by individual distance learners, they encourage discussion and collaboration. Rather than an institutional or teacher-centered approach to instruction, these educators take a more learner-centered approach.

Educators around the world are experimenting with and laying the foundation for new opportunities for learners to access education through connections and technologies that did not exist 10 years ago. How will these new options affect our understanding of the educational process? What provisions should we be making now to prepare ourselves and our students to use this new technology of CMC in the most pedagogically sound and cost effective ways? To begin to answer some of these questions, Justus Lewis, Janet Whitaker, and John Julian, identify models for distance education and discuss some of the issues raised and opportunities provided by computer communications within distance-learning environments. Morten Paulsen, an array of illustrative CMC applications for online classrooms and distance education programs. Each application is classified according to its predominant communication paradigm: one-alone, one-to-one, one-to-many, and many-to-many. Included in the one-alone section are applications that utilize online resources: information (online databases and online journals), software (online applications and software libraries), and people (online interest groups and individual experts). As examples in the section on one-to-one CMC, Paulsen includes learning contracts, mentorship, apprenticeship, and correspondence study. These applications are characterized by one-to-one relationships and by individualized learning.

In discussing one-to-many applications, such as lectures and skits, Paulsen differentiates them from other forms of CMC by their use of presentation techniques in which learners are not usually invited to interact. With many-to-many CMC applications, all participants have the opportunity to take part in the kind of interaction that can be facilitated in computer conferencing systems. In this section, Paulsen discusses such techniques as debate, simulation, role play, discussion groups, transcript-based assignments, brainstorming, the delphi technique, the nominal group technique, and project groups. In conclusion, Paulsen notes that the applications presented are by no means meant to constitute an exhaustive list. They represent, however, a comprehensive set of examples that show the range of techniques available for designers of CMC courses.

Effective design is essential to the success of an online course. Using their recent experience designing an online adult education graduate seminar as an example, Dan Eastmond and Linda Ziegahn outline essential issues, considerations, and tasks for instructional development with CMC to which the course designer must attend. These considerations include overall course design issues, resource allocation, syllabus creation, activity selection, online structure production, and evaluation planning. Appropriate attention to these items during the design phase informs the development and delivery phases of the online course, thereby creating a "good learning experience" for adult college students.

Morten Paulsen's, presents a review and analysis of the literature relevant to moderating educational conferences on computer networks. He suggests that moderators should identify their preferred pedagogical styles, based on their philosophical orientation, their chosen moderator roles, and their preferred facilitation techniques. The author assigns the moderator role three functions: the organizational, the social, and the intellectual. To help moderators improve their moderating skills, Paulsen organizes facilitation techniques recommended in the literature according to these three role functions. Finally, the author assists moderators in finding their pedagogical style by identifying some possible philosophies, roles, and facilitation techniques discussed in the literature.

Rae Wahl Rohfeld and Roger Hiemstra draw on their experience teaching in the Syracuse University Distance Education Program to examine the experiences of both course facilitators and students in courses delivered via CMC. They found that effective courses via CMC are based on a learner-centered approach to education in which facilitators and students share responsibility and participation in learning and teaching. To initiate such a process, facilitators must make sure they and their students have adequate training and support on the electronic system. They must also do a great deal of advance planning to teach a course via the new medium. By initiating a variety of activities, both on and off-line, facilitators can encourage an active, challenging learning environment. As the class conference progressed, Rohfeld and Hiemstra found that different strategies were necessary to keep energy high. Those involved in the Syracuse University Distance Education Program were highly satisfied with this mode of learning once they got past initial difficulties with technology. Because the courses were delivered by CMC, students were able to take considerable control over their learning in terms of how they scheduled both personal study time and group-interaction time, how much personal contact they had with the instructor and other learners, and how they contributed to the class. Rohfeld and Hiemstra are confident that courses delivered via CMC can meet immediate learning needs as well as help learners increase self-direction in their ongoing learning.

Morton Cotlar and James N. Shimabukuro describe their use of electronic guest lectures to stimulate thinking and interaction among students. This technique, like other applications of CMC in education, shows promise. However, the degree to which students interact in meaningful ways with the guest lecturers seems to be related to the style of the lecture. Three different lecturers addressed a graduate course (through text documents posted to the class discussion group, with the invitation for follow-up questions and discussion) and evoked markedly different degrees and types of responses. The authors analyzed the style of each lecture to explore the relationship between style and responsiveness. Extraordinary findings showed that the extent of personalization and readability in the lectures strongly influenced responsiveness. Cotlar and Shimabukuro invite others to replicate this kind of study to validate their findings.

Rachelle Heller and Greg Kearsley describe their experiences using a combination of instructional television and a computer bulletin board system (BBS) to teach graduate students in computer science and education. The television component provided a medium for lectures, guest interviews, and software demonstrations, whereas the bulletin board was used to stimulate interaction among students and the instructors. Heller and Kearsley used a variety of different strategies to encourage interaction on the BBS, including assignments, discussion questions, and team activities. Based on the evaluations completed by the students in their courses, the authors concluded that the combination of media works very effectively.

Alexander McAuley describes an innovative use of CMC to support cost-effective communication links across wide distances in the Baffin area of the Canadian North West Territories. The region's 3,100 kindergarten to Grade 12 students attend 20 schools, and approximately 90% of the students are Inuit and speak Inuktitut as their first language. The current heart of K-12 CMC on Baffin Island is an electronic bulletin board, with electronic mail and a conferencing system (supporting both synchronous and asynchronous communications) called "Takujaksat," which translates roughly from Inuktitut as "things you might like to see."

One of the most interesting and successful projects to make regional use of Takujaksat is an electronic newsletter called TGIF. Made up from contributions submitted by students from around Baffin, it is compiled, edited, and distributed electronically every Friday by students at Takijualuk School in Pond Inlet.

The Baffin School District's efforts to increase the use of CMC include providing an online component intended to follow up all face-to-face staff in-services and sponsoring projects that require student interaction via the online environment. The district also encourages interested teachers to coordinate and plan a project together through CMC and present it in the classroom. They then identify those teachers who are predisposed to work in this collaborative manner and attempt to match them with people and projects they will find rewarding and exciting. In justifying the support for CMC in Baffin schools, McAuley's examples also indicate a number of requirements for success: (a) CMC must have a strong user base at the local level before it can be widely used at a distance, (b) effective use of CMC demands specific conditions and skills, and (c) teachers and students must be supported in acquiring those skills. The author notes that future work will focus on all three of those areas.

Claire McInerney explores a method of integrating CMC within the curriculum of a course on communications technology designed for nontraditional students studying information management. Through anecdotal evidence drawn from student and faculty experiences, McInerney looks at some of the anticipated outcomes of CMC as well as the unanticipated benefits and limitations of CMC.

Ken and Carrie Loss-Cutler represent a growing group of homeschooling parents who are incorporating CMC into their curriculum and taking advantage of the resources available on the Internet. The Loss-Cutlers provide details on the various electronic discussion groups that deal specifically with alternative schoolers' interests and describe some of the beneficial network-supported activities available to homeschooled students. Since 1986 Jason Ohler has directed a Master's degree program in Education Technology at the University of Alaska, Southeast. Although the program seeks to empower teachers to be effective, creative, and socially responsible users of a wide range of new technologies, one area of instructional technology receives particular emphasis: educational applications of telecommunications and CMC. During the past six years, Ohler has taught, worked with, provided in-services for, and consulted on numerous projects by K-12 teachers and students in the field of educational telecommunications.

Ohler provides a vision as well as a practical road map for educators wishing to offer extended training in telecommunications to fellow K-12 teachers and their students. As the basis of this chapter, Ohler uses the syllabus of a 15-week course on educational telecommunications for the classroom teacher he has been teaching for the past five years. Christopher Baker and Thomas Buller observe that primary and secondary school systems are so burdened by a lack of funding that they usually cannot afford the tools and connections needed for CMC. Dedicated, wide-area computer network connections offer many features ranging from e-mail to peer discussions and have the potential to revolutionize education, but these dedicated connections are currently too costly for struggling K-12 schools. However, specialized access services such as NGS Kidsnetwork, CompuServe, and Argonne's NEWTON offer teachers and students a chance to experience the "global classroom" without the global price tag. Ava L. Fajen and J. Scott Christianson examine the use of Bulletin Board System (BBS) networks as an educational resource, specifically in primary and secondary classrooms. BBS networks are distributed group conferencing systems (Santoro, 1993) that allow teachers and students from around the world to interact with each other electronically in "virtual classrooms," sharing information and collaborating on learning projects. This chapter presents a brief history of BBS networks, explains the basic principles of BBS networking, and explores two BBS networks devoted to K-12 education: the Free Education Mail (FrEdMail) network and K12Net (a subdivision of the Fidonet BBS network). The authors also present a short summary of off-line mail readers, electronic mail tools used to decrease online time and costs.

Jill Ellsworth discusses not only specific sources of information useful to distance educators, but also covers some of the principle information management tools available on the Internet: Archie, Gopher, Veronica, and Worldwide Web. Scholars on the net can use these tools to locate a variety of information resources available through the Internet.

Online information about distance education comes from many sources and is available in many forms. There are several scholarly discussion groups distributed via LISTSERVs, for example, that focus on issues of concern to distance educators. In addition there are archives of papers, conference announcements, calls for papers, electronic journals, literature reviews, software, books, guides, library catalogs, resource databases and more-all accessible with a few keystrokes.

The key to accessing Internet information, says Ellsworth, is to gain familiarity with the sources and to use them regularly. Users need to take the time to keep up with the Internet, a dynamic system in which the resources can change every day, and to which new, more user-friendly search tools are constantly being added online.

Computer-mediated Communication

Computer-Mediated Communication (CMC) is defined as any communicative transaction that occurs through the use of two or more networked computers. While the term has traditionally referred to those communications that occur via computer-mediated formats (e.g., instant messages, e-mails, chat rooms), it has also been applied to other forms of text-based interaction such as text messaging. Research on CMC focuses largely on the social effects of different computer-supported communication technologies. Many recent studies involve Internet-based social networking supported by social software.

Scope of the Field

Scholars from a variety of fields study phenomena that can be described under the umbrella term of CMC. For example, many take a sociopsychological approach to CMC by examining how humans use "computers" (or digital media) to manage interpersonal interaction, form impressions and form and maintain relationships. These studies have often focused on the differences between online and offline interactions, though contemporary research is moving towards the view that CMC should be studied as embedded in everyday life. Another branch of CMC research examines the use of paralinguistic features such as emoticons, pragmatic rules such as turn-taking and the sequential analysis and organization of talk, and the various sociolects, styles, registers or sets of terminology specific to these environments. The study of language in these contexts is typically based on text-based forms of CMC, and is sometimes referred to as "computer-mediated discourse analysis". The way humans communicate in professional, social, and educational settings varies widely, depending upon not only the environment but also the method of communication in which the communication occurs (which, in this case, is through computers or other ICTs). The study of communication to achieve collaboration—common work products—is termed computer-supported collaboration and includes only some of the concerns of other forms of CMC research. Popular forms of CMC include e-mail, video, audio or text chat (text conferencing including "instant messaging"), bulletin boards, list-servs and MMOs. These settings are changing rapidly with the development of new technologies. Weblogs (blogs) have also become popular, and the exchange of RSS data has better enabled users to each "become their own publisher".

Characteristics

Communication occurring within a computer-mediated format has an effect on many different aspects of an interaction. Some of these that have received attention in the scholarly literature include impression formation, deception and lying behaviour, group dynamics, disinhibition and especially relationship formation.

Computer-Mediated Communication is examined and compared to other communication media through a number of aspects thought to be universal to all forms of communication, including (but not limited to) synchronicity, persistence or "recordability", and anonymity. The association of these aspects with different forms of communication varies widely. For example, instant messaging is prototypically synchronous, but rarely persistent since one loses all the content when one closes the dialog box unless one has a message log set up or has manually copy-pasted the conversation. E-mail and message boards are similar; both are prototypically low in synchronicity since response time varies, but high in persistence since messages sent and received are saved. Properties that separate CMC from other media also include transience, its multimodal nature, and its relative lack of governing codes of conduct. CMC is able to overcome physical and social limitations of other forms of communication and therefore allow the interaction of people who are not physically sharing the same space. Anonymity and in part privacy and security depends more on the context and particular program being used or web page being visited. However, most researchers in the field acknowledge the importance of considering the psychological and social implications of these factors alongside the technical "limitations".

Types

Computer-Mediated Communication can be divided into synchronous and asynchronous modes. In synchronous communications all participants are online at the same time, while asynchronous communications occurs without time constraints.

In *Datacloud: Toward a New Theory of Online Work,* Johndan Johnson-Eilola describes a specific computer-supported collaboriating space: The Smart Board. According to Johnson-Eilola, a "Smart Board system provides a 72-inch, rear projection, touchscreen, intelligent whiteboard surface for work". In *Datacloud,* Johnson-Eilola asserts that "[w]e are attempting to understand how users move within information spaces, how users can exist within information spaces rather than merely gaze at them, and how information spaces must be shared with others rather than being private, lived within rather than simply visited". He explains how the Smart Board system offers an information space that allows his students to engage in active collaboration. He makes three distinct claims regarding the functionality of the technology: 1)

The Smart Board allows users to work with large amounts of information, 2) It offers an information space that invites active collaboration, 3) The work produced is often "dynamic and contingent".

Johnson-Eilola further explains that with the Smart Board "…information work becom[es] a bodied experience". Users have the opportunity to engage with—inhabit—the technology by direct manipulation. Moreover, this space allows for more than one user; essentially, it invites multiple users.

Language learning

Computer-Mediated Communication is widely discussed in language learning because Computer-Mediated Communication provides opportunities for language learners to practice their language. For example, Warschauer conducted several case studies on using email or discussion boards in different language classes. Warschauer claimed that information and communications technology "bridge the historic divide between speech ... and writing". Thus, considerable concern has arisen over the reading and writing research in L2 due to the booming of Internet.

9

Communication Technology for Social Development

Introduction

Projects applying information and communication technology (ICT) to social development are rarely researched, evaluated or reported, and even when they are, the conceptualisation, design, conduct and reporting of this work often lacks quality.

There is a need for far more rigorous research into ICT projects at the national, organisational and practitioner levels, to achieve a body of research that can guide future planning and practice. Policy makers, planners and practitioners alike need to be involved in undertaking formative and summative evaluation, and quantitative and/or qualitative research, not only to improve their own knowledge and skills in ICT for social development, but to provide robust and strategically significant findings that can influence and guide governments, donors, and other key stakeholders. Research and evaluation of ICT for social development are needed at the:

1) National level:

- to enable governments, national agencies and other key decision makers to assess the quality, cost, relevance, effectiveness and potential of ICT projects; and

- to inform policy making, management and implementation in such projects.

2) Organisational level:

- to ensure that social development needs are understood and provided for;
- to satisfy the internal and external reporting requirements and assure quality in processes and outcomes; and
- to ensure that those engaged in the projects are granted the status, training and resources they need.

3) Practitioner level:

- to improve the understanding and practice of the managers, course and materials developers, teachers, trainers and technologists; and
- to persuade others to support such projects.

ICT for social development needs to be informed by:

- empirical inquiry, through which projects are analysed to guide future practice;
- theoretical inquiry, in which hypotheses and conceptual frameworks are developed to guide future thinking and action;
- formative research, which is conducted throughout projects to monitor what is occurring so that corrections and revisions can be made before it is too late;
- summative research, which is carried out at the conclusion of projects to measure the outcomes against the missions, goals and key performance indicators, and to report on what succeeded and what failed, and why;
- quantitative research, which involves collecting numerical data through surveys and questionnaires to inform the planning, implementation and review of projects; and
- qualitative research, which involves observing, questioning

and documenting processes, actions, behaviours, opinions, and values, to inform the planning, implementation and review of projects.

Or by any combination of these.

Let us consider the kinds of research needed in ICT for social development. Let us suppose we are devising a project using ICT to help farmers in remote/rural areas improve their farming methods. Before embarking on this project, we need to know who these farmers are, where they are, what their needs are, their levels of literacy, their circumstances and culture, the technologies they can access, afford and use, and the training methods that are most likely to work well for them. This work is *formative*. As we develop and deliver the ICT applications, we need constantly monitoring of the processes and outcomes, to see whether they are working or need changing. This research is also formative. At the conclusion of this project, we need to know and report on the outcomes, the numbers of farmers who took part, the dropout rate and its causes, the costs, cost benefits and cost savings, the effectiveness of the technology, any problems that arose, and any further work that is needed. This is *summative* research.

Some of our research will be *quantitative*. We need to find out what percentage of the targeted group of farmers signed up for the project, what percentage stayed the course, what percentage could access the technology, what percentage could operate the technology, what percentage found the ICT information and training useful, and so on. Some of our research will be *qualitative*. For example, we need to know what the farmers thought of the project, what they liked and disliked about it, what they found most useful, whether they put the new ideas into practice and whether they worked well, and whether they would take part in further projects.

All of the above is *empirical inquiry*. If we engaged in *theoretical inquiry*, we would try to work out what theory or model could be applied to training farmers via ICT, or what cultural, psychological and other factors needed to be embedded in this framework. Some of this work could be in the form of independent or *'third party research'*, carried out by outside experts who have nothing to gain or lose from their studies. Such research is strictly objective, usually 'once off', and primarily concerned with providing feedback to governments, donors and other providers on projects' quality, impact and value for money.

Some of this work may be in the form of 'practitioner research' undertaken by managers, teachers or trainers, instructional designers, ICT experts, and others involved in the project, in order to assess and improve their professional practice, test new ideas, methods and materials, share feedback with colleagues and decide which new approaches to carry forward. By its very nature, practitioner research is cyclical. As Woodley (2004) points out, the meaning of 'research' is "to search and search again". Situations are continually changing, there are always new depths and complexities to fathom, and new knowledge is forever throwing new light on our assumptions and practices. So there is always need for further research to support, extend, challenge or disprove our thinking and practices.

A Critical review of ODL and ICT Research and Evaluation

Much of the research into open and distance learning (ODL) and ICT comes in for criticism. The former Vice Chancellor of the UK Open University and President of the Commonwealth of Learning, Sir John Daniel refers (2002) to the mass of trivial and badly conceived research that has spawned, as ODL has become fashionable in conventional institutions. Professor Dianna Laurillard, head of the UK government's e learning strategy unit, observed (1994) that many evaluative studies of ICT are persistently and predictably inconclusive because they ignore the many complex factors that can support or undermine their use. Phipps & Merisotis (1999) referred to the paucity of original research dedicated to explaining or predicting phenomena related to ODL, and observed that little of this work allows for extraneous variables or evidences cause and effect. For example, many studies suggest that ODL courses compare favourably with classroom learning, but the quality of much of the research is questionable, so the findings are inconclusive. Naidu (2003), Passi & Mishra (2003) and Robinson & Creed (2004) have suggested that much ODL/ ICT research is reiterative, uses invalid and unreliable instruments, and yields little in the way of new information.

Reviewing the 374 editorials, articles and colloquia published in the 31 issues of the *British Journal of Educational Technology (BJET)* between January 2000 and November 2005, Latchem (2006) found that over 50% of them addressed issues in the university sector, that very few examined ODL/ICT in open schooling or technical and vocational education and training (TVET), that *none examined ICT for social development* or non formal adult and community education, and that the developing countries were barely represented. Galbraith (1967) defined technology as "the systematic application of scientific and other organised knowledge to practical tasks". This definition is probably the best organising concept for the development of educational technology and its evolution into a discipline.

Educational technology is defined by the US Association for Educational Communications & Technology (AECT) as "the theory and practice of the design, development, utilisation, management, and evaluation of processes and resources for learning". Despite having 'educational technology' in its title, however, the majority of articles appearing in *BJET* were more narrowly focused than the definition suggests, dealing only with hardware, software, course design and teaching methods. Very few of the articles dealt with the all important planning, managerial, organisational, resource, costing or student support issues.

The momentum of ODL/ICT research is certainly growing in the Asian region, in, for example, the Open University of Hong Kong's Centre for Research in Distance and Adult Learning (CRIDAL), the Indira Gandhi National Open University's Staff Training and Research Institute (STRIDE), and at the Commonwealth Educational Media Co operative/Centre for Asia (CEMCA). Research carried out in the region is disseminated through national journals such as the *Indian Journal of Open Learning*, the *Turkish Online Journal of Distance Education*, and in international journals such as the Asia Pacific Educational Research

Association's *Educational Research for Policy and Practice,* and the Asian Society of Open and Distance Education's *Asian Journal of Distance Education.* Conferences organised by the Asian Association of Open Universities (AAOU) and other organisations also help to advance the research agenda, as do events organised by international agencies such as the ASEAN Foundation, the Asian Development Bank, UNESCO, the Commonwealth of Learning (COL), and the International Development Research Centre (IDRC) of Canada. Asian research also comes in for a fair degree of criticism. Reviewing research at the national level, the UNESCO Forum on Higher Education, Research and Knowledge concluded that it tends to be top down, that government funded research on national reforms often lack assessment, relevance and quality, and that rather than being undertaken prior to policy making, the research is often used to justify or amend policies that are already in place. Reviewing research and evaluation in India, gaps between the research that was needed and that actually undertaken; most of the research was piecemeal and lacking in a theoretical basis; and it lacked quantitative and qualitative rigour.

Reviewing the proceedings of the Asian Association of Open Universities (AAOU) Conferences held between 1995 and 1998, only 38% of the 178 papers were based upon empirical research. The majority of papers theorised about ODL/ICT, were descriptive, were re workings of familiar ground, and relied heavily on western theories, models and findings. As with the *BJET* articles discussed above, the majority of the AAOU papers focused on instructional technology and design, and were from the university sector. Few of the writers reported on student needs, characteristics and performance. Fewer still investigated student support and quality assurance, and only a small number dealt with non completion and failure rates, staff development, course evaluation, policy making, management, admissions, credit, costs, cost benefits, cultural and social factors, gender issues, library and information services, or plagiarism. There were *no papers on ODL/ICT for social development*.

The above findings clearly show that many significant aspects of ODL/ICT are not being researched or reported. From the performance improvement perspective, it is also noteworthy that many of the studies reported at the AAOU conferences were by managers or researchers rather than by those directly involved in developing and delivering the programmes or services. This may well lead to a failure to feed findings back into the workplace. If research is to inform practice, it is far better if those implementing the projects also do the research and evaluation. The lack of reliable data on success and completion rates in Asian ODL. It is equally difficult to find any cost efficiency, cost utility, cost effectiveness and cost benefit studies that would convince politicians, donors, administrators and providers of the values of ODL/ICT.

As in the international arena, most Asian research papers about ODL/ICT derive from the university sector. Very few deal with open schooling, colleges and non formal adult and community education, and *ICT for social development barely receives a mention*. This is extremely disappointing in a region where ODL/ICT are bringing education, training and information to millions of previously disadvantaged people, and are enabling women's groups, ethnic minorities and other previously unheard voices to build coalitions, share information, and find solutions to their problems in ways never possible previously. It is also disappointing to find so little research into any differences that may exist between 'Asian' and 'Western' styles of learning and their implications for ODL/ICT. Most research of this kind is carried out by Western researchers. How much better it would be if Asian researchers were researching and reporting on these issues. International organisations such as the ASEAN Foundation, World Bank, Japan International Cooperation Agency, the Commonwealth of Learning, private sector providers such as Microsoft, non profit organisations such as Grameen Bank, and national agencies, *are encouraging and supporting ICT projects for social development*.

It is important to develop a strong base of evidence to justify and inform the establishment and operation of these initiatives and to generate evidence about the kinds of interventions that work best. The meta surveys on behalf of international donor agencies interested in the quality and outcomes of their Asian ICT for social development projects, they discovered that many of the projects lacked key performance indicators by which they could be judged, that few of the team members had training in research and evaluation, and that there was a general reluctance to admit to what had been occurring or going wrong. This made it difficult for the researchers to provide useful feedback to the donors who had commissioned these meta surveys.

The ODL in Asia is most successful when systems are developed that are appropriate to local needs and circumstances. Whilst accepting that the current lack of indigenous theory and expertise will make the evolution of Asian models slow and difficult to achieve, he argues that as products of Asian conditions, they will have greater strength and relevance. Such an evolutionary process challenges managers and practitioners to move beyond their time honoured thinking and practices. This may not be easy where organisations are hierarchical, roles and functions are bound by tradition, consensus and harmony are valued over individualism and candour, criticism is deemed unseemly, and self criticism leads to 'loss of face'.

However, if governments, donors and other important stakeholders are to be convinced of the value of ICT for social development, all of their processes and outcomes must be open to public scrutiny and their quality assured – and this can only be done through rigorous, honest and frank research and reporting.

Failure is a stepping stone, not a stumbling block

In ICT for social development, it is sometimes the case that costs spin out of control, technologies fail, teaching methods turn out to be inappropriate, learners drop out, management systems falter, and territorial disputes arise between providers.

These failures are rarely admitted in journal articles and conference presentations, however. They may only become apparent to those who have first hand experience of the projects or who can talk with the participants. Only then may it emerge that the project management was poor, that the learners did not really 'buy in' to the project, that the technology was inappropriate, or that conflicts arose as soon as key personnel departed or the donors withdrew their funding.

Such omissions and cover ups are particularly worrisome because, as Koul (1998) observes, politicians, managers and practitioners new to ODL/ICT are easily misled by over optimistic accounts of what occurs, and fail to appreciate the complexities involved. The dangers of focusing on success alone. They suggest that organisations can learn as much from their failures as from their successes, and that failure needs to be seen as a stepping stone to improvement, not as a stumbling block to be ignored or covered up.

Researching and reporting on failure requires imagination, diligence, courage and a willingness to ask awkward questions. This may be difficult to achieve in some contexts, but it is important to develop an organisational culture in which people are encouraged to admit what went wrong, and to do something about it.

A Research and Evaluation Agenda for ICT for Social Development

ICT for social development calls for research into the needs and circumstances of the end users, the services provided, the methods and technologies employed, the outcomes and the benefits. Research is also needed into the policies and procedures that are needed to achieve successful outcomes. The following research and evaluation agenda is proposed for those concerned with ICT for social development.

National Level

Governments, donors and other national agencies need to be able to draw upon the following in order to develop well informed plans, policies and procedures:

a) Meta surveys (surveys of a range of initiatives) and meta analyses (findings derived from a number of research studies) that provide robust evidence of system wide gains in access, economy, efficiency, effectiveness and impact, the factors that support or prevent the achievement of these outcomes, and ways to overcome any barriers to change that may arise in the process.

b) Environmental scanning to establish:

- The needs and opportunities for using ICT to achieve, for example, the UN's Millennium Development Goals of eradicating extreme poverty and hunger, achieving universal primary education, promoting gender equality and empowering women, reducing child mortality, improving maternal health, combating HIV/ Aids, malaria and other diseases, ensuring environmental sustainability, and developing a global partnership for development; and
- ways to bridge the digital divide.

c) Research findings on:

- the political actions, policies and systems needed to achieve project sustainability;
- the technology, infrastructure and logistics needed for such projects;
- the funding and resource requirements;
- the staff training requirements;
- the potential for collaboration and partnership; leadership and management issues; and
- key performance indicators needed to measure the short term and longer term benefits of projects. d) Formative and summative evaluation to provide robust information on:
- the appropriateness of projects; and
- the impact, efficiency, cost and cost effectiveness of projects.

Organisational Level

ICT based social development projects take many forms, from improving adult literacy and helping poor farmers to adopt new practices, to providing disadvantaged communities with ICT through community telecentres.

Many of these initiatives are experimental and new to the providers as well as the end users.

A number of stakeholders individuals or groups (including the end users) are interested in influencing the projects, achieving the outcomes, and ensuring the projects' viability. Organisations supporting such projects need to be accountable to these stake holders and to undertake or commission research ensuring that:

- the end users' needs and circumstances have been correctly defined;
- the projects have been appropriately resourced, managed, implemented, provided and evaluated and delivered;
- the goals, targets and performance indicators have been met;
- problems have been resolved; and that
- dissemination and diffusion methods have informed all stakeholders of the projects' outcomes and benefits.

Practitioner Level

Managers and staff engaged in such projects need to undertake:

a) Personal inquiry to inform their understandings of:

- the theoretical basis of ODL/ICT, lifelong learning and non formal adult and community education;
- global developments and trends in ODL/ICT;
- adult and distance learners and their learning;
- constructivist, independent, collaborative and problem and work based learning; • cultural, gender and individual differences in learning;
- curriculum, course and instructional design;
- materials development;
- learner support;
- quality assurance; and

- leadership and management.

b) Action research (work based research by individuals or groups that proceeds through a cycle of planning, action, observation and reflection and provides evidence that informs practice) regarding:

- equity and access;
- end users' needs, circumstances, behaviours and achievements;
- curriculum, course and materials development and delivery;
- instructional design and technology;
- learner support; and
- assessment and evaluation.

c) Formative and summative research into:

- the effectiveness of the policies, planning and project management;
- the effectiveness and cost effectiveness of the projects;
- the effectiveness and cost effectiveness of the technology;
- the effectiveness of the teaching/training and learner support systems;
- the end users' views on the methods and technologies employed;
- the benefits to the end users; and
- the social development benefits for the wider community.

Performance Indicators and Research

Key performance indicators (KPIs), sometimes known as Performance Indicators or Key Success Indicators, are essential in defining and measuring progress toward a project's goals.

KPIs are observable, quantifiable and agreed to processes and outcomes that reflect the critical success factors in projects. They vary according to the projects' missions and goals. Let us consider, for example, a project whose mission is "to improve health awareness in rural communities", and whose goals are "to use ICT to motivate and educate village communities in health care", and "to achieve more effective and cost effective ways of improving community health care". To evaluate the progress and outcomes of this project, we need something more specific than its overall mission and goals.

We need to specify the number of village communities to be targeted, who is to be involved (e.g., the village heads, the mothers, the younger generation, or the entire community), the methods and technologies to be used, the intended cost savings and cost benefits, the intended short term outcomes and longer term benefits, and how the project compares with other, more traditional approaches.

We then need to set targets for each performance indicator. For example "Involve all villages", or "Involve all mothers in improving health care", or "Reduce the costs of delivery by at least fifty percent" are clear targets that everyone will understand and be able to act on.

Next we need to mandate a person or persons to be accountable for qualitatively and/or quantitatively evaluating and reporting on the steps taken to achieve these targets, and on what has been achieved.

We also need to establish causal links. For example, if the village mothers fail to stay the course or do not adopt the recommended approaches, we need to find out why. Such an approach provides a sound basis and framework for research and evaluation of ICT for social development.

Disseminating Research

Unfortunately, research findings do not always result in greater understanding or improved practice. The researchers may lack credibility, the dissemination methods may be inappropriate, the findings may be ignored, there may be disagreement on the problems or proposed solutions, the recommendations may be too costly, or they may have political ramifications that threaten the *status quo*.

It is therefore important to consider who the research findings are intended for, and how to disseminate the research findings in ways that will attract the attention and support of the key decision makers and will result in the necessary actions .

Training in research and evaluation

Until recently, knowledge and skills in research and evaluation have been limited to academics and key practitioners in other sectors. Relatively few people have been trained in researching ICT for social development, particularly in the developing world.

Researchers and would be researchers can now receive excellent online training through the Practitioner Research and Evaluation Skills Training Programme (PREST) developed by the Commonwealth of Learning (COL) and the International Foundation for Open Learning (IRFOL).

Written for ODL practitioners by ODL practitioners, the PREST training resources provide convenient access to training in research and evaluation that can be of immediate relevance to those working in the field, and can also be a resource for formal study.

Conclusions

This chapter has argued the need for:

- a stronger research and evaluation culture in ICT for social development;
- providers and practitioners in this field to engage in research and evaluation, to be self critical, and to be committed to quality assurance;
- researchers to collaborate with policy makers in educational, training and donor organisations, and to help create a body of research to guide future planning and practice;

- environmental scanning, meta surveys, meta analyses and overviews of current thinking, needs and developments; and
- formative and summative evaluation, with robust strategically significant findings to inform and influence decision makers. A prime reason for the current Symposium is the desire of the ASEAN Foundation and its Canadian donors for more and better research and evaluation in ICT for social development. It is hoped that the Symposium delegates will now seize the many opportunities that present themselves for research activities that can help to improve the quality and extent of ICT for social development in Asia.

10

Automatic Communication

Automatic data communication as a development strategy.

To get a lead on your competitors.

To avoid duplication of effort.

To reduce costs.

To reduce boring and repetitive work.

To avoid having to remember technical details.

Automatic communication is both for professionals and amateurs. It helps keep your costs down. Also, it lets you do the job faster and safer. Sometimes, it is the only way to get the job done. We all have Different Needs. Automation will never be the same for everybody. Our needs are too different. Some get excited when a program can dial a bulletin board, retrieve a program, and then disconnect without having to touch the keyboard. Some want an "answering machine" that can respond to and forward email when he or she is away from the office. Others want a communications system that can tap selected news sources, search databases, and do post-processing on the retrieved material.

For most professionals, doing things manually takes too much time. Time is better spent reading, digesting, and using, rather than on stupid technical retrieval work. Computers can do that. To others again, automation is a question of being able to use the online resource at all. If it takes 60 seconds to get a piece of information, it may be possible to get before running for the next meeting. However, if it takes 15 minutes, there may not be enough time. If you must also read a help text to find out how to do it, you may not even consider doing it. Your mind is so full of other things right now. *When using a system for automatic communication, you do not have to learn and remember online commands. The system will do it for you.*

The Minimum Solution

Automatic data communication in its simplest form entails the following:

- One keystroke to get the communications program to dial a number, and send user name/password when the online service requests this information.
- Macro commands (like in a word processor) for navigating through an online service, searching, and to send complex commands by pressing one key.

Most communication programs have a macro language or a script language. There are also macro programs designed to be used with Microsoft Windows. In many instances, users are taking advantage of these features without even knowing it. This is the case for many of those connecting to the Internet with a simple mouse click. If this has not been done for you, then you will probably never regret time spent on learning how to use these features. At a minimum, you should be able to have your system log on automatically to your favourite service provider. Autologon spares you the task of remembering your user name and password. Besides, most people are only able to use the keyboard at a low speed. They easily get frustrated by having to correct typing errors.

Macros

Above, we used a script to log on automatically to a service. When Procomm gives us access to the keyboard again, we must continue manually. What we want to do online varies. Sometimes, we want to read new messages in conferences. In other cases, the purpose is to check new programs in the file library. If we find programs of interest, we may want to download them.

Shorthand macros can help you do this faster and safer. For example, one macro can take you quickly to a conference for new messages. You can make Procomm start this macro whenever you press ALT-0 (keep the ALT key down, then press 0). You can have the macro key ALT-1 send other commands when in the file archives. When I started using MS-DOS computers for data communications, PC-TALK became my favourite program. It has many of the same macro capabilities that Procomm has.

With PC-TALK, I did autologon to the now defunct NewsNet service. Macro number one sent commands that gave me the contents of various newsletters. Macro #2 picked up the contents in another group. Macro #3 picked up stories from my mailbox, and macro #4 logged me off the service. My mission was completed by pressing four or five keys. The bookmark files of Netscape's Navigator and Microsoft Explorer are also nice macro features.

Automating the Full Task

It's a long way from automated logon scripts and the use of macros to full automation. The major difference is that with full automation, you do not have to look at the screen while the script is working. You can do other things. Sometimes, you may not even be present when the job is being done. On a typical morning in my house, I go directly from bed to my office to switch my communications computer on. While I visit the bathroom, my communications program calls two Internet service providers to retrieve and send information.

When the script has disconnected, it analyses the received data. I want important mail highlighted. Some information is to be automatically appended to storage files. Retrieved news menus are to be analyzed to see if there are any articles that I want to read (compared with a set of keywords). "Spam" messages (unsolicited advertisements) are to be deleted automatically, etc.

Sometimes, the unexpected happen. There may be noise on the phone line, or a sudden disconnect. Usually, my script can solve this without manual intervention. It is therefore allowed to work unattended most of the time. When I get to my office after breakfast, it is all done. My communications program is set for reading and responding to today's email. I can sit down, and immediately get to work.

After having written all my replies, I say "send" to my system. For me, it's time for another cup of coffee. I am not needed by the keyboard while mail is being sent. This is what an automatic communications system can do. My scripts also help plan and prepare online visits, and ease my work by postprocessing results.

When your communication is fully automated, you need not read incoming data while it scrolls over your screen, and then again after logging off the service. You do it only once.

How to get it? Here are some alternatives:

Alternative 1: Write your own system

You can write procedures for powerful script-driven programs like ProYam (from Omen Technology) and Crosstalk MK IV for DOS.

I started writing scripts for ProYam way back in 1985. The system is constantly expanded to include new services, refined to include more functions, and enhanced to become more robust. My system work like an autopilot. It calls online services, navigates, retrieves, sends data, and logs off. Postprocessing includes automatic reformatting of retrieved data, transfers to various internal databases, statistics, usage logs, and calculation of transfer costs. Such scripts can do quite complex operations online. For example, it can

- Buy and sell stock when today's quotes are over/under given limits,
- Select news stories and other types of information based on information found in menus or titles.

Script writing is not for everybody. It is complicated, and takes a lot of time, so it may not be for you.

On the other hand, those going for it seldom regret, and you may find systems offered by others that you automate more of your work. Tailor-made communication scripts give a wonderful flexibility. The software does not cost much, but it sure takes a lot of time!

Hints for script writers:

Do not use large and complex script files before you know the online service well. The scripts let you do things quicker and safer, but there is always a possibility for unexpected problems.

Test your scripts for a long time to make them robust by "training" them to handle the unexpected. Leave them to work unattended when you are reasonably certain that they can do the job.-It may take months or years to get to that point.

Build a timeout feature into your scripts, so they do not just hang there waiting for you after a meeting with fate.

Alternative 2: Use scripts made by others

Some script authors generously let others use their creations. Earle Robinson of CompuServe's European Forum, share his ProYam scripts for automatic usage of CompuServe with others. They are available from the PC Communications Forum library (GO PCCOM).

Enter GO XTALK on CompuServe to find advanced script files for Crosstalk Mk.4.

ZCOMM and ProYam scripts for visiting my board automatically can be freely downloaded there. They split access up into these three phases:

Phase 1: Menu driven offline preparation.

Phase 2: Automatic logon, navigation through the system, and automatic disconnection.

Phase 3: Automatic offline postprocessing.

You will find scripts for other programs on many online services.

Alternative 3: Special software

Several online services sell communication programs with built-in functions that provides you with automation. They can have offline functions for reading and responding to mail. The degree of automation varies. There are also many programs written by third parties. Most programs assume that you use 'expert' as your default operating mode on the online service.

TapCIS, NavCIS, Autosig (ATO), OzCIS, CISOP, CompuServe Navigator (for Macintosh), CSNav/Win, AutoPilot (for Amiga), ARCTIC (for Acorn Archimedes), and QuickCIS (for Atari) are popular choices on CompuServe. The DOS program TapCIS is my personal favourite. (CIM does not offer much automation!)

Journalist is an interesting program that creates a personalized newspaper view of CompuServe for Windows users. It automatically logs on to retrieve the information necessary to fill the frames in your document, and formats it according to your specifications.

LEXIS-NEXIS News Plus has pull-down menus and detailed selection of commands. This MS-DOS program helps users set up detailed search commands before logging on to the LEXIS-NEXIS service. Your search results will be downloaded automatically.

Alternative 4: Offline readers

The alternatives above have one important weakness. Noise on the line can prevent the "robot" from doing the job. All it takes is for noise to give a prompt another content than is expected by your program or script (as in "En@er a number:" instead of "Enter a number:").

You can avoid noise problems by using grab or get commands, and by making the online service use its minimum prompts ('expert mode'). Still, this does not give full protection.

The best is to let the online service do the navigation. Think of it as logging on to run a batch file on the remote computer. Combine this with automatic transfers of your commands, sent in of one stream of data with automatic error correction (in the software and in the modem), and you have a very robust system.

The program logs on to the service. Then the service takes over. It registers your user identity, checks your user profile for personal interests, retrieves and packs all messages, news and files into one compressed file, and sends it to you at high speed. Your outgoing messages, search commands, commands to join or leave conferences, and more, are transferred to the remote computer in a similar packet (compressed file). When received by the remote computer, it unpacks the transfer file and distributes messages and commands to various services following your instructions. Your "physical" contact with the service is when your modem is disconnected. The help menus that you read belong to your program, and not the online service. You read and respond to mail in a reading module (ref. the term "offline reader"). Some offline readers give the caller access to more tools than is available on the online service itself. They may have spelling checkers, multimedia support, let you use your favourite editor or word processor, and offer various storage, search, and printing options. They may let you sort incoming conference mail by "threads," and permit you to place obnoxious writers on a "kill" list.

Using offline readers is probably the easiest, cheapest, and safest way of using online services. You even risk writing more concise and thoughtful messages. The "readers" are popular among bulletin board users, and some commercial services are also starting to accommodate them. There are many offline reader programs. The most advanced take over completely upon logon, and manage transfers of commands and compressed information files to and from the host. (Example: Binkley Term on FidoNet) Global Link is an offline reader for EcoNet. Bergen By Byte offers the BBS/CS Mail Grabber/Reader, a script system used with the communications program Telix and the service's "auto-get" function. NUPOP (MS-DOS), Eudora for Windows (Windows and Macintosh), and WinQVT/Net (Windows) are offline readers for use when calling Unix hosts. The most popular systems on the PCBoard based Thunderball Cave BBS are Offline Express, Megareader, Session Manager, Rose Reader and EZReader. Freddie is a reader for Macintosh. These readers are used with scripts written for various communication programs. Some of them have built in communications (and script) modules.

EZReader from Thumper Technologies (P.O. Box 471346, Tulsa, OK 74147-1346, U.S.A.) lets users retrieve mail from several online systems using transfer formats such as QWK, PCBoard capture files, ProDoor ZIPM files, XRS, MCI Mail, and others.

1stReader from Sparkware (Post Office Box 386, Hendersonville, Tennessee 37077, U.S.A.) is my personal favourite for accessing Qmail based online systems.

Note: Some offline readers contain all the features required for fully automated communications. Some bulletin boards allow up- and downloading to start right after CONNECT.

Off-Line Xpress, an offline mail reader for QWK (Qwikmail) packets, does not contain a communications module. It just does pre-and postprocessing of mail packets. You can use the Off-Line Xpress as one element in a larger automated system. For example, a system for access to PCBoard bulletin boards may consist of Off-Line Xpress software, PKZIP and PKUNZIP (popular shareware programs to compress/decompress mail packets), the QMODEM communications program, and a script to navigate to/from the QWK packet send and receive area on the BBS.

1stReader contains a powerful script based communications module. It let you compose replies, set search commands, subscriptions to services, add and drop conferences, and enter download commands offline.

Automatic Automation

We have explained how to write scripts with Procomm. However, there are simpler and quicker ways. Many communications programs can make scripts automatically using a learning function. It goes like this: Start the learning function before calling the online service. Then log on, navigate to the desired services, do what you want to automate, and disconnect. The learning feature analyses the received data and builds a script file for automatic communication.

If you call again with the new script, it will "drive the same route one more time."

ZCOMM and ProYam have a learning feature. This is how I made a script for accessing Semaforum BBS using ZCOMM:

ZCOMM asked for a phone number. I entered +47-370-11710. It asked for speed, and I entered 14400 bps. Next, I had to choose one of the following:

(1) System uses IBM PC (ANSI) line drawing

(2) 7 bits even parity

(3) 8 bits no parity

My choice was 1.

ZCOMM dialed the number. When the connection was set up, I entered my name and password, navigated to the message section, read new messages, browsed new files in the library, and entered G for Goodbye. This was the "tour" that I wanted to automate.

When disconnected, I pressed the F1 key. This prompted the learning process based on a record of the online tour. The log described everything that had happened in detail, including my pauses to think. Now I was prompted by the following question:

'newscr.t' exists. Append/replace/quit?

I selected append. Then:

Do you want this script file as a new entry in your

telephone directory (y/n)?

I entered "y," and named it "semaforum." After a few seconds, my new script was ready:

Your new script is in the file 'newscr.t' !! You can append the file to your current script file (for example PHODIR.T) or have the commands executed by entering:

call semaforum.newscr.t

It was time to test the new wonder. I entered

call semaforum.newscr.t

at the ZCOMM command line, hit the ENTER key, and off it went. ZCOMM called the BBS and repeated everything-at far higher speed than I had done it manually. It went on-hook as planned when done.

Limitations

Auto-learn programs can create a script file that let you "drive the same route." For some applications this is enough. For others, it's just part of the way. You have to refine the script manually to get what you want.

Example: *If you some bulletin boards with an auto-learned script made yesterday, chances are that everything works well. If you call twice on the same day, however, you may be in for a surprise as the board may greet you differently on your second visit. If this is the case, then your script must take this into account.*

On most online services, many things can happen at each "junction of your road." At one point in one of my scripts, up to twenty things may happen. Each event needs its own "routing."

Twenty possible events are an extreme, but three to four options at each system prompt is not unusual. All of them need to be handled by your script, if you want it to visit online services unattended while asleep.

It is quicker and simpler to use other people's scripts and programs, although this might force you to use a different program for each service.

Personally, I prefer offline readers on services where they can do the job. On other services, I usually depend on my own tailor-made scripts.

11

Organizational Communication

Organizational communication, broadly speaking, is: the transactional, symbolic process in which the activities of a social collective are coordinated to achieve individual and collective goals.

Discipline History

The modern field DOES NOT have a more recent lineage through business information, business communication, and early mass communication studies published in the 1930s through the 1950s. Until then, organizational communication as a discipline consisted of a few professors within speech departments who had a particular interest in speaking and writing in business settings.

Through the World War II and post-war years, particularly 1942 through about 1949, studies of effective communication practices in group and organizational settings became particularly salient. Great numbers of servicemen (and some service women) underwent communication training, first in the military, and then in colleges and universities. A concern with effectiveness in transmitting messages soon broadened into concern with environmental factors, characteristics of the people involved in the communicative activity, and differences in utility of different transmission media.

Several seminal publications stand out as works broadening the scope and recognizing the importance of communication in the organizing process, and in using the term "organizational communication". Nobel Laureate Herbert Simon wrote in 1947 about "organization communications systems", saying communication is "absolutely essential to organizations". In 1951 Bavelas and Barrett wrote An Experimental Approach to Organizational Communication in which they stated that communication "is the essence of organized activity".

In 1953 the economist Kenneth Boulding wrote The Organizational Revolution: A Study in the Ethics of Economic Organization. While this work directly addressed the economic issues facing organizations, in it he questions the ethical and moral issues underlying their power, and maintains that an "organization consists of a system of communication." In 1954, a young Chris Argyris published Personality and Organization. This careful and research-based book attacked many things, but singled out "organizational communication" for special attention. Argyris made the case that what passed for organizational communication at the time was based on unstated and indefensible propositions such as "management knows best" and "workers are inherently stupid and lazy." He accused the emerging field of relying on untested gimmicks designed to trick employees into doing management's will.

Assumptions Underlying Early Organizational Communication

Some of the main assumptions underlying much of the early organizational communication research were:

- Humans act rationally. Sane people behave in rational ways, they generally have access to all of the information needed to make rational decisions they could articulate, and therefore will make rational decisions, unless there is some breakdown in the communication process.
- Formal logic and empirically verifiable data ought to be the foundation upon which any theory should rest. All we really need to understand communication in organizations is (a) observable and replicable behaviours that can be transformed into variables by some form of measurement,

and (b) formally replicable syllogisms that can extend theory from observed data to other groups and settings

- Communication is primarily a mechanical process, in which a message is constructed and encoded by a sender, transmitted through some channel, then received and decoded by a receiver. Distortion, represented as any differences between the original and the received messages, can and ought to be identified and reduced or eliminated.
- Organizations are mechanical things, in which the parts (including employees functioning in defined roles) are interchangeable. What works in one organization will work in another similar organization. Individual differences can be minimized or even eliminated with careful management techniques.
- Organizations function as a container within which communication takes place. Any differences in form or function of communication between that occurring in an organization and in another setting can be identified and studied as factors affecting the communicative activity.

Herbert Simon introduced the concept of bounded rationality which challenged assumptions about the perfect rationality of communication participants. He maintained that people making decisions in organizations seldom had complete information, and that even if more information was available, they tended to pick the first acceptable option, rather than exploring further to pick the optimal solution.

Through the 1960s, 1970s and 1980s the field expanded greatly in parallel with several other academic disciplines, looking at communication as more than an intentional act designed to transfer an idea. Research expanded beyond the issue of "how to make people understand what I am saying" to tackle questions such as "how does the act of communicating change, or even define, who I am?", "why do organizations that seem to be saying similar things achieve very different results?" and "to what extent are my relationships with others affected by our various organizational contexts?"

Research Methodologies

Historically, organizational communication was driven primarily by quantitative research methodologies. Included in functional organizational communication research are statistical analyses (such as surveys, text indexing, network mapping and behaviour modeling). In the early 1980s, the interpretive revolution took place in organizational communication. In Putnam and Pacanowsky's 1983 text Communication and Organizations: An Interpretive Approach. They argued for opening up methodological space for qualitative approaches such as narrative analyses, participant/observation, interviewing, rhetoric and textual approaches readings) and philosophic inquiries.

During the 1980s and 1990s critical organizational scholarship began to gain prominence with a focus on issues of gender, race, class, and power/knowledge. In its current state, the study of organizational communication is open methodologically, with research from post-positive, interpretive, critical, postmodern, and discursive paradigms being published regularly.

Organizational communication scholarship appears in a number of communication journals including but not limited to Management Communication Quarterly, Journal of Applied Communication Research, Communication Monographs, Academy of Management Journal, Communication Studies, and Southern Communication Journal.

Organizational Communication

Organizational communication can include:

Flow of Communication, e.g.,

- formal, informal
- internal, external
- upward, downward, horizontal
- networks.

Induction, e.g.,

- new hire orientation
- policies & procedures
- employee benefits

Channels, e.g.,

- electronic media such as e-mail, intranet, internet
- teleconference
- print media such as memos, bulletin boards, newsletters etc.
- face-to-face

Meetings, e.g.,

- briefings
- staff meetings
- project meetings
- town hall meetings

Interviews, e.g.,

- Selection
- Performance
- Career

More recently, the field of organizational communication has moved from acceptance of mechanistic models (e.g., information moving from a sender to a receiver) to a study of the persistent, hegemonic and taken-for-granted ways in which we not only use communication to accomplish certain tasks within organizational settings (e.g., public speaking) but also how the organizations in which we participate affect us.

These approaches include "postmodern", "critical", "participatory", "feminist", "power/political", "organic", etc. and draw from disciplines as wide-ranging as sociology, philosophy, theology, psychology, business, business administration, institutional management, medicine (health communication), neurology (neural nets), semiotics, anthropology, international relations, and music.

Thus the field has expanded or moved to study phenomena such as:

Constitution, e.g.,

- how communicative behaviours construct or modify organizing processes or products
- how the organizations within which we interact affect our communicative behaviours, and through these, our own identities
- structures other than organizations which might be constituted through our communicative activity (e.g., markets, cooperatives, tribes, political parties, social movements)
- when does something "become" an organization? When does an organization become (an)other thing(s)? Can one organization "house" another? Is the organization still a useful entity/thing/concept, or has the social/political environment changed so much that what we now call "organization" is so different from the organization of even a few decades ago that it cannot be usefully tagged with the same word--"organization"?

Narrative, e.g.,

- how do group members employ narrative to acculturate/ initiate/indoctrinate new members?
- do organizational stories act on different levels? Are different narratives purposively invoked to achieve specific outcomes, or are there specific roles of "organizational storyteller"? If so, are stories told by the storyteller received differently than those told by others in the organization?
- In what ways does the organization attempt to influence story-telling about the organization? Under what

conditions does the organization appear to be more or less effective in obtaining a desired outcome?

- When these stories conflict with one another or with official rules/policies, how are the conflicts worked out? In situations in which alternative accounts are available, who or how or why are some accepted and others rejected?

Identity, *e.g.,*

- Who do we see ourselves to be, in terms of our organizational affiliations?
- Do communicative behaviours or occurrences in one or more of the organizations in which we participate effect changes in us? to what extent are we comprised of the organizations to which we belong?
- Is it possible for individuals to successfully resist organizational identity? what would that look like?
- Do people who define themselves by their work-organizational membership communicate differently within the organizational setting than people who define themselves more by an avocational (non-vocational) set of relationships?

Interrelatedness of organizational experiences, *e.g.,*

- How do our communicative interactions in one organizational setting affect our communicative actions in other organizational settings?
- How do the phenomenological experiences of participants in a particular organizational setting effect changes in other areas of their lives?
- When the organizational status of a member is significantly changed (e.g., by promotion or expulsion) how are their other organizational memberships affected?

Power *e.g.,*

- How do the use of particular communicative practices within an organizational setting reinforce or alter the various interrelated power relationships within the setting? Are the potential responses of those within or around these organizational settings constrained by factors or processes either within or outside of the organization-- (assuming there is an "outside"?

- Do taken-for-granted organizational practices work to fortify the dominant hegemonic narrative? Do individuals resist/confront these practices, through what actions/ agencies, and to what effects?
- Do status changes in an organization (e.g., promotions, demotions, restructuring, financial/social strata changes) change communicative behaviour? Are there criteria employed by organizational members to differentiate between "legitimate" (i.e., endorsed by the formal organizational structure) and "illegitimate" (i.e., opposed by or unknown to the formal power structure)? Are there "pretenders" or "usurpers" who employ these communicative behaviours? When are they successful, and what do we even mean by "successful?"

Sociolinguistics

Sociolinguistics is the study of the effect of any and all aspects of society, including cultural norms, expectations, and context, on the way language is used. It also studies how dialects differ between groups separated by certain social variables, e.g., ethnicity, religion, status, gender, level of education, etc., and how creation and adherence to these rules is used to categorize individuals in social class or socioeconomic classes. As the usage of a language varies from place to place (dialect), language usage varies among social classes, and it is these sociolects that sociolinguistics studies.

The social aspects of language was in the modern sense first studied by Indian and Japanese linguists in the 1930s, but did not receive much attention in the West until much later. Sociolinguistics in the west first appeared in the 1960s and was pioneered by linguists such as William Labov in the US and Basil Bernstein in the UK.

Applications of Sociolinguistics

For example, a sociolinguist might determine through study of social attitudes that a particular vernacular would not be considered appropriate language use in a business or professional setting; he might also study the grammar, phonetics, vocabulary, and other aspects of this sociolect much as a dialectologist would study the same for a regional dialect.

The study of language variation is concerned with social constraints determining language in its contextual environment. Code-switching is the term given to the use of different varieties of language in different social situations.

William Labov is often regarded as the founder of the study of sociolinguistics. He is especially noted for introducing the quantitative study of language variation and change, making the sociology of language into a scientific discipline.

Sociolinguistics differs from sociology of language in that the focus of sociolinguistics is the effect of the society on the language, while the latter's focus is on the language's effect on the society.

Sociolinguistic Variables

Studies in the field of sociolinguistics typically take a sample population and interview them, assessing the realisation of certain sociolinguistic variables. Labov specifies the ideal sociolinguistic variable to

- be high in frequency,
- have a certain immunity from conscious suppression,
- be an integral part of larger structures, and
- be easily quantified on a linear scale.

Phonetic variables tend to meet these criteria and are often used, as are grammatical variables and, more rarely, lexical variables. Examples for phonetic variables are: the frequency of the Glottal stop, the height or blackness of a Vowel or the realisation of word-endings.

An example of a grammatical variable is the frequency of negative concord (known colloquially as a double negative).

Fundamental Concepts in Sociolinguistics

While the study of sociolinguistics is very broad, there are a few fundamental concepts on which most sociolinguistic inquiries depend.

External vs. Internal Language

Sociolinguistics is different from many of the other branches of linguistics in that it studies external as opposed to internal language. Internal language applies to the study of language on the abstract level; put simply, in the head. External language applies to language in social contexts, or outside the head. This distinction is important, because internal language analyses, such as syntax and semantics, operate on the assumption that all native speakers of a language are quite homogeneous in how they process and perceive language. External language fields, such as sociolinguistics, attempt to explain why this is in fact not the case. These two approaches, while distinct, complement each other in practice.

Conversation Analysis

Conversation analysis (commonly abbreviated as CA) is the study of talk in interaction. CA generally attempts to describe the orderliness, structure and sequential patterns of interaction, whether this is institutional (in the school, doctor's surgery, courts or elsewhere) or casual conversation. Thus, use of the term "conversation" to label this disciplinary movement is misleading if read in a colloquial sense, as many have. In light of this, one of CA's principal practitioners, Emanuel Schegloff, has more recently identified "talk-in-interaction" as CA's topic. Perhaps for this same reason, others (e.g., Jonathan Potter) who use CA methods identify themselves as discourse analysts (DA), though that term was first used to identify researchers using methods different from CA (e.g., Levinson, 1983), and still identifies a group of scholars larger than those who use only CA methods.

Inspired by ethnomethodology, it was developed in the late 1960s and early 1970s principally by the sociologist Harvey Sacks and, among others, his close associates Emanuel Schegloff and Gail Jefferson. Sacks died early in his career, but his work was championed by others in his field, and CA has now become an established force in sociology, anthropology, linguistics, speech-communication and psychology. It is particularly influential in interactional sociolinguistics, discourse analysis and discursive psychology, as well as being a coherent discipline in its own right. Recently CA techniques of sequential analysis have been employed by phoneticians to explore the fine phonetic detail of speech.

Basic Structures

Turn-taking Organization

The nature by which a conversation is done in and through turns. Turn-taking is one of the fundamental organizations of conversation. According to CA, the turn-taking system consists of two components: the turn constructional component and the turn allocational component. The turn-taking organization is described in Sacks, H., Schegloff, E. A., & Jefferson, G. (1974). A simplest systematics for the organization of turn-taking for conversation.

While CA does not explicitly claim that turn-taking is universal, as research is conducted on more languages, it is possible that if there were any basis for a claim to universality in language, turn-taking is a good candidate. The turn-taking model for conversation was arrived at inductively through empirical investigation of field recordings of conversation and fitted to such observationally arrived at fact as overwhelmingly, participants in conversation talk one at a time. This can be illustrated by the game ping-pong, where the people conversing are players and their turns are represented as they hit the ball.

Turn Constructional Component

The turn constructional component describes basic units out of which turns are fashioned. These basic units are known as turn constructional units or TCUs. Unit types include: lexical, clausal, phrasal, and sentential. These are grammatically and pragmatically complete units, meaning that in a particular context they accomplish recognizable social actions. Note that not all unit types may exist in all languages. Further, it is possible that there are units in other languages, such as particles in Asian languages, that may not exist in English.

Turn Allocational Component

The turn allocational component describes how turns are allocated among participants in a conversation. The three ordered options are: Current Speaker selects Next Speaker; Next Speaker Self-selects as Next; or Current Speaker Continues.

Sequence Organisation

This concerns how actions are ordered in conversation.

- **Adjacency Pairs:** Talk tends to occur in responsive pairs; however, the pairs may be split over a sequence of turns.
- **Pre-sequences:** Use of sequences of talk prior to purposeful talk.
- **Preference Organisation:** There are structural (i.e. practice-underwritten) preferences for some types of actions (within sequences of action) in conversation over other actions.
- **Repair:** Repair organization addresses problems in speaking, hearing, or understanding in conversation. Repair has two broad classes: self-repair and other repair. Code-switching is a way to communicate to prevent the need for repair by using words fitted for a specific audience.
- **Action Formation:** This concerns the description of the practices by which turns at talk are composed and positioned so as to realize one or another actions. Generally, women find it easier to read others non-verbal communication than men do.
- **Contrasts to Other Theories:** In contrast to the research inspired by Noam Chomsky, Conversation Analysis only

examines natural talk. In contrast to the theory developed by John Gumperz, CA maintains it is possible to decode a conversation based on its transcript alone. In CA there is no belief that the researcher needs to consult with the talk participants or members of their speech community.

Cognitive linguistics

In linguistics and cognitive science, cognitive linguistics (CL) refers to the school of linguistics that understands language creation, learning, and usage as best explained by reference to human cognition in general. It is characterized by adherence to three central positions. First, it denies that there is an autonomous linguistic faculty in the mind; second, it understands grammar in terms of conceptualization; and third, it claims that knowledge of language arises out of language use.

Cognitive linguists deny that the mind has any module for language-acquisition that is unique and autonomous. This stands in contrast to the work done in the field of generative grammar. Although cognitive linguists do not necessarily deny that part of the human linguistic ability is innate, they deny that it is separate from the rest of cognition.

Thus, they argue that knowledge of linguistic phenomena--i.e., phonemes, morphemes, and syntax--is essentially conceptual in nature.

Moreover, they argue that the storage and retrieval of linguistic data is not significantly different from the storage and retrieval of other knowledge, and use of language in understanding employs similar cognitive abilities as used in other non-linguistic tasks. Departing from the tradition of truth-conditional semantics, cognitive linguists view meaning in terms of conceptualization. Instead of viewing meaning in terms of models of the world, they view it in terms of mental spaces.

Finally, cognitive linguistics argues that language is both embodied and situated in a specific environment. This can be considered a moderate offshoot of the Sapir-Whorf hypothesis, in that language and cognition mutually influence one another, and are both embedded in the experiences and environments of its users.

Areas of Study

Cognitive linguistics is divided into three main areas of study:

- Cognitive semantics, dealing mainly with lexical semantics
- Cognitive approaches to grammar, dealing mainly with syntax, morphology and other traditionally more grammar-oriented areas.
- Cognitive phonology.

Aspects of cognition that are of interest to cognitive linguists include:

- Construction grammar and cognitive grammar.
- Conceptual metaphor and conceptual blending.
- Image sachems and force dynamics.
- Conceptual organization: Categorization, Metonymy, Frame semantics, and Iconicity.
- Construal and Subjectivity.
- Gesture and sign language.
- Linguistic relativism.
- Cognitive neuroscience.

Related Work that Interfaces with Many of the above Themes:

- Computational models of metaphor and language acquisition.
- Psycholinguistics research.
- Conceptual semantics, pursued by generative linguist Ray Jackendoff is related because of its active psychological realism and the incorporation of prototype structure and images.

Cognitive linguistics, more than generative linguistics, seek to mesh together these findings into a coherent whole. A further complication arises because the terminology of cognitive linguistics is not entirely stable, both because it is a relatively new field and because it interfaces with a number of other disciplines. Insights and developments from cognitive linguistics are becoming accepted ways of analysing literary texts, too. Cognitive Poetics, as it has become known, has become an important part of modern stylistics. The best summary of the discipline as it is currently stands is Peter Stockwell's Cognitive Poetics.

History of Organizational Communication

The field traces its lineage through business information, business communication, and early mass communication studies published in the 1930s through the 1950s. Until then, organizational communication as a discipline consisted of a few professors within speech departments who had a particular interest in speaking and writing in business settings. The current field is well established with its own theories and empirical concerns distinct from other communication subfields and other approaches to organizations.

Several seminal publications stand out as works broadening the scope and recognizing the importance of communication in the organizing process, and in using the term "organizational communication". Nobel Laureate Herbert Simon wrote in 1947 about "organization communications systems", saying communication is "absolutely essential to organizations".

In the 1950s, organizational communication focused largely on the role of communication in improving organizational life and organizational output. In the 1980s, the field turned away from a business-oriented approach to communication and became concerned more with the constitutive role of communication in organizing. In the 1990s, critical theory influence on the field was felt as organizational communication scholars focused more on communication's possibilities to oppress and liberate organizational members.

Assumptions Underlying Early Organizational Communication

Some of the main assumptions underlying much of the early organizational communication research were:

- Humans act rationally. Sane people behave in rational ways, they generally have access to all of the information needed to make rational decisions they could articulate, and therefore will make rational decisions, unless there is some breakdown in the communication process.
- Formal logic and empirically verifiable data ought to be the foundation upon which any theory should rest. All we really need to understand communication in organizations is (a) observable and replicable behaviours that can be transformed into variables by some form of measurement, and (b) formally replicable syllogisms that can extend theory from observed data to other groups and settings
- Communication is primarily a mechanical process, in which a message is constructed and encoded by a sender, transmitted through some channel, then received and decoded by a receiver. Distortion, represented as any differences between the original and the received messages, can and ought to be identified and reduced or eliminated.
- Organizations are mechanical things, in which the parts (including employees functioning in defined roles) are interchangeable. What works in one organization will work in another similar organization. Individual differences can be minimized or even eliminated with careful management techniques.
- Organizations function as a container within which communication takes place. Any differences in form or function of communication between that occurring in an organization and in another setting can be identified and studied as factors affecting the communicative activity.

Herbert Simon introduced the concept of bounded rationality which challenged assumptions about the perfect rationality of communication participants. He maintained that people making decisions in organizations seldom had complete information, and that even if more information was available, they tended to pick the first acceptable option, rather than exploring further to pick the optimal solution.

Through the 1960s, 1970s and 1980s the field expanded greatly in parallel with several other academic disciplines, looking at communication as more than an intentional act designed to transfer an idea. Research expanded beyond the issue of "how to make people understand what I am saying" to tackle questions such as "how does the act of communicating change, or even define, who I am?", "why do organizations that seem to be saying similar things achieve very different results?" and "to what extent are my relationships with others affected by our various organizational contexts?"

In the early 1990s Peter Senge developed a new theories on Organizational Communication. This theories were learning organization and systems thinking. These have been well received and are now a mainstay in current beliefs toward organizational communications.

Communications Networks

Networks are another aspect of direction and flow of communication. Bavelas has shown that communication patterns, or networks, influence groups in several important ways. Communication networks may affect the group's completion of the assigned task on time, the position of the de facto leader in the group, or they may affect the group members' satisfaction from occupying certain positions in the network. Although these findings are based on laboratory experiments, they have important implications for the dynamics of communication in formal organizations.

There are several patterns of communication:

- "Chain",
- "Wheel",

- "Star",
- "All-Channel" network,
- "Circle".

The Chain can readily be seen to represent the hierarchical pattern that characterizes strictly formal information flow, "from the top down," in military and some types of business organizations. The Wheel can be compared with a typical autocratic organization, meaning one-man rule and limited employee participation. The Star is similar to the basic formal structure of many organizations. The All-Channel network, which is an elaboration of Bavelas's Circle used by Guetzkow, is analogous to the free-flow of communication in a group that encourages all of its members to become involved in group decision processes. The All-Channel network may also be compared to some of the informal communication networks.

If it's assumed that messages may move in both directions between stations in the networks, it is easy to see that some individuals occupy key positions with regard to the number of messages they handle and the degree to which they exercise control over the flow of information. For example, the person represented by the central dot in the "Star" handles all messages in the group. In contrast, individuals who occupy stations at the edges of the pattern handle fewer messages and have little or no control over the flow of information.These "peripheral" individuals can communicate with only one or two other persons and must depend entirely on others to relay their messages if they wish to extend their range.

In reporting the results of experiments involving the Circle, Wheel, and Star configurations, Bavelas came to the following tentative conclusions.

In patterns with positions located centrally, such as the Wheel and the Star, an organization quickly develops around the people occupying these central positions. In such patterns, the organization is more stable and errors in performance are lower than in patterns having a lower degree of centrality, such as the Circle. However, he also found that the morale of members in high centrality patterns is relatively low. Bavelas speculated that this lower morale could, in the long run, lower the accuracy and speed of such networks.

In problem solving requiring the pooling of data and judgments, or "insight," Bavelas suggested that the ability to evaluate partial results, to look at alternatives, and to restructure problems fell off rapidly when one person was able to assume a more central (that is, more controlling) position in the information flow. For example, insight into a problem requiring change would be less in the Wheel and the Star than in the Circle or the Chain because of the "bottlenecking" effect of data control by central members.

It may be concluded from these laboratory results that the structure of communications within an organization will have a significant influence on the accuracy of decisions, the speed with which they can be reached, and the satisfaction of the people involved. Consequently, in networks in which the responsibility for initiating and passing along messages is shared more evenly among the members, the better the group's morale in the long run.

Direction of Communication

If it's considered formal communications as they occur in traditional military organizations, messages have a "one-way" directional characteristic. In the military organization, the formal communication proceeds from superior to subordinate, and its content is presumably clear because it originates at a higher level of expertise and experience. Military communications also carry the additional assumption that the superior is responsible for making his communication clear and understandable to his subordinates.

This type of organization assumes that there is little need for two-way exchanges between organizational levels except as they are initiated by a higher level. Because messages from superiors are considered to be more important than those from subordinates, the implicit rule is that communication channels, except for prescribed information flows, should not be cluttered by messages from subordinates but should remain open and free for messages moving down the chain of command. "Juniors should be seen and not heard," is still an unwritten, if not explicit, law of military protocol.

Vestiges of one-way flows of communication still exist in many formal organizations outside the military, and for many of the same reasons as described above. Although management recognizes that prescribed information must flow both downward and upward, managers may not always be convinced that two-wayness should be encouraged.

For example, to what extent is a subordinate free to communicate to his superior that he understands or does not understand a message? Is it possible for him to question the superior, ask for clarification, suggest modifications to instructions he has received, or transmit unsolicited messages to his superior, which are not prescribed by the rules? To what extent does the one-way rule of direction affect the efficiency of communication in the organization, in addition to the morale and motivation of subordinates?

These are not merely procedural matters but include questions about the organizational climate, pr psychological atmosphere in which communication takes place. Harold Leavitt has suggested a simple experiment that helps answer some of these questions. À group is assigned the task of re-creating on paper a set of rectangular figures, first as they are described by the leader under one-way conditions, and second as they are described by the leader under two-way conditions.(A different configuration of rectangles is used in the second trial.) In the one-way trial, the leader's back is turned to the group. He describes the rectangles as he sees them. No one in the group is allowed to ask questions and no one may indicate by any audible or visible sign his understanding or his frustration as he attempts to follow the leader's directions. In the two-way trial, the leader faces the group. In this case, the group may ask for clarifications on his description of the rectangles and he can not only see but also can feel and respond to the emotional reactions of group members as they try to re-create his instructions on paper.

On the basis of a number of experimental trials similar to the one described above, Leavitt formed these conclusions:

1. One-way communication is faster than two-way communication.
2. Two-way communication is more accurate than one-way communication.
3. Receivers are more sure of themselves and make more correct judgments of how right or wrong they are in the two-way system.
4. The sender feels psychologically under attack in the two-way system, because his receivers pick up his mistakes and oversights and point them out to him.
5. The two-way method is relatively noisier and looks more disorderly. The one-way method, on the other hand, appears neat and efficient to an outside observer.

Thus, if speed is necessary, if a businesslike appearance is important, if a manager does not want his mistakes recognized, and if he wants to protect his power, then one-way communication seems preferable. In contrast, if the manager wants to get his message across, or if he is concerned about his receivers' feeling that they are participating and are making a contribution, the two-way system is better.

Interpersonal Communication

Another facet of communication in the organization is the process of face-to-face, interpersonal communication, between individuals. Such communication may take several forms. Messages may be verbal (that is, expressed in words), or they may not involve words at all but consist of gestures, facial expressions, and certain postures ("body language"). Nonverbal messages may even stem from silence.

Managers do not need answers to operate a successful business; they need questions. Answers can come from anyone, anytime, anywhere in the world thanks to the benefits of all the electronic communication tools at our disposal. This has turned the real job of management into determining what it is the business needs to know, along with the who/what/where/when and how of learning it. To effectively solve problems, seize opportunities, and achieve objectives, questions need to be asked by managers—these are the people responsible for the operation of the enterprise as a whole.

Ideally, the meanings sent are the meanings received. This is most often the case when the messages concern something that can be verified objectively. For example, "This piece of pipe fits the threads on the coupling." In this case, the receiver of the message can check the sender's words by actual trial, if necessary. However, when the sender's words describe a feeling or an opinion about something that cannot be checked objectively, meanings can be very unclear. "This work is too hard" or "Watergate was politically justified" are examples of opinions or feelings that cannot be verified. Thus they are subject to interpretation and hence to distorted meanings. The receiver's background of experience and learning may differ enough from that of the sender to cause significantly different perceptions and evaluations of the topic under discussion. As we shall see later, such differences form a basic barrier to communication.

Nonverbal content always accompanies the verbal content of messages. This is reasonably clear in the case of face-to-face communication. As Virginia Satir has pointed out, people cannot help but communicate symbolically (for example, through their clothing or possessions) or through some form of body language. In messages that are conveyed by the telephone, a messenger, or a letter, the situation or context in which the message is sent becomes part of its nonverbal content. For example, if the company has been losing money, and in a letter to the production division, the front office orders a reorganization of the shipping and receiving departments, this could be construed to mean that some people were going to lose their jobs — unless it were made explicitly clear that this would not occur.

A number of variables influence the effectiveness of communication. Some are found in the environment in which communication takes place, some in the personalities of the sender and the receiver, and some in the relationship that exists between sender and receiver. These different variables suggest some of the difficulties of communicating with understanding between two people. The sender wants to formulate an idea and communicate it to the receiver. This desire to communicate may arise from his thoughts or feelings or it may have been triggered by something in the environment. The communication may also be influenced or distorted by the relationship between the sender and the receiver, such as status differences, a staff-line relationship, or a learner-teacher relationship.

Whatever its origin, information travels through a series of filters, both in the sender and in the receiver, before the idea can be transmitted and re-created in the receiver's mind. Physical capacities to see, hear, smell, taste, and touch vary between people, so that the image of reality may be distorted even before the mind goes to work. In addition to physical or sense filters, cognitive filters, or the way in which an individual's mind interprets the world around him, will influence his assumptions and feelings. These filters will determine what the sender of a message says, how he says it, and with what purpose. Filters are present also in the receiver, creating a double complexity that once led Robert Louis Stevenson to say that human communication is "doubly relative". It takes one person to say something and another to decide what he said.

Physical and cognitive, including semantic filters (which decide the meaning of words) combine to form a part of our memory system that helps us respond to reality. In this sense, March and Simon compare a person to a data processing system. Behaviour results from an interaction between a person's internal state and environmental stimuli. What we have learned through past experience becomes an inventory, or data bank, consisting of values or goals, sets of expectations and preconceptions about the consequences of acting one way or another, and a variety of possible ways of responding to the situation. This memory system determines what things we will notice and respond to in the environment. At the same time, stimuli in the environment help to determine what parts of the memory system will be activated. Hence, the memory and the environment form an interactive system that causes our behaviour. As this interactive system responds to new experiences, new learnings occur which feed back into memory and gradually change its content. This process is how people adapt to a changing world.

Communication Approaches in an Organization

Informal and Formal Communication are used in an organization. Informal communication: Informal communication, generally associated with interpersonal, horizontal communication, was primarily seen as a potential hindrance to effective organizational performance. This is no longer the case. Informal communication has become more important to ensuring the effective conduct of work in modern organizations.

Top-down approach: This is also known as downward communication. This approach is used by the Top Level Management to communicate to the lower levels. This is used to implement policies, gudelines, etc. In this type of organizational communication, distortion of the actual information occurs. This could be made effective by feedbacks.

Research in Organizational Communication

Research Methodologies

Historically, organizational communication was driven primarily by quantitative research methodologies. Included in functional organizational communication research are statistical analyses (such as surveys, text indexing, network mapping and behaviour modeling). In the early 1980s, the interpretive revolution took place in organizational communication. In Putnam and Pacanowsky's 1983 text *Communication and Organizations: An Interpretive Approach*. they argued for opening up methodological space for qualitative approaches such as narrative analyses, participant-observation, interviewing, rhetoric and textual approaches readings) and philosophic inquiries.

During the 1980s and 1990s critical organizational scholarship began to gain prominence with a focus on issues of gender, race, class, and power/knowledge. In its current state, the study of organizational communication is open methodologically, with research from post-positive, interpretive, critical, postmodern, and discursive paradigms being published regularly.

Organizational communication scholarship appears in a number of communication journals including but not limited to Management Communication Quarterly, Journal of Applied Communication Research, Communication Monographs, Academy of Management Journal, Communication Studies, and Southern Communication Journal.

Current Research Topics in Organizational Communication

The field of organizational communication has moved from acceptance of mechanistic models (e.g., information moving from a sender to a receiver) to a study of the persistent, hegemonic and taken-for-granted ways in which we not only use communication to accomplish certain tasks within organizational settings (e.g., public speaking) but also how the organizations in which we participate affect us.

These approaches include "postmodern", "critical", "participatory", "feminist", "power/political", "organic", etc. and adds to disciplines as wide-ranging as sociology, philosophy, theology, psychology, business, business administration, institutional management, medicine (health communication), neurology (neural nets), semiotics, anthropology, international relations, and music.

Currently, some topics of research and theory in the field are:

Constitution, e.g.,

- how communicative behaviours construct or modify organizing processes or products

- how the organizations within which we interact affect our communicative behaviours, and through these, our own identities
- structures other than organizations which might be constituted through our communicative activity (e.g., markets, cooperatives, tribes, political parties, social movements)
- when does something "become" an organization? When does an organization become (an)other thing(s)? Can one organization "house" another? Is the organization still a useful entity/thing/concept, or has the social/political environment changed so much that what we now call "organization" is so different from the organization of even a few decades ago that it cannot be usefully tagged with the same word—"organization"?

Narrative, e.g.,

- how do group members employ narrative to acculturate/initiate/indoctrinate new members?
- do organizational stories act on different levels? Are different narratives purposively invoked to achieve specific outcomes, or are there specific roles of "organizational storyteller"? If so, are stories told by the storyteller received differently than those told by others in the organization?
- in what ways does the organization attempt to influence storytelling about the organization? under what conditions does the organization appear to be more or less effective in obtaining a desired outcome?
- when these stories conflict with one another or with official rules/policies, how are the conflicts worked out? in situations in which alternative accounts are available, who or how or why are some accepted and others rejected?

Identity, e.g.,

- who do we see ourselves to be, in terms of our organizational affiliations?

- do communicative behaviours or occurrences in one or more of the organizations in which we participate effect changes in us? To what extent do whe consist of the organizations to which we belong?
- is it possible for individuals to successfully resist organizational identity? what would that look like?
- do people who define themselves by their work-organizational membership communicate differently within the organizational setting than people who define themselves more by an avocational (non-vocational) set of relationships?

Interrelatedness of organizational experiences, e.g.,

- how do our communicative interactions in one organizational setting affect our communicative actions in other organizational settings?
- how do the phenomenological experiences of participants in a particular organizational setting effect changes in other areas of their lives?
- when the organizational status of a member is significantly changed (e.g., by promotion or expulsion) how are their other organizational memberships affected?
- what kind of future relationship between business and society does organizational communication seem to predict?

Power e.g.,

- how does the use of particular communicative practices within an organizational setting reinforce or alter the various interrelated power relationships within the setting? Are the potential responses of those within or around these organizational settings constrained by factors or processes either within or outside of the organization—(assuming there is an "outside"?
- do taken-for-granted organizational practices work to fortify the dominant hegemonic narrative? Do individuals resist/

confront these practices, through what actions/agencies, and to what effects?

- do status changes in an organization (e.g., promotions, demotions, restructuring, financial/social strata changes) change communicative behaviour? Are there criteria employed by organizational members to differentiate between "legitimate" (i.e., endorsed by the formal organizational structure) and "illegitimate" (i.e., opposed by or unknown to the formal power structure)? Are behaviours? When are they successful, and what do we even there "pretenders" or "usurpers" who employ these communicativemean by "successful?"

Business Communication

Business Communication: communication used to promote a product, service, or organization; relay information within the business; or deal with legal and similar issues. It is also a means of relying between a supply chain, for example the consumer and manufacturer.

Business Communication is known simply as "Communications." It encompasses a variety of topics, including Marketing, Branding, Customer relations, Consumer behaviour, Advertising, Public relations, Corporate communication, Community engagement, Research & Measurement, Reputation management, Interpersonal communication, Employee engagement, Online communication, and Event management. It is closely related to the fields of professional communication and technical communication.

In business, the term communications encompasses various channels of communication, including the Internet, Print (Publications), Radio, Television, Ambient media, Outdoor, and Word of mouth.

Business Communication can also refer to internal communication. A communications director will typically manage internal communication and craft messages sent to employees. It is vital that internal communications are managed properly because a poorly crafted or managed message could foster distrust or hostility from employees.

Business Communication is a common topic included in the curricula of Masters of Business Administration (MBA) programs of many universities. AS well, many community colleges and universities offer degrees in Communications.

There are several methods of business communication, including:

- Web-based communication-for better and improved communication, anytime anywhere...
- e-mails, which provide an instantaneous medium of written communication worldwide;
- Reports-important in documenting the activities of any department;
- Presentations-very popular method of communication in all types of organizations, usually involving audiovisual material, like copies of reports, or material prepared in Microsoft PowerPoint or Adobe Flash;
- telephoned meetings, which allow for long distance speech;
- forum boards, which allow people to instantly post information at a centralized location; and
- face to face meetings, which are personal and should be succeeded by a written followup.

Organizations

- Founded in 1936 the Association of Business Communication (ABC), originally called the Association of College Teachers of Business Writing, is "an international organization committed to fostering excellence in business communication scholarship, research, education, and practice."
- The IEEE Professional Communication Society (PCS) is dedicated to understanding and promoting effective

communication in engineering, scientific, and other environments, including business environments. PCS's academic journal, IEEE Transactions on Professional Communication, is one of the premier journals in professional communication. The journal's readers are engineers, writers, information designers, managers, and others working as scholars, educators, and practitioners who share an interest in the effective communication of technical and business information.

Written Communication in an Organization

Business communication is a process of transmitting information between different parts of an organization. Organizations use various forms of communications such as in-house magazines, journals, reports and bulletin boards to transmit ideas, thoughts and information.

Communication is a process of transmitting information between different parts of an organization. It is one of the basic functions of management in any organization. For communication with the outside world, organizations use advertising material, news releases and audio-visual aids. However, for communication within organization and with employees, different forms of communications are used such as in-house magazines, journals, reports and bulletin boards to transmit ideas, thoughts and information.

Forms of Communication in an Organization

Employee handbook: Employee handbook is given to the new employee at the time of induction or orientation program. It provides complete information of the organization with details on nature of the business, its customers, products, policies, benefits and services available to its employees. Some organizations use charts, photographs, and cartoons to make it more interesting for reading.

In-house Magazines & journals: Organizations publish quarterly or monthly in-house magazines to keep employees updated about the latest development in the business, activities conducted in the company like social or cultural and achievements by the sales team. Management can unite with employees in an informal or direct way through these magazines. It also contains promotions, retirements, honours and awards with pictures of employees receiving award from management.

Financial reports to employees: Financial reports published for shareholders & general public with all the technical accounting language & its terminologies, do not serve any purpose for the employees. So, some organizations publish financial reports specifically for employees with details on expenses, income, profits and distribution of income, which gives the idea about financial standing of the organization to the employees.

Information racks or display stands: Information racks or stands are usually placed at places like front lobby, factory gate, cafeteria, shop or at a place which is most frequented by employees. These stands are used to display books dealing with wide range of topics such as help yourself, hobbies, sports, accident prevention etc.

Bulletin boards: Bulletin boards in attractive colours & types can be used for display of clippings from newspapers, magazines, clippings on retirements, honours, marriages and other events in the lives of employees.

Museums & exhibitions: Small museum or an exhibition can be used to display quality control ideas, old photographs of the factory, old designs and good quality products. It can create interest among the employees in their own work.

Posters: Posters are used to display topics related with health and safety, hygiene, improvement in production process, etc. Along with text matter, it should contain pictorial diagrams, charts, and photographs to explain the topic in a simple way.

Notice Boards: Notice boards are usually placed at the factory gate or in front lobby. These are used to display notices and circulars issued by the management for administrative purposes, circulars related with hours of work, factories act and any new rules and regulations.

Suggestion system: Some organizations use suggestion system to provide an opportunity for a working communication with the management. Employees can use this system to give positive proposals for improvement in machines, devices, techniques and procedures or to express their dissatisfaction with existing facilities or particulars.

Memo: Memos are business letters but used within an organization and only for employees. Memos are used to give information to employees such as changes in some procedures or rules, policy change or for specific purpose like request to attend a meeting. The format of the memo differs from business letter format.

Business writing softwares can be used while writing any business communication to check and correct English grammar and spellings and for proofreading. Some software programs also enrich your text with adjectives & adverbs, which enhances the simple sentence into more professional and sophisticated one & suggest context related synonym for repeated words.

Communications-enabled Application

A communications enabled application (CEA) is a set of information technology (IT) components and communication technology components that are integrated using a particular service-oriented architecture (SOA) to increase the productivity of an organization and/or improve the quality of users' experiences.

Communication enablement adds real-time networking functionality to an IT application. Providing communications capability to an IT application:

- removes the human latency which exists when (i) making sense of information from many different sources, (ii) orchestrating suitable responses to events, and (iii) keeping track of actions carried out when responding to information received;
- enables users to be part of the creative flow of content and processes.

What distinguishes a CEA from other software applications is its intrinsic reliance upon communications technologies to accomplish its objectives. A CEA depends on real-time networking capabilities together with such network oriented functions as location, presence, proximity, and identity.

Another distinguishing characteristic of a CEA is the implicit assumption that network services will be available as callable services within the SOA frameworks from which the CEA is constructed. To provide callable services, the network services which are available today must be made virtual and component-like. CEAs apply to business processes as well as instances where no obvious business process which requires improvement exists (e.g., games, entertainment video). CEAs that apply to business processes are referred to as communications enabled business processes or communications enabled business solutions.

Importance

CEA are important for at least four reasons:

1. The convergence of (i) CEA, (ii) broadband and (iii) millions of different devices connected to the network is expected to significantly affect the communications industry.
2. CEA introduce a fundamental change in the way that information communications technology (ICT) applications and services are designed, developed, delivered, and used. To date, SOA has focused on building IT applications only and the network has been mostly deemed to be a transport pipe. CEA incorporate communications capability into any application. This requires that network services must be made virtual and component-like as well as callable within a SOA framework. CEA implementation entails a significant reorganization of present network management functionality.
3. CEA bring together the richness of IT applications with the sophistication and intelligence of communications networks. This enables greater customization, greater simplification of interactions, and automatic adaptation to users' environments and preferences.

4. Making network components from multiple vendors work in a mashup will be a major challenge. The service level agreements (SLAs) for these mashups will be difficult to define and deliver upon.

Examples

- A tech savvy entrepreneur can integrate highly secure services such as messaging, voice, conference call, authentication and inbound short message service into an IT application for the purpose of delivering a customized solution in hours or days at a fraction of the cost of large packaged applications or custom development projects.
- A patient is discharged more quickly because the patient care application used by authorizing medical personnel can reach out to the discharge application, wherever they are.
- A new policy is processed and approved more quickly because the client's insurance agent initiates real-time communications with people who have reviewed the policy and are required to approve it.
- Faster and more effective emergency response is provided because the first responder application recognized the availability and location of key resources.
- An industrial customer problem is resolved more quickly because the project management application scheduled the earliest possible conference call with all key available stakeholders and delivered all relevant information to them.
- A data centre backup package that runs overnight must be complete by 8 a.m. when the network turns back to daytime operations. The application recognizes that it will not complete in time-so it makes a request of the network for more capacity. The network can apply logic to translate the request into a set of commands to the various nodes to do whatever is required for the task to be completed by 8 a.m. (e.g., change the priority, provision more capacity, allocate more wavelengths).

Integrated Marketing Communications

Integrated Marketing Communications is a term used to describe a holistic approach to marketing communication. It aims to ensure consistency of message and the complementary use of media. The concept includes online and offline marketing channels. Online marketing channels include any e-marketing campaigns or programs, from search engine optimization (SEO), pay-per-click, affiliate, email, banner to latest web related channels for webinar, blog, micro-blogging, RSS, podcast, and Internet TV. Offline marketing channels are traditional print (newspaper, magazine), mail order, public relations, industry relations, billboard, radio, and television. A company develops its integrated marketing communication programme using all the elements of the marketing mix (product, price, place, and promotion).

Integrated marketing communication is integration of all marketing tools, approaches, and resources within a company which maximizes impact on consumer mind and which results into maximum profit at minimum cost. Generally marketing starts from "Marketing Mix". Promotion is one element of Marketing Mix. Promotional activities include Advertising(by using different medium), sales promotion (sales and trades promotion), and personal selling activities. It also includes internet marketing, sponsorship marketing, direct marketing, database marketing and public relations. And integration of all these promotional tools along with other components of marketing mix to gain edge over competitor is called Integrated Marketing Communication.

Reasons for the Growing Importance of IMC

Several shifts in the advertising and media industry have caused IMC to develop into a primary strategy for marketers:

1. From media advertising to multiple forms of communication.
2. From mass media to more specialized (niche) media, which are centered around specific target audiences.
3. From a manufacturer-dominated market to a retailer-dominated, consumer-controlled market.

4. From general-focus advertising and marketing to data-based marketing.
5. From low agency accountability to greater agency accountability, particularly in advertising.
6. From traditional compensation to performance-based compensation (increased sales or benefits to the company).
7. From limited Internet access to 24/7 Internet availability and access to goods and services.

Selecting the Most Effective Communications Elements

The goal of selecting the elements of proposed integrated marketing communications is to create a campaign that is effective and consistent across media platforms. Some marketers may want only ads with the greatest breadth of appeal: the executions that, when combined, provide the greatest number of attention-getting, branded, and motivational moments. Others may only want ads with the greatest depth of appeal: the ads with the greatest number of attention-getting, branded, and motivational points within each.

Although integrated marketing communications is more than just an advertising campaign, the bulk of marketing dollars is spent on the creation and distribution of advertisements. Hence, the bulk of the research budget is also spent on these elements of the campaign. Once the key marketing pieces have been tested, the researched elements can then be applied to other contact points: letterhead, packaging, logistics, customer service training, and more, to complete the IMC cycle.

Integrated Communication: From Theory to Performance

The Renaissance Communicator

As organizations of all types are rapidly transforming their business processes and management styles, the traditional roles of internal communication professionals may well become obsolete. Landes (1992) described the conventional roles of organizational communicators as "reporters, promoters, and corporate apologists", and numerous researchers and practitioners have critiqued typical practice models as being reactive, not strategically aligned with management, and oriented towards narrow, technical, production-centered solutions such as producing newsletters and videos (c.f. D'Aprix, 1977). As communication has developed in terms of both theory and practice, separate specialties and departments within organizations were created: employee communication, public relations and public affairs, advertising and marketing, audiovisual media, training and development, event and meeting planning, and information systems. These separate "islands of communication" (Gayeski, 1993b) have grown and moved further apart, often resulting in fragmented, redundant, or even contradictory communication programs and messages. This can lead to information overload, a loss of credibility, and wasted resources.

However, a new model for organizational communication is emerging: Gayeski (1993b) calls this more integrated and strategic archetype the "Renaissance Communicator" and defines corporate communication quite broadly as the professional practice of developing and implementing communication "rules and tools" to enhance the dissemination, comprehension, acceptance, and application of information in ways which help to achieve an organization's goals. Grates (1995) states that the lines between communication disciplines as well as those between communication and other related types of consulting are blurring. "In this new era, communication professionals in public relations and advertising will be asked less frequently for specific advice as it relates to their individual disciplines and more frequently for solutions". Similarly, Freeland (1994) maintains that the successful communicator will become identified with cost control and performance improvement and that perhaps titles like "communication director" will be dropped in favour of "director of change management". Finally, Kreps (1989) expands on the traditional theoretical perspective of PR as being external communication-oriented to include the role of internal communication as change agents who promote increased organizational reflexivity and who are involved in organizational development.

Although few practitioners would reject a more strategic and integrated role, there are not yet many real-life examples of "Renaissance Communicators". Many forward-looking professionals in public relations, training and development, marketing, employee communications, and information systems are attempting to break out of their narrow specialties, but find it to be a long and difficult process to work outside of institutional "silos", to learn new cross-functional skills, and to gain credibility with management. For example, Smalley, et. al. (1995) report that it took three years for Amway's training department to become involved in their first real project employing the more holistic approach of "performance technology". However, given the current business climate, it may not be feasible for communicators to wait for three years to redirect their efforts; case studies and models for practice need to be shared and adopted rapidly so that professional communicators retain positions of value in their organizations.

Conceptual Foundations

A new model for organizational communication management is needed to encompass emerging theories of management, learning, and communication — as well as new realities of an increasingly competitive marketplace and rapidly merging and emerging technologies. One such model is "integrated communications". Although this term has been used to describe combined advertising / marketing / public relations campaigns (Schultz, 1993b), we define integrated communications more broadly as the application of analysis, communication, and evaluation techniques to create and manage integrated, multi-faceted interventions combining information, instruction, collaboration, business process design, feedback, and incentive systems to improve human performance in the workplace in order to achieve organizations' desired missions and visions. Traditional models of communication practice (including public relations, instructional design, and employee communications) are based on a number of assumptions that are no longer valid: · Although they generally include audience and message analysis, traditional models of communication practice assume that one type of well-designed intervention will solve the problem — be it training, promotion, or information-retrieval.

They do not help practitioners determine what types of problems are potentially not solvable by these interventions, nor do they incorporate the other types of support that are generally necessary for any long-term change to occur. For example, employee communication and training systems may promote safe work practices, but if the work design and performance appraisal systems do not reinforce these messages, they are likely to be ineffective. The traditional linear models of communication analysis and message design reflect early linear models of communication: assume the "sender" crafts a well-designed message, the "receiver" will "get it".

They do not reflect the complex interplay of interpretation and negotiation among all parties in a communicative situation, nor the impact of environmental and social influences. · Conventional models assume that the client or requester has correctly identified the problem and the appropriate intervention — for example, that a performance gap is due to poor morale or that a two-day training course is needed. Traditional practice is reactive rather than proactive. Moreover, there is evidence that clients and sponsors often "do not ask us to deliver what they need; they ask us to deliver what they believe we can provide. . . . We do not do what we are not asked to do — improve human performance in the workplace". · Finally, traditional communication practice measures the outcomes of communication projects by satisfaction indicators — how much the audience "liked" a meeting, newsletter, or course, or by readership or attendance. These statements of satisfaction are assumed to relate to the effectiveness of an intervention in terms of organizational goals. Few models for evaluation actually link interventions to the "bottom line". The model we propose for integrated communication is based upon several new approaches:

Market-based strategic communication

This term represents the approach of designing proactive communication programs that candidly inform employees about the requirements of their customers and the realities of the marketplace, and focus on organizational strategy.

Performance technology or performance engineering

These terms describe systematic processes for solving organizational problems by analyzing and improving selection, communication, instruction, work design, feedback, and incentive systems. The theoretical foundation for this approach is found in behavioural theories of psychology, including motivation and learning. This approach centres around identifying and solving "performance gaps" which are defined as "discrepancies between an organization's expectations and its actual performance".

Business process reengineering

This phrase represents the approach of radical reinvention of business processes rather than merely "tweaking" current, obsolete systems. Although this has been used as a euphemism for downsizing, the original intent of this model is to carefully scrutinize and re-design basic business systems around work processes rather than bureaucratic "silos" and departments.

ComADD model

The communication analysis, design, and development model is a system for identifying and operationalizing performance gaps and for selecting and assessing communication-based solutions. It consists of five phases: initiating, descriptive, conceptual, prototypic, actual, and continuous improvement. This model is iterative rather than linear, and emphasizes the development of a number of alternative solutions that are selected by a process of rapid prototyping and determining optimum potential return-on-investment of time and money.

A Model for Developing Integrated Communication Interventions

The integrated communication model proposed here reflects the theories and perspectives described above: an examination of customer and market needs, an identification of performance goals and gaps, an examination and possible re-design of basic business processes to meet those goals, and the systematic identification, implementation, and evaluation of a coordinated set of communication solutions.

Communication Resources and Perspectives Required

In order to offer integrated communication interventions, a team or a multidisciplinary communication professional with competencies in message design, training, persuasion, incentive systems, business process reengineering, media/information technology, marketing, employee selection and performance assessment is needed. This team or person works with the client and a representative constituency of the target audience to analyse the situation and to prototype and evaluate interventions. The team may exist within one department, or may be an interdepartmental work group. The analysis and development steps for an integrated approach are listed below:

Problem identification

- Identify market and customer needs / perceptions
- Describe and operationalize the performance goal for the target group
- Are there examples of exemplary performers? If not, are you sure that the goal is attainable?
- Describe and operationalize the current performance of the target group
- What is the "gap" between ideal and current performance?

Determine cause(s) of the gap and identify potential solutions

- Did the target group ever meet the performance goal in the past? If so, why has the performance slipped?
- If the target group really had to, could they exhibit the desired level of performance? If they could not, is it a lack of skill, or are there other barriers? If they could exhibit the desired performance, they do not need training — look for other barriers.

- Are the best performers recruited and selected for the job?— If not, investigate public relations, recruiting, and testing interventions.

- Do they understand the business and its goals and values?— If not, investigate employee communication systems, better methods of orientation, training in basic business concepts, articulation of mission and vision.

- What are the barriers or disincentives to performing well?— Look for opportunities to change the culture to one that values high performance and doesn't inadvertently reward poor performance.

- What are the incentives for performing well? Do they "work" for your target group? — Investigate what kinds of rewards and feedback are actually meaningful to your target group (i.e. publicity, monetary incentives, job "perks", etc.).

- Could the job, work process, or environment be re-designed? — Could the job be made less complex? Could jobs be divided up differently? Are all the steps really valuable?

- Is the environment conducive to the type of work performed and to the personal styles of the workers?

- Does a new skill need to be learned or concepts / facts memorized? — Investigate various methods of training and development if memorization is necessary. Otherwise, consider job aids, performance support systems, data banks, etc..

- What are the important sources of feedback, social support, and coaching? — Can you redesign the performance appraisal system, make families and communities more supportive of employees, teach managers to be better coaches?

Select, Prototype, Implement, and Evaluate Interventions

- What types of interventions fit the organizational culture?
- Which have the best chance of showing a positive return on investment?
- How do these interact with other existing communication and performance systems?
- Develop a rough rapid prototype, or pilot the interventions on a small group
- Measure and document results, tweak, maintain, and revise as necessary.
- What was the bottom-line result in performance?

Although we do not represent this as a lock-step "formula" for approaching communication projects, the protocol and mindset of performance-based analysis and consideration of an integrated set of communication interventions can, and has been, successfully applied.

Organizational Implementation of Integrated Communication

Although most organizations' communication systems and interventions are not yet "integrated" as we define them, there are a number of examples that demonstrate that this model of organizational communication can be applied creatively in a number of diverse settings. In some cases, integrated communication models are used on an ad hoc basis by a communication professional or team when faced with a particularly significant or difficult problem. A particular project may provide the opportunity to employ broader, more strategic methods. For example, Smalley et. al. (1995) report the results of an integrated performance-based approach to improving the performance of a telephone order-taking department: the intervention gained approximately $1 million in "saved sales" each year, and the time it took new clerks to become comfortable with their jobs was reduced from 90 days to 30 days. The intervention was designed by the training department as one step in their strategic plan to becoming a "performance improvement" department.

The training, advertising, public relations, and documentation groups at Apple Computer are now coordinating their efforts to provide information to the company's 20,000 salespeople. One specific outcome has been the creation of an on-line database on new products called Apple's Reference Performance and Learning Expert (ARPLE). "The PR, advertising, documentation, and training departments pool their information to eliminate redundancies before sending the information out to salespeople. It wastes less time and money on the corporate end, and saves the salespeople from wading through useless information" (Geber, 1994).

ISVOR Fiat, the subsidiary that provides training to the international conglomerate Fiat, has recently found a decline in interest for traditional classroom training among its internal clients. Not only has it embraced new forms of media production, such as multimedia and video, but it has also worked with one of the authors to expand upon its services to include knowledge capture and engineering and design and documentation of corporate meetings. The training department at a utility also transformed its mission, changing its name to "professional development resources", and adding to its repertoire the creation of sales aids, a database of company expertise, and the facilitation of "brown bag" information lunch seminars given by company employees (Gayeski, 1993a).

Other organizations are re-structuring key roles and departmental teams related to communications and learning. Among the clients of one of the authors, one national restaurant chain charged a cross-functional team called FutureCom with investigating and designing a plan for the future of internal communication. The results of the initial study not only recommended new technologies, but made clear that more coordination of communication was necessary to attempt to control "information overload". A prototype daily e-mail update integrating information across various departments, is now being developed. A new job description for their manager of corporate communication was developed and a new individual hired into that position who has a background in both mass media and new training technologies.

The authors have also worked with a large regional healthcare organization whose leadership team was interested in the concept of the "learning organization". The CEO established a strategic planning committee to investigate organizational development and performance technology, to identify gaps and barriers to learning, and to recommend a new organizational structure and policy. The work of this committee is still in progress, but the proposal currently being drafted integrates the human resources, staff development, and media production departments into one team which will be self-managed with a group of advisors including representatives from information systems, finance, and corporate communications.

Entirely new job titles and descriptions are being crafted. For example, Millbrook Distribution Services has recently created a position of Chief Learning Officer with a small staff of communication, graphic arts, media production, and instructional design specialists. The responsibilities and structure of this position were designed, in part, based on Gayeski's (1993b) concept of the "Renaissance Communicator". The Chief Learning Officer at Millbrook has stated, "Management of the formal communication processes of the organization as part of the Chief Learning Officer's responsibilities is believed to be a leading edge innovation... In times of non-stop change, it is essential to bridge the traditional 'islands of corporate communication' such as training and development, employee communications, public affairs, corporate media, documentation, library systems, policies and procedures, and advertising and marketing to create integrated, consistent, and coherent messages to stakeholders". Coca-Cola has also created a similar position of "CLO" (Willis and May, 1996).

Barriers to Adopting Integrated Communication

Despite the documented interest in and success of an integrated communication model, this approach is still not yet widely accepted. In our research and practice, we have found that there are significant barriers that organizational communication professionals face when they attempt to employ models of integrated communication and performance technology: · Current jobs and departments related to organizational communication often pigeonhole professionals into narrow roles. Professionals in training often assume that their job is to "produce courses", just as employee communication professionals believe that their job is to organize newsletters and meetings, and perhaps to somehow increase morale. In order to provide what they feel is "good service", they produce what they are asked for: videotapes, meetings, courses, electronic bulletin boards, and so forth. Because these separate "islands of communication" (Gayeski, 1993b) actually are often engaged in internal competition for resources and credibility, there are few incentives to work together and more incentives to protect "turf".

External suppliers, such as ad agencies, also tend to specialize in advertising or PR or direct marketing or media production — generally not truly an integrated approach (Schultz, 1993c).

Organizational communicators often suffer from a lack of credibility, especially when they attempt to recommend some intervention that is outside their usual specialty. They often have little access to management, and are not a part of the executive decision-making team. Integrated communication models require new approaches that often require significant change and resources— often more than the typical employee communication specialist, PR agent, or trainer can martial.

As Schultz (1993c) points out, "Some of the difficulty in integration is a result of many organizations never viewing communication as important to their overall success."

Because integrated communication interventions are often "high risk, high gain", there is a necessity for rigorous evaluation in terms of bottom-line return on investment. Dozier (1990) argues that program research, the use of quantitative and qualitative research techniques to plan and evaluate communication programs, is still considered something new to most practitioners. Although such "hard" measures may still be considered innovative and are not well-established in traditional practice, he insists that they are essential to the progress of the field. However, communicators often lack the skills to develop business plans and conduct formal program evaluation, and such rigorous evaluation carries the risk of pointing out failure.

An even more important consideration is how communicators themselves are evaluated and compensated. Now, professional communicators are often evaluated and rewarded on the quantity rather than quality of their output — how many brochures and newsletters they produced, how many hours of training they designed, or how many ads they placed. Clients and managers need to alter the current system. "Agencies must move to media neutrality. That simply means they must move away from being driven by media commissions and find a new method of compensation".

Opportunities and Strategies

As organizations are attempting to "re-engineer" and strive to become "learning organizations", communication professionals should look for opportunities to employ new integrated communication approaches. Some specific approaches we recommend are:

- Focus communication strategies on teaching the audience how to better learn about and respond to the needs of their customers. Meeting marketplace expectations can be a differentiating factor and a competitive edge. An analysis of customer needs can be done through business processing mapping. Then, all communication to the audience can be integrated and aligned (training, incentive plans, marketing materials, etc.), so that people don't have to put fragments of uncoordinated messages together for themselves.
- When confronted with a potential communication-related project, explore all the factors that can impact the performance of the target audience. For example, in our work and research in sales training, we have often found that performance gaps that initially look like training problems are actually a result of incentive programs that are not aligned with the business objectives, or or caused by suboptimal business process design. In one situation, a time analysis of sales representatives' work was performed and it was found that reps were spending

almost half of their time doing technical service instead of selling. Their frustration was high because they could not meet their customers' expectations and because they were not trained to be technicians. In this case, technical reps were added to the sales team, freeing up sales reps' time to sell. Neither typical motivational nor sales training programs would have truly addressed this performance gap.

- Communicators should network and collaborate with other communication-related professionals within their organizations. Look for opportunities to share resources and information and to develop integrated approaches to major performance gaps. For example, in a sales organization, marketing, training, and field service personnel could form an integrated team to understand how to best meet customer needs and how to support sales representatives in the selling process. This team should be seamless: although reporting lines still may remain functional, the team supports a common goal and is self-directed in its mission.
- Managers should work towards identifying and quantifying performance gaps and presenting those gaps— rather than "work orders"— to teams of professionals in employee communications, public relations, human resources, training, and marketing / advertising. Specific deficiencies should be defined and operationalized and goals should be set so that communicators can target a specific objective. In our experience, communicators can often easily respond to specific problems with appropriate interventions, but too often, there are no data about performance gaps, and no direction regarding what the most crucial and expensive organizations problems may be. If no gaps are defined, it is impossible to produce return-on-investment analyses.
- Executives should form teams or committees to investigate new approaches to communication. Leadership and support from the top of the organization is crucial to the

kinds of systemic changes that integrated communication demands. "Integration cannot be accomplished by middle managers or from those in the lower levels of the organization. It must come from the top, and it can't be just a memo or a directive... There must be a commitment from top management to integrate and to remove the barriers which prevent integration. Moreover, while integrated teams of communication professionals to explore new models and to execute interventions are essential, organizations should also consider appointing a high-level executive to provide leadership and guidance in integrated communication and to make sure that communication and learning resources are a part of the critical path for all new projects.

- Communication educators need to prepare young professionals who are skilful not only in message design and media production, but who also are analysts, managers, evaluators, and strategic partners. They need to understand a broad range of communication tools and interventions, and to be able to apply theory and research methods (Gayeski, 1994). The research of Dozier (1990) concludes that public relations professionals' roles in management decision-making increase when they play the "manager role" and conduct program research. Further, he finds that the diffusion of this innovation of "program research" is slowed down by a perception of complexity of these methods, and is accelerated when practitioners have formal training in the social sciences, statistics, and computer use. Neff (1989) found that academic programs in public relations are shifting away from a concentration on journalism to a more complex integration of communication theory and social science. These are not just requirements of the "ivory tower", but increasingly they are demanded by organizations of all types.

- Academics and practitioners must collaborate in generating and testing theory, and in sharing case studies both of success and failure with their professional community.

> When clients ask who else is applying new approaches and upon what conceptual foundation we are basing our proposals, we need better answers. Ideally, practitioners should be teaching partners with professors, and academics should be represented on the teams that are redesigning organizations' information and learning systems and shaping the communication philosophy.

We are hopeful that the model and cases presented here will encourage more collaboration and learning among communication professionals within organizations, and strengthen the ties between organizational communication theory and practice.

12

Mass E-mail and Effective Electronic Communication

Introduction

Electronic communications (including e-mail, websites, listservs, and voice mail) are used extensively at Iowa State University. In particular, e-mail is a powerful electronic communication tool when it is used effectively. Recognizing that, the university seeks to enable the distribution of e-mail across campus as efficiently as possible and to have e-mail be beneficial rather than disruptive to people in their work. Because of the high volume of e-mail as well as our dependence on its reliable delivery, it is important that we observe best practices to ensure effective use of e-mail on campus in a manner that benefits all of the Iowa State University community, from both the technical and personal aspects.

When e-mail is used for large-scale distribution it has the potential to disrupt normal operations by overloading the network, decreasing the efficiency of the mail servers, or disrupting routine network traffic. Following guidelines for large-scale or mass e-mail can help smooth out e-mail traffic so it continues to flow smoothly for everyone. The first section of this document notes existing electronic communication channels that should be used when appropriate. The second section notes best practices for e-mail. The third section covers policies and procedures for large-scale mailing. We encourage the inclusion of the best practices noted here in departmental and college guidelines.

Objectives

- Ensure University resources are used effectively.
- Preserve e-mail as an effective communication tool.
- Maintain accessibility to network by all users.

Using Existing Communication Channels

The most effective communication method is often one that uses an existing communication channel. Presenting your news or information in a publication that your target audience is already reading can increase the probability of your item being read. Combining smaller items of interest together can yield greater effect to the overall communication. A key point is that the news or announcement must be relevant to the publication and, thus, to the audience.

To assist with effective communication to the university community, Iowa State University has many existing electronic communications or publications that are published or updated regularly. When you want to disseminate an announcement to the university community, you should use one of these methods if it is appropriate to the publication rather than doing your own mass e-mail.

E-Mail Best Practices

Effective Communication

E-mail is a quick and easy way to send a message but that doesn't ensure it's the most effective method for communication. If you send a short e-mail to 400 people, it may take only one minute of your time. On the receiving end, however, that same e-mail can take 400 minutes of time to read. Consider the following points to help determine if using e-mail to convey your message is the best choice for effective communication.

- Appropriate method. E-mail is not always the appropriate or best method to disseminate information to your intended audience, especially if you're not able to target a specific audience. For some announcements, other methods (newsletters, online postings, etc.) may be more effective in reaching the audience.
- Content of mailing. When mailing to a diverse group of individuals, it is likely that some recipients don't need or want the mailing. Complaints from a large number of individuals can temporarily load down the e-mail system and/or your e-mail inbox.
- Perceived importance to recipient. If the recipient does not care to get unsolicited communications of the type you are sending, it may persuade them to ignore future communications from you or others.
- Segment intended audience. Targeting a pre-defined or specific group will yield better results than if you send an e-mail to a non-specific or generic audience.
- Repeated or frequent contacts. If you will be making repeated contacts, it is more effective to only contact those people who have opted to receive those notifications rather than blanketing a group of whom only some are interested. Also, you should offer individuals the ability to easily opt out of the mailing when it is no longer of interest to them.
- Relevant to University business. Is the e-mail relevant to the University's core missions, or is it important in protecting physical, financial, or human assets? If not, distributing a mailing to a university e-mail list may not be appropriate.

E-Mail Etiquette

- Use the blind carbon copy field for addressing when the list of recipient addresses is lengthy. If you use the blind carbon copy field for the recipient list, the names and addresses of all the recipients won't appear in the received e-mail. When the recipient list is lengthy, your intended reader might not scroll through the long list of names to get to the message. Also, sometimes, it is best not to reveal the identity of the recipients to each other (e.g., when the nature of the e-mail may be sensitive or personal).

- When it is important for those receiving the e-mail to know who else is receiving that e-mail, enter the recipient addresses into the "To" and/or "Cc" fields. Otherwise, enter the recipient list into the "Bcc" field.

Minimizing the Load on the Network and Servers

Mailings that have a small distribution list usually don't have a noticeable impact on network traffic, although best practices should still be observed. Mailings that have a large distribution list (more than 1,000 addresses) can have a significant impact on the network traffic. Following the guidelines below will help minimize the impact on the network. Information on large-scale electronic mailings is also contained in the following section of this document. E-mail messages should be short since each copy of e-mail takes up disk space until read. Long documents should not be included in a mass e-mailing. Reference longer documents by using URL pointers to Web pages.

- Sending a large mailing during off-hours is highly recommended since these kinds of mailings impose a heavy load on the mail system. "Off-hours" is defined as midnight to 8:00 a.m. on weekdays; all day Saturday; and midnight to noon on Sunday. Avoid doing a large mailing (more than 1.000 addresses) during the normal 8:00 a.m. to 5:00 p.m. business day.

- Break a large mailing into smaller chunks (100-250 addresses each) if mass e-mail is determined as a suitable method to reach the audience. This helps to spread out the load on the network. IT Services maintains a utility for doing this automatically with big mailings.

- Setting up the addresses correctly is extremely important. For large mailings, don't put a list name or list of addresses in the To: field. Instead, you should put your own e-mail address in the To: and From: fields and place the list name or list of e-mail addresses in the Bcc: field. Using this method keeps the list of recipients from being displayed with the e-mail and keeps anyone replying to the e-mail from sending his or her response to the entire list, creating more traffic than was originally intended.

Mass E-mail Policies and Procedures

Approval

All electronic communications are expected to comply with relevant federal and state laws, as well as University regulations and policies, including those governing public computing resources, security considerations, and ethics in computing.

Permission to mail to a group is not needed if you are the authorized agent for the group or are conducting normal University business (e.g., reminders to Library patrons about book due dates). The role of approval is delegated to specific governing groups (e.g., P&S Council may mail to P&S staff; Faculty Senate may mail to faculty). Before using a list that someone else owns, you must ask permission to use it. Access to a list does not necessarily imply permission to use.

If you wish to do a large mailing to a group and are from outside of the unit, area, or division, you must get approval from the office authorized to give permission to mail to that audience. Exceptions or requests that fall outside the scope of this table will be handled on a case-by-case basis. Direct your request to the head of the division or unit for the intended audience.

Procedures

- After obtaining approval to do a mass mailing, obtain authorization to use the appropriate mailing list. All list owners are encouraged to consider the benefits of moderating or otherwise controlling access to large lists. This applies whether a list has been created for one-time use or is maintained as a standing list, whether compiled manually or from the central database, and whether membership is involuntary or by subscription. Authorization to use a mailing list is given by the list owner or the person/office empowered to give such permission.

- If a list needs to be extracted from an IT Services database, the person authorizing the use of the list must send approval to the appropriate IT Services analyst, who will process the actual request for list extraction.
- Using a utility to assist with a large mailing can be useful in spreading out the load on the resources. IT Services has a script called "bigmail" for such a use. There also are instructions for using bigmail. The bigmail script runs on Unix systems but Macintosh/Windows users can telnet to a suitable machine and run the script. The script takes a flat file of e-mail addresses (one address per line) and sends out the same text message to each e-mail address in that file. Bigmail mails in units of 100 every 2 minutes (for example, mailing 1,000 messages would take a minimum of 20 minutes).
- In some situations (e.g., administrative uses) there may be some charges by IT Services for list extraction and processing. After obtaining approval to use a list, the requestor should send e-mail to solution@iastate.edu to initiate the process; include "Text for mass mailing" in the subject line.
- Remember that while e-mail is a good mechanism for short-term communication, it is not instantaneous when one is mailing to a large group. It can take several hours to send a message to a large group and up to 15 hours to send a message to all of the campus community.

Supported E-mail Clients

Eudora

- Click on New Message.

- Enter your e-mail address in the To: field (or that of the person who should receive the replies).
- Enter a descriptive subject in the Subject: area.
- Enter the recipient e-mail addresses in the Bcc: area, separating each with a comma.
- Type in the message.
- Click on Send, as usual. The receivers will not see who else the message was sent to.

Outlook

- Create a new message.
- Click on the View Menu.
- Click on the BCC Field Option.
- A box with the button BCC will come up in the header area. Enter the recipient e-mail addresses, separating each with a semicolon.
- Type your message.
- When finished typing the message, send the message as usual. The receivers will not see who else the message was sent to.

Mass E-mail Checklist

Before you send a large-scale mailing, you should ensure you can answer "yes" to each of the following questions:

- Is e-mail the best or appropriate method to get information to your intended audience?
- Have you clearly identified the intended audience and the appropriate mailing list to use to reach them?
- Is the message relevant to the university's core missions?
- Have you included in the content of the message:

- A "From:" address where replies will be received
- The office, organization, or individual sending the message
- Contact information if there is a question, comment, or complaint about the message
- An explanation of why the recipient is receiving the message
- Required information presented succinctly
- Pointers to Website or elsewhere for additional information, if applicable
- An approval notice

- Have you included only plain text in the message body (and no attachments)?
- Do you have authorization to use the mailing list?
- If your mailing will go to more than 1,000 recipients, do you have approval to do a mass mailing to your intended audience?
- If your mailing will go to more than 1,000 recipients, are you using a mailing method to minimize the load on the network?

Communication-based Train Control

Communication-based train control (CBTC) is an automated control system for railways that ensures the safe operation of rail vehicles using data communication between various control entities that make up the system. CBTC is a modern successor of the traditional railway signalling systems which provide a limited control using track circuits, interlockings, and signals. CBTC technology is part of the same convergence engineering field as the automotive traffic automation systems. Even though the principles of control between the 2 transportation domains are quite different they both are part of the telematics: a CBTC system is based on basic principles from both the automation and telecommunication.

Communication-based train control is the culmination point of a long parallel history of two important technologies that stimulated the development of each other and marked profoundly the development of our society in the last century: railways, telecommunications.

There are multiple generations of CBTC systems based on multiple variations and configurations depending on the providers and operators.

A CBTC can provide different levels of railway automation, grouped in the following major functionalities:

- Automatic Train Protection (ATP)
- Automatic train operation (ATO)
- Automatic Train Supervision (ATS)

CBTC systems range in complexity based on the functionality provided from CBTC systems that provide only the ATP functions to CBTC that provide both the ATP and ATO functions and CBTC that on top of that provide also the ATS functions. All CBTC systems operate in the same basic way. An off board computer can track all trains operating on track linked to the computer. This allows trains to be spaced closer together than on a manually controlled line. The computer sends information to the computers aboard the train. This differs from normal Automatic Train Operation (ATO) systems in that the train is actually controlled by the on board computers. Older ATO systems, such as San Francisco's BART, use a system where the off board computers control the train. Based on the media used for communication the CBTC are categorized in:

- radio-based
- rail-based
- loop-based

The older of the three, rail-based, has been in use in a few systems. Train control signals are sent through the tracks to the train. RF, which has yet to be used on an in service heavy rail Metro application, transmits the signal from wayside equipment.

Deployments

MTA New York City Subway in the United States. The New York City Subway 14th Street-Canarsie Local route (line L) is nearing the completion of tests on the new control system. Communication-based train controlC has started commercial operation in Line 6 of Metro de Madrid (Spain): and is about to start (spring 2009) in Line 1. The CBTCs deployed on transit systems as the SRT line from Toronto, and SkyTrain from Vancouver are based on loop communication. Trans-Gabon Railway for Hughes satellite based train control system. Singapore's two MRT lines, North East Line and Circle Line are completely Communication-based train control based.

13

Managerial Communication

Content and Significance

Interest has been shown in the art of communication since the classical age, the Greeks being those who developed specific communication methods and techniques that conferred it the status of science. In the contemporary age, the theory of communication has known an impressive growth, being a major preoccupation for many specialists in extremely different domains (psychology, philosophy, marketing and public relations, management etc.). Along the time the concept of communication has been ascribed numerous and very different meanings. In the specialty literature the exact meaning of the notion is still vividly debated, the approach perspectives and the tackling methods being varied. Communication is the process of sending a message, via a communication channel, towards a receptor, whereas the communication "as establishing univocal correspondence between a space and time A-transmitter universe and a space and time B – receiver universe which includes the notion of understanding, transfer and which takes place from the field of phenomena to the field of symbols connected in a structure".

To define communication as an exchange of messages between a transmitter and a receptor is the simplest reflection of the essence of this process. Among the general elements to be found in most of the communication theories must be retained those which mention that, in essence, communication is a psychosocial process, a social relation of informational, interpersonal transfers between individuals and the group, but also between groups. The analysis of the message exchange shows that it is equally useful for one to know that the message transmitter tends to influence and modify the receptor's behaviour in all the aspects of his/her actions, in the sense of the receptor getting adapted to the context generated and promoted by the transmitter. As a matter of fact, from a broader perspective, the purpose of communication is to perform changes, to influence an action. Communicative competence is assessed based on the way in which, by means of using the adequate means of communication, one influences the behaviour of one's interlocutor. The existence of a feedback system, which indicates how correctly the information goes from the transmitter to the receptor is necessary because the information may often be distorted or modified.

Managerial communication has a special status, which derives from the organizational framework in which it is performed, from its goals, purpose and role. It represents the decisive means by which the manager fulfils his/her tasks and duties and employs the competences and skills pertaining to his/her role in the company and in the relations with the business partners. The manager sends information to the members of the organization and the business partners, and their response influences his/her decisions and behaviour. The quality of the communication channels, formal or informal, depends on the functionality of the communication system. This system needs to be conceived as a dynamic organism, capable of adapting to the information needs of the company at any moment, at all the levels and in all senses, laying the stress on the problems that influence and condition its normal functioning. Within the company, the individual and the group performance of the employees while fulfilling tasks largely depends on the quality of the managerial communication process.

The manager communicates for the purpose of sending and receiving information, of triggering the adequate answers and, implicitly, of influencing the receptors' decisions and their response to the transmitted messages. The efficient management of the communication process when acting as a contact person who ensures interpersonal communication with the employees in the company, but also with the business partners, outside the company, is a tough responsibility for a manager, and the way he/she fulfils it is decisive for the good business and the success of the company. On one hand, the manager needs to inform all the employees with respect to the company mission and goals, the costs of such, the quality and economy issues, the tasks that need to be fulfilled to attain the set goals. The manager is also interested to get information on the way in which such tasks are fulfilled, suggestions and opinions on the well-being of the company, as seen by the employees. At the same time, the members of the managerial team must exchange information with regard to the main technical, economic and social problems of the company, to the management techniques and methods that need to be used to increase the efficiency of the activity. Thus, a system of reciprocal cooperation is created, which facilitates for the fundamental objectives of the company to be attained.

Managerial communication acts as an integrating factor of the relations from inside the company, as well as those from outside the company, with the business partners, pursuing to harmonize interests and creating the premises needed to attain the set goals. Competitive companies have understood this, and have promoted communicative competence as a philosophy assumed by the management and the entire team. In many such companies, communication is considered to be and is used as one of the most valuable instruments of managerial strategy. At the opposite pole, the defective transmission of information, communication breakdowns and the lack of transparency and honesty most often account for business failure.

Models of Approach of the Managerial Communication

The managerial communication process becomes more and more complicated as the complexity of the company activities and that of the manager's responsibilities increases. The manager's communication behaviour is the one that may generate adequate behaviour on the part of all the members of the organization, mobilizing them around the values tied to performance and the competitive spirit.

In time, several models of approach of the communication process have been built. According to specialists, four of these models are the most significant and most widely used in the managerial practice: the one-way communication model, the circuit communication model, the interactive communication model and the behavioural model. The one-way communication model of approach is a classical model of the communication process. It was developed by the Engineer Claude Shannon in 1949. The managers who choose the classical model of approach (from transmitter to receptor), which Phillip Clampit called "the arrow approach", start from the presupposition the receptor's feedback is not needed as long as the information and decisions transmitted were clearly formulated, in a language that is adequate and clear to those whom they are addressed to. This idea relies on the belief that if the message is clear for the 2 In 1949 Engineer Claude Shannon elaborated the classical model of the communication (one-way communication); in 1954, Wilbur Schramm built the interactive communication model, while David Campbell and Dale Level developed, during the early 1980s, the behavioural model of communication.

By taking up this type of communication, the manager considers that, by using a clear and precise language, the decision that he/she transmits will be correctly understood and complied with by the receiver, without a feedback being needed. The person receiving the message is regarded as a passive receptor, without taking into account the fact that he/she decodes the message and interprets it based on his/her own system of values and on the context in which he/she acts. This type of communication is a model that, in many cases, proves defective, as it generates problems at the organizational level. The employees often complain about the lack of information or about the fact that the information reaches them distorted. In the absence of a response, this sort of information can no longer be corrected. The inadequate distribution of the information from the upper level of management to the lower levels by the fact that, when taking up the one-way communication model, the managers ignore the receptor. Communication is incomplete if the information is not understood, many theorists considering that we may speak of communication only when the receiver gives feedback. As long as there is no response from the part of the receiver, there is no certainty that the message (the arrow) has attained its target, i.e. being received, decoded and correctly understood. This type of communication is preferred by those managers who prefer the formal, rigid, plain and authoritarian style and who do not develop interpersonal communication relations within the organization. Mention must be made that, apart from the aforementioned advantages, the classical model of approach of the managerial communication has the advantage that it shortens the path from decision to action.

The managers concentrate over the short and specific messages, transmitted firmly, avoiding any collateral discussion over the topic of the message. On the other hand, the employees execute or comply with the decision as soon as they receive it. Taking into account these positive aspects and starting from the idea that the expression of a clearly stated message is a compulsory and sufficient condition for efficient communication, many managers appreciate this model of communication. Obviously that is true provided the receiver uses the same system to decode the message he/she receives as the one the transmitter used when encoding or sending the message. We must specify that we do not entirely impart this point of view. We believe that, under the conditions of the ever-increasing complexity of the company activities, the efficiency of the managerial communication process is not fully sustained by adopting the one-way communication model. Communication is a process of transmission and receipt of the information – facts, intentions, attitudes etc. – having the purpose of getting a reaction from the interlocutor. Consequently, the existence and quality of the feedbacks is of extreme importance, communication being incomplete unless the receiver confirms having received and correctly understood the message. Organizational practice has shown that efficient managerial communication relies on a plurality of factors. Among them, the employees' feedback to the messages received from the company management certifies the correct understanding of the act of communication and makes possible the adaptation of the employees' behaviour to the manager's requirements and expectations. Overlooking the employees' responses may have negative effects upon the effectiveness of the communication process, especially over the results of the company in general.

Another model of approach of the managerial communication is the circuit communication, which supposes the existence, in all the cases, of the receptor's response (reaction) to the received message. Unlike the "arrow" approach, this type of communication starts from the presupposition that the manager must know all the problems that the employees are facing in fulfilling the tasks assigned, all their opinions and views in connection with the activity they carry within the company. This approach of the communication is specific of the managers having an open style of management, a free and understanding one, those managers who are interested in providing a harmonious organizational environment and in cultivating agreeable relations with their subalterns. For this type of manager interpersonal communication with all the employees, the understanding of the employees, the adaptation of the messages based on each employee's personality and the certainty that the message sent was correctly understood are of utmost importance. The manager relies on the positive response of the employees to this sort of behaviour and, by way of consequence, on the increased quality of the work generated by this state of affairs. The success of this type of managerial approach depends on the manager's skills of fine psychologist, of his/her ability to stimulate the employees' devotion towards the company. The disadvantage of approaching this sort of communication comes from the large amount of time spent in discussions and debates, which may negatively reflect in the effectiveness and efficacy of the activity.

Interactive communication is another way of approaching the managerial communication. Apart from the other two models presented above, interactive communication supposes an exchange of ideas between those who communicate, each having, in turn, the role of receptor and transmitter. This model of communication is particularly characteristic of the organizations in which the employees' creative skills are appreciated and their participation into solving the problems that the company faces is stimulated. The manager trusts the subalterns' professional competence and has them informed and consulted about the occurring problems and the solution of such. Interactive communication relies on group creativity, the valorisation of the proposals, suggestions and ideas expressed by the members of the organization and on the possibility to identify the best solutions generated by the exchange of ideas. The effectiveness of this type of communication is conditioned by the compatibility of those who communicate, from the perspective of the level of knowledge, experience, share values and type of behaviour.

A more complex model of managerial communication – the behavioural model. The two researchers analyse the managerial communication process from the perspective of the way in which the transmitter expects the receptor to react after receiving the message. The anticipation of the possible response of the employee upon receipt of the message helps the manager structure and adapt the message in such a way as to get a positive response from the receiver. The determination of the receiver's behaviour subsequent to the communication must be, in the two researchers' view, the transmitter's first goal, while taking into account the interferences that might occur during the process of communication and the influences that other communication processes, occurring in parallel, might have upon the receptor's final behaviour.

Even though companies have gone through massive changes with respect to the way they approach managerial communication, none of the models presented above is close to perfection. Each has, as shown, both advantages and disadvantages. In essence, managerial communication must be approached in a manner that best suits the set purpose, the stress being laid on the manager's competence of good communicator. The manager must ensure the smooth going of the communication process on all the channels, both formal and informal, both inside and outside the company.

Development of the Managerial Communication Competence

While performing, the manager takes different roles in which his/her communicational competence is decisive. Upon analysing the activity of some managers with good business results, many specialists have placed communicational competence to the centre of the managerial success. Reflecting on the qualities that underlie the managerial success, John C. Maxwell (2002, p. 101) ranks the manager's ability to communicate efficiently first in importance, with a rate of 38% (it is noticeable that the importance that Maxwell gives to the other components is lower: creation – 31%, management knowledge – 19%, relations – 12%). In turn, Peter Drucker (1977, p. 262) urged the managers to improve their communicative competence, so as to make themselves remarked for "the ability to communicate with the people and to introduce to them their own thoughts and ideas in such a way as to get them to understand and be persuaded", as "this ability to express oneself may be the most important aptitude one can have".

The consolidation of the constructive actions oriented towards the values of the dialogue partners, the exploitation of the informal network of communication in a way that is positive for the company and the maintenance of a climate of open-mindedness and trust, lacking in conflicts and tension, all depend on the manager's ability to constantly improve his/her abilities of good communicator. Apart from the innate qualities that are important in the communication process, the manager may also develop his/her communicative competence by stimulating those abilities that allow the understanding of the subtle mechanisms of the communication act. Communicating or transmitting unpleasant news or information with diplomacy and courtesy, diverting the conflicting discussions tactfully or solving the problems with firmness and authority when required are aspects that reflect the ability to communicate efficiently, and this is a vital quality for a capable manager.

Business partners may have divergent interests, views or positions. The open and positive attitude, the honesty, the appeal to rational or emotional arguments based on the interlocutor's personality are manifestations that can be found in the communicational behaviour of a responsible manager who is interested to keep the channels of communication open, irregardless of how complicated or controversial the problem in discussion is.

This desideratum is possible through a correct appropriation of the communication techniques and the perfecting of their use. By using argumentation as a communication technique, the manager may influence the interlocutor's actions and options through well-grounded evidence that can support his/her assertions and objectives. Through solid arguments that rely on real facts, figures, judgments and incontestable reasoning one can get the adhesion of the dialogue partner to the ideas sustained. Obviously, the arguments need to be relevant, credible, verifiable, correctly understood by the interlocutor and they must come in support of the goals set. The more the problem tackled is complicated and harder to solve, the stronger the arguments used must be. The argumentation strategy needs to be built taking into account the interlocutors' personality, attitude (favourable, less favourable, indifferent) to the ideas presented. In order to achieve the convergence of interests and agreement one must use, apart from the logical arguments, arguments that appeal to feelings, cultural values and beliefs. We need to mention that there are situations when the resort to emotional, affective arguments constitutes a strong support in persuading the business partners. The same may be true in the communication within the company. Often, the manager's force of persuasion grows when appeal is made to arguments of emotional nature, aimed at the employees' sentimental side (loyalty towards the company, beliefs, moral consciousness, honesty, enthusiasm etc.) For a long time, the affective side of the communicational behaviour was entirely ignored. During the more recent years, numerous studies have brought to light the relationship between the quality of the communication process and the degree of emotional intelligence of the people involved in the process. In order to indicate the influence of the degree of emotional intelligence over the success attained in most of the human actions, the American specialists speak of the emotional intelligence quotient (EQ), whose importance in the success or failure of the human actions is decisive.

The implications of the emotional intelligence over the effectiveness of the communication process within the company is a relatively new concept in business, which some managers find hard to accept. However, one cannot build an efficient communication system in which the EQ is minimized. The research conducted has shown that businesspeople with a high EQ have better communicative abilities and grasp better the meaning of the messages transmitted by the interlocutor, whereas emotional intelligence deficiencies tend to jam the communication channels. Correlatively, at least three applications of the emotional intelligence (EI) may be identified in business management: the possibility to motivate, to dissipate conflicts and to build an efficient communication network. These are three trumps for a businessperson, out of which derive several qualities that are important for a good communicator such as intuition, self-control, involvement, the listening ability, the persuasion ability, perseverance and flexibility in communication.

A high EQ favours empathy, the ability to perceive the interlocutor's feelings and emotions, to anticipate his/her intentions, reactions and behaviour, by transposing into his/her psychology and role. In this sense, businesspeople and all the people involved in social relations should take into account the piece of advice given by Tadeuz Kotarbinski (1976) who recommended: "whatever you do, be able to imagine yourself in the stead of your partner, of your interlocutor… be able to examine the matter from his/her point of view, before making any gesture and, most importantly, before uttering a word." In a very deceptive world, as the one of business and trade, empathy is a communicative skill that proves its efficiency chiefly in the process of negotiation. The development of the capacity to communicate empathically allows a deeper understanding of the attitude and conduct of the interlocutor, of the system of values on which he/she founds his/her actions and behaviour, thus increasing the efficiency of the communication act.

A business meeting or a negotiation apparently destined for failure may often be saved by virtue of the mastery, tact and utmost diplomacy with which the partners may change the communicative register. In fact, the adoption of a flexible style of communication, adapted to the situation and the interlocutor's personality, along with tact and diplomacy are indispensable abilities in business practice. Influencing the business partner's behaviour, getting some favourable reactions from his/her part by resorting to certain communication techniques might be perceived as a form of manipulation. Manipulation by means of communication is considered, to a certain extent, natural, particularly in the process of negotiation, when each party pursues to influence the other party's behaviour and decision in the direction most favourable for his/her own interest. Modern management resorts to effective psychological techniques of communication in business. These techniques allow a certain sort of manipulation of the interlocutor or partner's behaviour. We are speaking about the Transactional Analysis (commonly known as TA) and the Neuro-linguistic Programming (NLP). These techniques allow interlocutors to establish an efficient communication rapport and they currently have very good applications in business negotiations and in the harmonizing of interpersonal communication in business relations.

Through specific instruments of analysis and action they allow a better understanding of the interlocutor and, as mentioned already, even a certain form of manipulation of his/her 5 Transactional analysis (TA) was founded by the American psychiatrist Eric Berne during the late 1950s as a new theory of the human personality. At present, the applications of the TA have started being used in business management, particularly in communication and business negotiation. An excellent means of analysis and action in business communication, the transactional analysis makes available for entrepreneurs and managers certain techniques and instruments which allow them to understand their dialogue partner and helps loose fear and negative emotions. 6 The study of Neuro-linguistic Programming (NLP) was initiated by Richard Bandler and John Grinder at the University of Santa Cruz, California in 1972. They started from the structure of what they called "excellence in interpersonal relations". NPL was defined as a corpus of means of study of interpersonal communication and of the structure of positive experience of such. NPL constitutes a mean of effective interpersonal communication in business relations, as it allows to influence the interlocutor's behaviour and to assess the impact of the message transmitted over the interlocutor.

The difficult challenges that the business manager faces and the complex activities that the manager has to carry out in a tougher and tougher concurrent environment have consecrated the use of the competitive communication techniques as a subtle means of knowing the business and action partners for the purpose of harmonizing the interpersonal communication relations in this domain. That way, certain communication abilities are developed that make it easier to overcome negative emotions and tensions that may arise in the relationship with the business partners. At the same time, in a good partnership relation, they favour the attaining of the set goals.

Managerial Communication of Analytical Work

When students graduate and enter or reenter the workforce, many will find themselves performing analytical work. Their ability to communicate the meaning of this work in nontechnical terms will be critical to their ability to influence their organizations and advance their careers. Unfortunately, many students struggle to give effective managerial presentations of analytical work. The difficulty lies not in "general" presentation skills, but in extracting from the numbers a coherent story that is meaningful in a business context.

We believe that the ability to create and deliver effective managerial presentations of analytical work is a vital component of students' analytical education. What we mean by "effective managerial presentation" is a clear, compelling, and persuasive presentation of the business insights and decision guidance that result from the analytical process, meaningfully integrated with the surrounding business context, that is credible to and easily understood by a nontechnical audience of managers and executives. A managerial presentation is distinct from a technical Presentation, in which the purpose is to discuss the analytical process and numerical results. Our sense is that technical presentation skills are much better developed than managerial presentation skills.

The ability to give effective managerial presentations is essential for analytical work to have the appropriate level of impact on a company, and for our graduates to advance their careers using our tools. This ability is vital for students taking a business school course in management science or quantitative analysis, and for students in an OR degree program. Unfortunately, we have a dearth of teaching materials; furthermore, we have little systematic understanding of the difficulties students have, why they struggle, and what we can do to help students learn from their ineffective presentations or prepare them to present effectively in the first place. Even worse, faculty are often ill-prepared to teach managerial presentation skills. Graduate education in operations research or related fields provides little training to future faculty members in communications, and even less in managerial communication of analytical work. These skills reside primarily in the business and practitioner community, where they seem to be transferred informally over a period of several years of practice. However, faculty often have insufficient professional work experience to adequately develop these skills, if they have any nonacademic work experience at all. Bennis and O'Toole (2005) explain the pressures militating against practical business experience in the professoriate, and point out that "the road to tenure does not run through field work in business."

It is challenging for faculty who themselves have inadequate training and experience in these skills to deliver them to students. They need support, which should include a conceptual framework to integrate their area of expertise (OR technology) with areas where they are less experienced (the broader business context and managerial communication), as well as materials and techniques they can use to teach their students.

Contribution

The purpose of this paper is to take a first step towards equipping management science faculty to teach students how to give effective managerial presentations of analytical work. The contributions of this paper are to:

1. Raise the issue of managerial presentation of analytical work, and argue that it is important and merits further research;

2. Share our experience and some examples of difficulties encountered by students when they attempt to communicate managerially;
3. Propose that a central problem is the students' tendency to give a "narrative presentation" rather than a "managerial presentation," and discuss the differences between the two;
4. Present the "business analysis lifecycle" as a conceptual framework to help explain why students give narrative presentations and enable faculty and students to understand the relationship between analysis and communication; and
5. Provide suggestions for faculty to improve students' ability to deliver managerial presentations. We hope this paper will stimulate readers to notice the communications abilities of their students, provide a framework to understand their abilities, and above all motivate efforts to develop new materials. For simplicity, this paper will focus on business students. However, we believe that many insights generalize to students in engineering students focusing on operations research and perhaps students in other engineering fields.

Overview. In §2 we discuss why we believe the managerial communication of analytical work is important. We identify a strange disconnect between the importance of the topic and its absence from introductory management science textbooks. In §3 we discuss our experience with student presentations of their analytic work and the many ways they reduce the effectiveness of their communications.

In §4 we identify a common theme, the tendency of students to give a "narrative presentation" about how they did an analysis rather than a presentation about the meaning of that analysis, and provide a table that contrasts the two types of presentations.

In §5 we present the "business analysis lifecycle" that provides a conceptual framework for understanding why students give narrative presentations, and provides guideposts for helping students and faculty think about the purpose of analysis and what types of communication are appropriate at different phases. We consider the normative assumption of the idealized decision maker, and argue that this assumption needs to be relaxed.

In §6 we describe the vital role of Microsoft PowerPoint presentation software. In §7 we explore actions that management science faculty can take to help their students give managerial presentations of analytical work. We conclude in §8, discussing the approaches and teaching materials currently available, and calling for new teaching materials that ideally are grounded in research on communication in the working world.

The Importance of Communicating Analytical Work

It is well known that effective communication is important to success in business. The learning goal for an undergraduate quantitative methods course is the ability to "communicate findings in terms meaningful and useful to management." The communication of results using PowerPoint in all assignments, with the final integrative assignment including "communication of the model assumptions, structure, and usefulness to management." It is suggests that "students' ability to effectively communicate ideas can be supported by including student presentations" in a business school statistics course, and that instructors develop business students' "ability to communicate technical material to a general audience." Carraway and Clyman (2000) frame the importance nicely: "Recommendations that cannot be sold are seldom implemented. And if they cannot be implemented, then the analysis is a failure." The traditional business school management science courses fail to provide "meaningful guidance in how to use analytical insights to communicate, persuade or drive change in the business," and indicates that students are grateful to a teacher who can enable them to use numbers to communicate effectively.

The Association to Advance Collegiate Schools of Business (AACSB, 2007) Standards for undergraduate programs include learning experiences in "communication abilities" and the intellectual ability to "make and communicate sound decisions." The standards for MBA programs are much less detailed and do not mention communication explicitly.

We have over many years had extensive interactions with OR hiring managers, project managers, junior OR consultants, and OR clients. We frequently hear of the importance of communication for selling OR projects, obtaining client buy-in, getting OR results used in the client organization, and in the professional development of OR consultants.

The ability to effectively and persuasively communicate the results and meaning of analytical work to nontechnical managers is essential to a student's ability to apply ir to influence an organization. Yet in conversations with or practitioners, it is evident that many young or professionals struggle to communicate the meaning and importance of their work to nontechnical people. The development of managerial communications skills is an important part of the development of junior analysts and is a hallmark of the transition from "coding analyst" to vitally important client-contact and selling roles. This seems to be a component of informal on-the-job training and mentoring of junior OR professionals. Systematic research on the career development of entry-level OR analysts would be welcome.

Discussion of Communication in Management Science Textbooks

We examined several management science textbooks for content related to communication and found very little. We found a single instance in the form of a memorandum from "the management science team" to "Profit snd Gambit management." Because there is essentially no textbook material, it is unlikely that the managerial presentation of analytical work is being systematically taught to students in their management science classes.

The Contribution of Research on Engineering Communication

For the purposes of this paper, *workforce communication* refers to communication between and among senior executives, engineers, and managers in the workforce.

In spite of its importance, there seems to be no widely available information or materials relevant to the managerial presentation of analytical work. Fortunately, there has been recent research on workforce communication in engineering organizations that is directly relevant to our problem. Engineers routinely perform analytical work that needs to be presented in managerial terms. This is closely related to presentations of operations research or business analytic work performed by OR specialists and business students.

Over the past six years, researchers at Georgia Tech's Stewart School of Industrial and Systems Engineering Workforce Communication Program have performed empirical research on managerial communication of analytical work. Researchers conducted extensive standardized personal interviews with senior executives, engineers, and managers in engineering firms regarding communication skills and the creation of documents and presentations. To our knowledge, the instruction resulting from the interviews is unique because the workforce interviews served as the sole basis for the instruction. Although these interviews focused on engineering professionals rather than OR specialists or business school graduates, their findings provide powerful insight into the general question of how to give managerial presentations of technical and analytical work. Business students, as well as engineering students, need effective workforce presentation skills. Both business students and engineering students need to develop the skill of explaining their ideas and recommendations to managers in order to get them implemented. Such skills are essential for career advancement.

Students Struggle to Communicate Managerially

We want our students to be able to perform analytical work, and without external support or guidance create and deliver an effective managerial presentation. Without this skill, much analytical work will be a waste of time.

How effective are our students and graduates at communicating the managerial implications of an analysis? To our knowledge, the literature contains no systematic investigation of this question.

However, we have reasons to be concerned. We have extensive experience observing business students giving presentations in a required quantitative analysis course. We have taught business students in undergraduate and MBA programs in a large public university, an elite private top-10 programmes, and a nonelite private university. We have observed over one hundred business student presentations of cases studies, and over one hundred business student presentations of field projects. We generally instruct students to prepare a "business presentation" or "managerial presentation" regarding their case or project and let them decide what to do. We often tell them the audience for the presentation (e.g., "the protagonist of the case and his boss, the president of the company"). We see the same problems occurring independent of the setup, unless we require students to use an outline that we provide.

It is possible these problems occur because we are lousy teachers. However, they show up not only in our classrooms but also in the classrooms of our colleagues at the same schools. We believe that we observe these problems because we look for them. If we did not require our students to give managerial presentations (as opposed to technical presentations), their skill deficiencies would have simply remained undiscovered.

Our sense is that work experience has a positive effect on how students present analytic work, but it is modest. MBA students with many years experience often struggle to explain their analytic results in managerial terms. There are exceptions. Broadly speaking, students with many years experience in a consulting firm or investment bank sometimes do very well, perhaps because they have acquired the necessary skills on the job. The training that students receive in their communications course (if they take one) is valuable, but the particular challenges of managerial communication of analytical work are not covered in these courses.

Examples of Problems with Student Presentations

Our observations of the problems students have fall into two categories. The first category can be observed from the visual aids used by the students during their presentations. Students invariably prepare their presentations using Microsoft PowerPoint. PowerPoint is so widely used that the terms "presentation" and "PowerPoint" are used interchangeably. For the past few years we have asked students to provide their slides to us. These artifacts can be examined, and we present some examples below.

The second category is elements that do not appear in the artifacts, such as the students' choice of words, and the times at which they switch from Power-Point to Excel. These behaviours do not leave artifacts behind, but we summarize what we have seen.

Examples from Presentations

Students sometimes use ineffective techniques to make presentations for managerial communication. Students frequently provide a tour of their spreadsheet model, switching from PowerPoint into Excel, showing large spreadsheets, and giving rapid-fire tours of these spreadsheet models; these tours are virtually impossible to understand, even if the audience just built their own versions of the same model. Spreadsheets will often be presented with so many cells that individual numbers cannot be read by the audience. Students focus on particular cell formulas, range names, or other programming aspects that they found particularly helpful, exciting, or challenging. Students tend to speak frequently about "the model." They often anthropomorphize the model and make statements that begin "the model says" when it is more effective to say "our analysis indicates" or "we believe."

Students might mention, sometimes repeatedly, how hard they worked, how late they stayed up, or how they struggled with a particular aspect of the work. These statements sometimes seem to be offered should be sure not to do what we did and double check the absolute references before copying." Such statements often seem to be accompanied by pride in overcoming challenges. However, such statements are not effective in managerial presentations. The blunt reaction of a senior executive to similar comments in a student presentation:

"No one wants to hear how hard you have worked; that is taken for granted and is the reason professionals are well compensated. What decision makers want to hear is what they should do and why."

The Problem: Narrative Presentations Instead of Managerial Presentations

We have noticed a common factor in poor managerial presentations by business students. Students tend to give a presentation about *what they did and how they did it*, rather than *why they did it and what it means*. We are not alone in noticing this. Writing a paper regarding an MBA elective course on professional decision modeling, notes the students' tendencies to create narrative presentations and prefers managerial presentations:

"Students' initial presentations and memos tend to be 'book reports.' We did this, then we ran that, and 'the model says' this is the result. So keep the plant. Or invest the money. I remind them that models don't say anything and that no one is convinced to invest millions of dollars by a book report. They are convinced by credible insights conveyed by effective advisors who demonstrate an understanding of complex situations."

When presenting analytical work, students tend to deliver what we term a "narrative presentation" that chronicles how they went about their analysis. Such narrative presentations are excessively detailed and cannot reasonably be understood by an audience who is not as close to the analysis as are the presenters. This is quite different than a "managerial presentation" that reports a set of insights and recommendations supported by analysis. A managerial presentation can easily be understood by someone with no prior knowledge of the underlying analytical work.

We summarize the differences between narrative and managerial presentations, which consists of three sections: Planning Assumptions, Analytical Aspects, and Communication Elements. We want students to avoid the characteristics in the "Narrative Presentation" column, and to deliver instead the characteristics in the "Managerial Presentation" column. Planning

Assumptions, considers six assumptions implicit in the presentation. If the author's mind is on the *performance* of the analytical work, he will plan to discuss how he went about that work, share aspects that were challenging or controversial in his group, and discuss low-level issues related to the analysis rather than high-level issues related to the business. He will tend to focus on "the solution" which is the "right answer" to a narrowly defined question. The talk will be of more interest to fellow students or analysts. Social and political issues tend to be ignored or "assumed away" in the form of an idealized decision-maker. In contrast, if the author's mind is on the *meaning* of the analytical work he will plan to discuss the importance of the work at a higher level. He will focus on evaluating the implications and likely results of different courses of action.

He will seek to influence the organization's social and political decision-making process by presenting information and conclusions that are interesting and relevant to an audience of managers and executives.

Analytical Aspects

Analytical Aspects, considers four issues regarding the analytical work. Students usually expend great effort devising, programming, and debugging their model. They are excited about it and want to talk about it, and this can cause them to focus on the model and the spreadsheet, rather than on the function and utility of the model. The resulting behaviours include cell-by-cell tours of spreadsheet models (which are inevitably incomprehensible to an audience); asides about how hard they (the students) worked; and presentations of cell formulas of which students are particularly proud. In contrast, a managerial presentation spends little time on the details of the model. The need is to explain the function of the model—what outputs it produces—and to provide a sense of how those outputs are computed. There is little or no discussion of how the creators built the model; at most the presenter can briefly mention the resources required to build the model or mention the approach taken if it is unusual.

The presenters work to establish their credibility as skilled and trustworthy analysts, seeking to enroll the audience in the quality of the speakers rather than the quality of the model. Communication Elements, considers four different types of communication in the presentation. In a narrative presentation, the presenter's attention is on the fascinating (to him) complexity and rich model insights that emerged in the analysis. Vocabulary tends to be technical. Numbers are presented with mathematical precision (excessive significant digits) because that level of detail matters when programming a spreadsheet. Numeric results are presented in dense tables of numbers or overly complex charts. In contrast, in a managerial presentation the presenter's focus is on clarifying complexity and providing rich managerial insight. Vocabulary is managerial. Numbers are presented with limited significant figures. Numeric results are presented in the form of a modest amount of carefully selected numbers or with simple charts. If complex charts are necessary to tell a compelling managerial story, the presenter carefully develops the charts to be understood by people not familiar with the analysis.

The Business Analysis Lifecycle

Business analysts need to engage in a variety of activities in order to influence the actions taken by their organization. It is essential that students have a conceptual framework that identifies these activities and explains how they relate to each other. We provide this conceptual framework in the form of the "business analysis lifecycle". Powell and Baker start with a "problem statement," whereas we start with a "business situation" from which a problem statement must be extracted during formulation.

The phase of "Formulate" to create "assumptions and model structures," we use two phases in order to distinguish between the conceptual activity of model formulation and the computer programming activity of implementing the model as a spreadsheet computer program. Thus, we "Formulate" a "mathematical model," and then "Engineer" a "spreadsheet model." The Powell and Baker figure uses the word "solution" where we use "managerial insights." Where we have the words "Communicate: Recommend,

Influence, Persuade, Decide and Act," the Powell and Baker figure is blank.

The Real World, the Model World, and the Idealized Decision Maker

It is helpful to conceptualize a "Model World" and a "Real World." The Model World is an idealized and rational place where problems are well defined and ambiguity is absent. In the Model World, we are concerned with the details of a model, its computer implementation, how to analyse that model, and the exact numeric values that emerge from the analysis. In the Model World, we can (with analytical effort) discover the "solution" to a well-defined problem.

In contrast, the Real World represents the messy, ambiguous, and sometimes irrational realm of human organizations. In the Real World we are concerned with the practical, social, and political issues that affect business actions. There might not be agreement on what the problem is, and although circumstances can (one hopes) be improved, a "solution" is all too often elusive or unobtainable.

One of the foundations of OR is a set of normative decision-making principles centered on a "decision maker" who is rational, consistent, and empowered to irrevocably commit resources. The classic idealized decision maker makes his home in the Model World. In the Model World, the analysts' task is to generate exact numeric values for consumption by this mythical creature of power.

The idealized decision maker is an important tool and a valuable invention because it allows us to focus our attention on analytical issues and exclude (or at least control) hard-to-model social and political concerns and ambiguities. However, it is essential to remember that the decision maker is a (very useful) fiction that functions to establish a boundary between the clean Model World and the messy Real World. In the Real World analysts need to contend with the social, political and interpersonal realities of a business. In the Real World the analysts' task is not to generate exact numeric values, but to influence the complex, ambiguous, and sometimes irrational decision-making processes common to real organizations.

It is essential for a business analyst to be able to work in both the Model World and the Real World. More important, the analyst needs to be able to cross the boundary between the two.

Phases in the Business Analysis Lifecycle

The business analysis lifecycle is the five-phase loop. It begins, as all analytical projects should begin, with a *business situation*—something that is of great interest to the organization.

From Real World to Model World

The analyst uses his understanding of the business situation to *formulate* a *mathematical model* that captures the quantitative relationships inherent in the business situation. The act of formulation is the bridge between the Real World and the Model World. It is here that the analyst makes assumptions about what to include and exclude from the model and which data will be necessary. The act of formulation effectively eliminates ambiguity and imprecision by dint of creating a precise mathematical model. Formulation determines what the spreadsheet model will do.

The analyst must then *engineer* a *spreadsheet model* (or more generally, write code) to implement the mathematical model as a computer program. Because the spreadsheet is a powerful modeling environment, many people will combine the acts of formulating a mathematical model and engineering the corresponding spreadsheet model. (It is important to distinguish between formulation and engineering. O'Beirne 2005 recommends a design and specification process prior to programming. Grossman 2002 cautions that formulating or exploratory modeling in a spreadsheet can lead to a poorly engineered spreadsheet computer program.)

The analyst next will *analyse* the spreadsheet model using one or more structured techniques or algorithms to generate *model insights* that summarize the analytical results. Model insights are framed in the Model World and therefore are numeric, exact, and use technical terminology.

Back to the Real World

The analyst's next step is to *interpret* the model insights and articulate them as *business insights* that summarize the meaning of the analytical results. Business insights are framed in the Real World and therefore are verbal, approximate (the model is only an approximation to reality), and use business terminology.

The act of interpretation is the bridge between the Model World and the Real World. It is here that the analyst must revisit any elements of the business situation that were assumed away when formulating the model and consider how the model results might affect different aspects of the business (particularly those not represented in the mathematical model). The act of interpretation requires letting go of the security of mathematical exactness and stepping into the ambiguity of a real business. An analytical "solution" in Model World might not translate into a "solution" in the Real World, but it might yield a model insight that suggests a course of action that would have particular benefits. For example, in a simple raw material-constrained product-mix problem, the model insight *build 100 of product A, 200 of product B, and 0 of* product C" might be converted into the managerial insight "use all available motors and all available housings to build products A and B, forget about product C.

Finally the analyst *communicates* the business insights to influence and guide real-world actions that ultimately affect the business situation. This requires leadership and managerial skills to craft a message that can be understood by various constituencies and individuals and to persuade the organization to take a particular course of action.

When a model is used successfully to influence an organization, there can be motivation for further study—that is, to again perform the formulateengineer-analyse-interpret-communicate loop.

The Lifecycle and Managerial Presentations

In terms of the business analysis lifecycle, a managerial presentation is based in the Real World, whereas a narrative presentation is based in the Model World. This helps explain the origin of narrative presentations: Students are anchored in the Model World and do not easily make the transition back into the Real World to present their results.

After completing an analysis, presenters must leave behind the niceties of the Model World and address two tasks: how to convert model insights into business insights and how to communicate these insights effectively. These are difficult challenges that require substantial thought and effort beyond the analytical work already performed in the Model World. It is much easier to simply stay in the Model World and give a narrative presentation. Students may be encouraged to do this by the strong Model World focus of business school management science courses and textbooks.

Classical Management Science and the Business Analysis Lifecycle

The impact and meaning of the analyst's work is not measured by the quality of his analysis. It is measured by his ability to get the organization to do something it would not otherwise have done. Therefore, success depends on the analyst's ability to influence the social, political, and interpersonal fabric of the organization. Many high quality analyses have foundered on the rocks of failed communication, sometimes because what was communicated were model insights rather than business insights. In our experience, senior OR practitioners have in mind the end goal of client communication during the beginning formulation stage of the analysis; this is supported by the scant research on expert modelers.

Management science textbooks are very strong on the "analyse" phase of the business analysis lifecycle. Books containing spreadsheets are forced into some consideration of the "engineer" phase of creating a spreadsheet model. Textbooks devote slight attention to the tricky art required during the "formulation" phase, which is poorly understood and not easily packaged in book form.

Management science textbooks tend to fall silent at the "interpret" phase where analysts must cross from Model World to

Real World and convert model insights to business insights. The role of classical management science would seem to be to generate plenty of high-quality model insights and stop at the boundary of the Real World. Any effort to make something actually happen in the organization is assumed away in the form of the idealized decision maker. The normative assumption of the idealized decision maker neatly sidesteps the messy complexities of getting an organization to take action. The idealized decision maker assumption is essential for algorithm researchers, because it allows them to isolate the precisely defined mathematical properties of a model from the poorly defined business context. However, it is problematic for people who want their analytical work to have an impact on a business because the business world is short of omnipotent idealized decision makers and long on complex social decision making processes. Substantial effort is required to bring analytical results to the organization, and if those efforts are inadequate then the value of the management science analysis is nil.

We find it helpful to teach students about the business analysis lifecycle and to help them integrate lifecycle ideas into their work. Students need experience and training to ask themselves where in the cycle they are and where in the cycle they should be. They also need experience in the skill, craft, and art of bringing model insights into the Real World as managerial insights, and then communicating them persuasively to influence real human organizations. Teaching this requires that we move beyond the boundaries of classical management science and leave behind the comfort of strong textbook support.

The Vital Role of PowerPoint

People can communicate analytical work in three ways:

(1) Communicate orally without the use of visual aids; this is commonly done in informal settings in the workplace.

(2) Give a "live" presentation, where a speaker provides visual aids and speaks to an audience that has convened to see and hear his presentation.

(3) Communicate asynchronously using a written document.

We know of no research on the relative workplace prevalence of oral communication without visual aids, live presentations, and written documentation for communicating analytical results. Certainly, this topic merits substantial research attention. As a practical matter visual aids seem to be developed primarily using Microsoft PowerPoint. Our students use PowerPoint exclusively, presumably because it is bundled with the ubiquitous Microsoft Office suite. Our observations in companies are similar. It is not unusual for the term "PowerPoint" to be used interchangeably with or in place of the generic term "presentation slides," similar to "Kleenex brand" and "facial tissue."

PowerPoint as Written Documentation, Not Solely Visual Aid

While conducting two independent empirical research projects we regularly encountered situations where PowerPoint is used as an important or even dominant method for documenting analytical results. In one company where interviews were conducted, PowerPoint was the main form of written business communication, and the slides were used without any accompanying reports.

In many situations, PowerPoint has a dual purpose: as a visual aid in live presentations and as written documentation. The documentation function occurs when the speaker makes copies for attendees at an oral presentation, or distributes a printed copy or computer file to people unable to attend. These copies can then be distributed independent of the speaker. We have observed PowerPoint slides being given to workers to help them learn their new jobs. Although these findings are at this time informal, they highlight the importance of PowerPoint for workforce communication of analytical results, both as visual aids to a presentation and as a written document that is distributed independent of the presentation.

We note that books on giving presentations tend to focus on PowerPoint slides as visual aids for a presentation and sometimes argue that slides should be kept scant to keep the focus on the speaker. This is inconsistent with our finding that people routinely use hardcopies or softcopies of the presentations for asynchronous communication. Research is needed on the role of asynchronous communication using presentation copies, and the implications for writing effective PowerPoint slides.

What Can Faculty Do?

There are several reasons a student may give a narrative presentation. A narrative presentation has emotional benefits because it focuses on the work the student has proudly accomplished. Doing a narrative presentation is easier than doing the additional work of crafting a managerial presentation. The textbook (and perhaps the entire course) is focused on Model World, which is the home of narrative presentations.

To be effective in the professional world students need to recognize these tendencies and make the effort to create managerial presentations. Because of the reasons in favour of narrative presentations, it is not obvious that students will do so without our help. They need faculty support to learn to not share the details of the difficult work they just did, to not share the analytical lessons they just learned, to not share the amount of effort they put in, and instead to undertake the distinct task of articulating managerial insights in a business context and communicating them persuasively. There are several steps that faculty can take.

14

Science Communication Movement in India

After Independence, a number of government agencies and non-governmental organisations (NGOs) took their cue from the constitution and became involved in science popularisation. In this way, science communication was taken up at various levels, institutional as well as individual. Nehru was a major force behind this advancement of science in independent India.

The National Institute of Science Communication (NISCOM)-previously the Publications and Information Directorate-began publishing of the Hindi popular science journal Vigyan Pragati (Progress in Science) in 1952. The Science Reporter (an English monthly) and Science Ki Dunia (an Urdu quarterly) followed soon after. Today, NISCOM also brings out 11 professional scientific journals and publishes various popular science books (often in Indian languages).

In 1980, science communication was given prominence in India's Sixth Five-year Plan, and two years later the National Council for Science and Technology Communication (NCSTC) was established. The Council has a mandate to integrate, coordinate, catalyse and support science communication and popularisation, at the micro as well as macro level. NCSTC's programmes include training in science and technology communication, software development, research, field-based projects, and creating information networks and databases.

Other Indian government initiatives include Vigyan Prasar-an autonomous organisation of the Department of Science and Technology set up in 1989-which plays an important role in coordinating efforts among various scientific institutions, educational and academic bodies, laboratories, museums, industry and other organisations for the effective exchange and dissemination of scientific information. *Vigyan Prasar* also develops and disseminates software materials and organises popular science events including workshops, debates and lectures.

The National Council of Science Museums, based in Calcutta, is the coordinating body of 26 science museums and science centres across the country. Science City in Calcutta has more than 1000 exhibits and attracts around 500,000 visitors a year. Based on the experiences and popularity of Science City, other such projects are being developed across the country.

Several NGOs have also pursued science communication programmes. The Indian Science Writers' Association (ISWA), for example, was founded in 1985 with a view to developing and nurturing the science writing profession in India. The association has around 200 members and undertakes a broad spectrum of activities including training courses, lectures and fellowships. ISWA also works with government agencies and NGOs in promoting science communication activities.

A Diversity of Science Communication Media

India's science communicators have used various modes of communication to reach out to the masses. As a result, a lot of infrastructure, software and human resources are available in the country. Each has its own significance and utility, given the vast diversities that exist in the country.

Print Media

In addition to the scientific journals (both popular and technical) published by the government, several national and regional daily newspapers have now started producing weekly science pages. In a unique initiative, Vigyan Prasar provides a weekly ready-to-print science page, in both Hindi and English, which some 21 newspapers use at a nominal cost.

Sadly, however, there are signs that interest in science communication is waning in the print media. For example, the Indian science magazines Science Today and Bulletin of Sciences have been discontinued, as have Indian editions of certain foreign magazines, such as La Recherche and Scientific American.

Audio-visual Media

A variety of science-based programmes are now available on All India Radio (AIR), such as Radioscope, Science Today, Science Magazine and Science News. In the early 1990s a landmark 144-part radio serial *Manav Ka Vikas* (Human Evolution) was jointly produced by NCSTC and AIR. The programme was broadcast simultaneously from more than 80 radio stations in 18 Indian languages with 100,000 children and 10,000 schools registered as dedicated listeners. A number of television channels have also been broadcasting science programmes for many years. For example, a 13-part film serial on the history of science and technology in the Indian sub-continent and its impact on the world, entitled Bharat Ki Chhaap, was produced by NCSTC and broadcast on the state-run Doordarshan channel in 1989.

Folk Media

It is a common observation that folk media-such as puppet shows, street plays, stage performances, and folk songs and dances-successfully reach segments of society where other forms of media have limitations. These traditional means of communication have all been exploited as alternative media for science communication. They are not only entertaining, but also offer two-way communication and are cost effective.

Several voluntary agencies, such as Kerala's Shastra Sahitya Parishad (People's Science Movement), are actively involved in taking science to the people, especially through folk forms. Where print and electronic media have limits rooted in literacy levels and accessibility, folk media can play a crucial role.

'Interactive' Media

Science exhibitions, science fairs, demonstrations, seminars, workshops, lectures, scientific tours, conferences and, more recently, digital software, have the advantage of being interactive forms of science communication. Perhaps the most impressive example is the Vigyan Jatha. During this massive event, science communicators march in groups from village to village, interacting with local people and spreading information about science relevant to their day-to-day lives. Catalysed by NCSTC, Vigyan Jatha could be considered the biggest science communication experiment anywhere in the world. Held in 1987 and 1992, themes have included health, water, environment, appropriate technology, superstitions, scientific thinking and literacy. Some 2,500 government agencies and NGOs have been actively involved, and the Jatha have covered nearly 40,000 locations in about 400 districts, touching almost a third of the country's population.

The annual Children's Science Congress-started in 1993 by the NCSTC Network-has become a highlight in the science communication calendar. The congress aims to extend classroom science teaching by providing 10-to 17-year-olds with an open 'laboratory' for enjoyable hands-on learning. Another very popular and important programme in India has been the 'scientific explanation of miracles'. This programme uses trained science 'activists' to demonstrate and explain so-called miracles. In 1995, for example, the author investigated and demonstrated the phenomenon of deities drinking milk on television, and exposed it as a hoax.

Information technology has given birth to a comparatively new form of interactive science communication-digital media-which includes the Internet and CD-ROMs. This is proving to be an effective way to illustrate difficult scientific concepts. It has also made science communication more accessible both to handicapped and less educated people. Though the reach of the technology is still a limiting factor, the government is working to extend this and reduce the costs of connectivity.

Present Challenges and Visions for the Future

Although much has been achieved in India, there is still an urgent need to make science communication activities more effective, both in terms of quality and quantity. We have yet to make a dent in wiping out superstitions that have prevailed throughout the ages, particularly in tribal areas where literacy levels are low and superstition is a way of life. Also, the general public is still largely ignorant about common scientific principles, such as the fact that the Earth orbits the Sun.

Mass Media

Science is not succeeding in attracting mass media interest. It rarely appears as a lead story, as editors and reporters do not consider science to be 'news' in the normal sense. On average, science only accounts for around three per cent of coverage by India's mass media. Additionally, readership of popular science magazines has declined-people no longer rely on print material as their only source of information.

For this reason, the Indian Science Writers' Association aims to encourage the editors of newspapers and magazines to regularly feature a science column. It also hopes to increase the readership of popular science magazines, for example by making them available through digital media. In addition, publications must cater to India's many languages. It is encouraging that radio, which is extremely popular in rural areas, has an increasing amount of scientific content. Television is following a similar pattern, with a few special channels on science and technology, and other channels featuring scientific discussions and interviews of scientists about their research. But it hasn't yet reached a satisfactory level as far as science communication is concerned.

Mass Education

There is no doubt that scientific information is becoming an essential and integral part of people's daily lives. Present and future science communication efforts have great potential in shaping the lives of the people and making their decisions more informative and rational.

However, illiteracy and ignorance are major challenges. While literacy levels are increasing (currently estimated at 52 per cent of the population), scientific literacy is still drastically low. Given India's large population, limited resources and multitude of languages,. mass science education faces particularly great challenges. There have been efforts to popularise science through our 18 regional languages, for example by producing some scientific publications in vernaculars and translating certain television and radio programmes. But without more attention on local languages, much of the population will miss out on science communication efforts.

In an ideal world science communication activities would be widespread right down to the village level. In order to create awareness among illiterates or the newly literate-and to maintain the knowledge they acquire-folk forms must be used more frequently. In this way, superstitious beliefs could be wiped from society and a scientific environment created even at the grassroots level.

Training of Science Communicators

Science writing still tends to be dry and boring, making it unsurprising that few science articles interest newspapers and magazines. The number of capable science communicators and voluntary scientific organisations is alarmingly low and hardly sufficient to cater to the country's large and diverse population.

That said, a number of science communicators are being trained through postgraduate degree and diploma courses in science communication, and short-term science writing and journalism workshops. Indeed, four Indian science communicators have won UNESCO's Kalinga Prize for their outstanding contributions to science communication and popularisation.

The way that scientific information is presented in the media needs to undergo a metamorphosis, with a new generation of the science writers and journalists presenting useful science in an interesting and innovative manner. For example, a science and technology news and features pool could be formed to allow writers and journalists to exchange information on scientific research and developments.

Networking

Most importantly, science communication activities must be conducted and governed in a systematically planned manner, under one umbrella organisation, and according to a properly defined national policy. To an extent this issue is already being addressed. An All India People's Science Network was created in the late 1980s, with 27 constituent voluntary organisations. The NCSTC Network started in 1991 with the objective of taking science popularisation activities to all the corners of the country. Presently it has around 100 members, including NGOs and government organisations. NCSTC has also started a countrywide project to compile information on science communication software, hardware, 'humanware' and agencies to facilitate further networking. But the formation of networks of organisations alone is not sufficient. A suitable mechanism must be evolved to ensure we work together in a more cohesive manner. I would also argue that we need a formal Science Media Network. In fact, moves have already been made towards a national database of science editors, writers, journalists, columnists, translators, 'scientoonists', illustrators, media-persons, producers, and media organisations interested in science coverage.

Conclusion

Following the industrial revolution in western countries, the level of science communication activities increased dramatically. In some ways, India is presently passing through a similar stage. As technology advances, the need for scientific information will also increase. Accordingly, an industrial India should soon witness a similar increase in science communication and popularisation. Indeed, the success of the information technology industry is proof of a growing scientific awareness in India. India has undertaken a large number of science communication initiatives, and has sometimes led the way in innovative approaches. However, we should also be open to new ideas, methodologies and programmes available in other parts of the world, and similarly share with others the successful strategies we have employed.

As far as science writing and journalism are concerned, there is ample scope for furthering such efforts in developing countries. India could take the initiative in mobilising like-minded people in South Asia to form Science Writers' and Journalists' Associations in each country, ideally with help from international organisations. The science communication scenario of our dreams is not unobtainable. Rather, it is based on technologies available today, which can be better utilised to carry scientific messages to the people. I believe that science communication in India has a bright future.

15

Communications: A Tool for Development

Prior to implementing a public communications campaign as part of a children's health program in Ecuador, only 28 percent of people surveyed had had their children vaccinated. After the campaign had been in effect for 18 months, the number jumped to 52 percent, according to a survey by the consulting firm HealthCom and the Academy for Educational Development (AED).

Similarly dramatic results were reported by the consulting firm the Manoff Group during a reproductive health project in Cochabamba, Bolivia. Before a communications campaign began, only 2 per cent of the women surveyed remembered that edema was a danger sign during pregnancy. After the campaign was underway, 64 percent remembered that fact.

"The question is not 'Does it work?'" said AED Executive Vice President Dr. William Smith in his keynote presentation, "it's 'What kind of problem do I have?' and 'What kind of communications [mechanism] should I use to address it?'" Dr. Smith was the keynote speaker at a seminar hosted by the IDB on the role of strategic communications in development. The seminar, held on July 1st at the IDB's headquarters in Washington, DC, brought together a panel of experts from the IDB, the Academy for Education Development, the World Bank, and USAID to discuss best practices for integrating communications into development projects and achieving social change.

Elena Suarez, Chief of the IDB's Special Programs Section in the Office of External Relations, mentioned a couple of ways that the IDB incorporates strategic communications into its activities. "We provide technical assistance to develop communications strategies for IDB-financed operations, carry out public awareness campaigns such as the Don't Call Me Street Kid and Natural Disaster Awareness campaigns, and produce television programming on development topics such as domestic violence to sensitize public opinion in Latin America and the Caribbean."

Communications in Development Projects

Communications can be used many ways to advance development, according to Silvio Waisboard, Senior Program Officer at the Academy of Educational Development. For example, development professionals can use communications to promote behavioral changes, to educate, to mobilize communities, to advocate policy changes, to spark a community dialogue or public debate, or to increase participation in a project. Integrating top-down approaches (i.e. mass media) and bottom-up ones (i.e. town hall meetings) is one of the most effective means of strategic communications for development projects, panel members agreed. One way of doing that, according to Waisboard, is to have a tool-kit approach and combine media and interpersonal communications. "You need to use techniques that fit your audience or target group, whether you use the mass media to mobilize large populations or do social marketing, or you use interpersonal communications to convince people to change their attitudes or behaviours." Waisboard continued, "Whatever you do, community empowerment should be the goal. If you want your project to be sustainable, you need to build community ownership."

The experts at the seminar also concurred that such communications efforts should be aimed at various levels-from individuals, families and communities to members of civil society organizations and governments from the municipal to the national level. Along those same lines, Cecilia Cabañero-Verzosa, head of knowledge and capacity building in the Development Communications Division of External Affairs at the World Bank, emphasized the importance of building partnerships in all sectors of society. "We've built partnerships at many levels, from internal networks at the World Bank, such as a 350 member development communications network, to sector-specific partnerships that focus on issues in the environment or the water sector, for example, to partnerships with civil society or the private sector," Cabañero-Verzosa said.

A Few Caveats

The Center for Population, Health and Nutrition's senior advisor on health communications and behaviour change at USAID, Elizabeth Fox, warned that communications managers need to keep an eye on the structure of and participation in communications.

"Who owns the media? How is it financed? How much competition is there [in each country in Latin America and the Caribbean]?" Fox asked. "The answers to those questions are going to influence who gets access to mass media communications and whether or not diverse opinions will get the chance to be heard." Experts also explained that investments in communications must be ongoing and long-term if they're going to bring sustained changes in behaviour.

"If you drop your communications campaign, results are going to drop, too," said Smith. He sited a campaign encouraging seat belt use in North Carolina called Click it or ticket. "Before the campaign began, 63 per cent of drivers used seat belts. Once the campaign was established, usage climbed to 80 per cent. The campaign was stopped for a time because local officials believed it had served its purpose. Afterward, usage dropped to 73 per cent. They quickly realized what had happened and reinstated the campaign. At that point, usage again increased to 81 per cent. The point is, using communications campaigns for short periods of time only brings short-term results."

Getting Results: Don't Call Me Street Kid Campaign

José Luís Lobera, a communications specialist in the Special

Programs Section, pointed out the specific impact that the Don't Call Me Street Kid campaign has already had in the region. "The campaign has created new links between groups-at least 15 new government-NGO partnerships and alliances per country." The IDB has taken the campaign to eleven countries.

> "The campaign has also expanded public debate," Lobera said, "including 3 televised national debates in Bolivia that have catapulted the issue to the top of the political agenda."
>
> "In Mexico," Lobera continued, "the campaign received an estimated $7 million in free on-air time, with our TV spot [on the campaign] airing 30,000 times and the video documentary 416 times."

Local policy changes that have resulted from the campaign include new local childhood policies in 50 municipalities in Colombia and the creation of action plans on the issue in Costa Rica, Honduras, El Salvador and Guatemala.

Development Communication: What Works

Alphabet soup of approaches in development communication

- Communication for development
- Communication for social change
- Information, education and communication
- Behaviour change communication
- Social mobilisation
- Media advocacy
- Strategic communication
- Participatory communication
- Strategic participatory communication

Common misconceptions about communication in development :

- ROLE

- Only necessary for a short period of time.
- Add-on to general planning and funding.
- IMPACT
- Information is enough to change behaviour.
- Unrealistic expectations about needed time for effects.
- STRATEGY
- Media training is sufficient to address communication problems.
- New communication technologies solve information and behaviour problems.

Development communication, definitions:

- Instrument in development projects.
- Methodologies and tools to spread information and contribute to behaviour change.
- The goal of development.
- Improve opportunities for community dialogue and access to information.
- Communication as citizenship, participation in political communities.
- Process of identifying, segmenting and targeting specific groups and audiences with particular strategies, messages and training programmes through various mass media and interpersonal channels, traditional and non-traditional (McKee 1992).
- A process of dialogue, information sharing, mutual understanding and agreement, and collective action (Rockefeller Foundation 2000).

Recent Changes in Practice

- Use data to set goals and strategies.

- Define target audiences.
- Conduct research on barriers, benefits and perceptions.
- Shift to strategic approaches

What Works: Five Key Ideas

Focus on Both Individual and Contextual Factors

- Comprehensive approach to address factors that affect behaviour.
- Consider behaviour at individual, family, community, and policy levels.

Integrate Top-down and Bottom-up Approaches

- Combination of actions by governments, donors, and civil society.
- Promote participation of actors at different levels.

Have a Tool-kit Approach

- Use techniques according to problems, priorities, and target groups.
- Take advantage of wide range of tools.

Uses of Tools

- Mass media to reach large populations.
- Social marketing for audience segmentation, to identify perceived benefits, build programme brand and create demand.
- Social mobilisation to bolster participation and support outreach efforts.
- Media advocacy to gain support from governments and donors, and put issues in public agenda.

- Popular/folk media to generate dialogue and activate information networks.

Combine Media and Interpersonal Communication Media

- Important to raise awareness and knowledge.
- Massive reach.
- Stimulate social networks and peer conversation.
- Mobilise those predisposed to engage in desired behaviours.

Interpersonal Communication

- Decisive for behaviour change.

Community Empowerment

- Community empowerment key for sustainability of projects.
- Promotes participation, which is intrinsic to any development project.
- Examples:
- Ciudadania en salud y municipios saludables en Peru.
- Community-based dengue prevention in El Salvador.

Challenges

- Attribution of effects.
- Development of indicators.
- Social norms.
- Community empowerment.
- Measurement of different kinds of effects.
- Long term or "Delayed" effects.
- Indirect or Unexpected effects.

• Replication of results and scaling up.

• Reaching "hard to reach" and "hard to convince" audiences.

Impact of Communication for Development

Historically development communication has gotten away with less rigorous measures of impact than other areas of investment in development. In part this is because it is difficult to measure the impact of communication. It often is hard to find a control group that has not been exposed to the message. It is even harder to control for the fact that people self select to see or listen to channels of communications-development communication does not occur in a laboratory, or even in a more controlled classroom setting. The development communication field often tests theories when it thinks it is testing impact, or relies on qualitative measures at the expense of harder evidence. Mostly, we fail to ask the right questions, or ask them over a long enough period of time.

Apparent past success in development communication-the green revolution, family planning-have given the field a green light to continue to apply past formulas uncritically to other areas such as HIV/AIDS without holding these formulas to very high standards of evidence on impact.

Evidence from several major studies is beginning to become available showing that our old assumptions about what works are wrong. One example of this is the recent report on the congressionally funded National Youth Anti-Drug Media Campaign, a five year approximately $1 billion effort, the largest public health communication program ever funded. The White House Office of National Drug Control Policy and the Congress allocated $35 million to undertake a careful, independently executed, evaluation of the Campaign. Through the fourth semi-annual evaluation, the result of the campaign are not positive, indeed there is a suggestion of a negative effect of the campaign. As managers, we need to ask the right questions and use the correct methodologies. We also need to require independent evaluations that uphold the most rigorous scientific standards.

Managing the Technology

As managers of communication for development, we hear a lot about new information technologies. I put this here as a footnote, partly because I do not think it should ever be our starting point. We do not start with a technology and try to fit it to a development application. Those of us who lived through the heady days of educational television, satellite delivered message to farmers, and distance learning to build math and reading skills to lower income children in Central America have learned that the technology will not sustain the effort and will disappear as soon as external funding or donated equipment gives out. Development communication starts with structure, participation and content and then finds the right technologies, or technologies. Technology is not the not the beginning and not the end, it is a tool. As an old friend taught me many years ago, you cannot blame the airplane for not getting you there on time.

Communication for Sustainable Development

"If development can be seen as a fabric woven out of the activities of millions of people, communication represents the essential thread that binds them together... A development strategy that uses communication approaches can reveal people's underlying attitudes and traditional wisdom, help people to adapt their views and to acquire new knowledge and skills, and spread new social messages to large audiences. The planned use of communication techniques, activities and media gives people powerful tools both to experience change and actually to guide it. An intensified exchange of ideas among all sectors of society can lead to the greater involvement of people in a common cause. This is a fundamental requirement for appropriate and sustainable development."

Colin Fraser and Jonathan Villet

In his paper, James Deane notes that the importance of communication in the development process has been acknowledged for many years by the development community. FAO has spent at least 30 years pioneering and promoting-both in thinking and practice-the centrality of communication in development.

The most essential ingredient of good communication-putting people at the centre of the communication process-has similarly been understood and documented for many years. Despite this, James Deane notes that the 2004 Communication for Development Round-table takes place against a background where resources for communication activities continue to be difficult to mobilize, where strategic thinking and implementation of communication in development are going through a period of some confusion, including within several bilateral and multilateral agencies, and where development organizations continue to find it difficult to put theory into practice in order to put people at the centre of the communication process. It also takes place at a time when the arguments for effective, professional and people-centered communication strategies have arguably never been as compelling.

He points out that one dominant global event since the last Round-table has shaped almost everything else-the attack on the US on September 11 2001. Never before has communication across boundaries and between cultures been more important, and never before has global security depended on the existence of channels that promote such communication. Arguably those channels have rarely been more fragile. The prevailing context for much development discourse before September 11 was focused on globalization and the associated interdependence and interconnectedness of all peoples, a process fundamentally dependent on and shaped by increasingly rapid flows of information around the world. The events of and following September 11 heralded a marked shift in international political attention away from globalization, a shift accompanied by an increased parochialism in communication channels.

At a time when the international community is so divided, these trends might have been expected to prompt an increase in support for organizations seeking to foster informed public discourse and communication at national and international levels. Much evidence suggests that the contrary has happened. At the international level, many of the main international NGOs dedicated to generating perspectives from developing countries and broader information flows across boundaries and cultures have suffered substantial uncertainty in funding. At the national level, decisions by many donor organizations to provide budget support to governments has often resulted in a shift of resources away from civil society organizations, many of them dedicated to fostering informed dialogue in society.

The central role of communication in the Millennium Development Goals: The paper notes that the principal strategic reference points for the global development community are the Millennium Development Goals (MDGs). Nearly all bilateral funding agencies, most multilateral agencies and many NGOs have explicitly aligned their medium-and long-term priorities to meeting the MDGs. The goal given the highest priority and around which many of the others are focused is to halve the proportion of people living on less than a dollar a day by 2015. The principal strategy adopted by the international community to achieve this goal is the development of poverty reduction strategy papers (PRSPs), a process initially promulgated by the World Bank and increasingly being used by most bilateral development agencies.

At the heart of the PRSP process, and indeed a founding principle informing all the MDGs and allied processes such as the New Economic Partnership for African Development (NEPAD), is the principle of ownership. The World Bank has repeatedly argued that unless there is a genuine process of ownership of these strategies within countries, and real participation and dialogue with all sections of society in drawing them up, they will fail.

Achieving such ownership requires, as the World Bank itself argues, a major focus on communication. "Participation, the keystone of PRSPs, relies on accurate, consistent and continuous communication that provokes response and encourages debate and dialogue leading to better understanding, the application of issues to one's own circumstances, and participation in all phases of a PRSP", argues the World Bank in its PRSP source book on communication.

A frequent complaint made by the communication community over many years, says James Deane, is that communication strategies are designed as an afterthought (rather than integrated from the start into development strategies), are accorded too few resources and implemented with insufficiently trained personnel. Certainly the central development strategy designed to meet the primary development objective of our times-halving poverty by 2015-appears to back up the complaint. The evidence of the last five years suggests that the level of ownership, participation and public discourse required for PRSPs to be successful requires a fundamental reassessment and reprioritization of the role of communication in meeting the MDGs.

Beyond Nicaragua: The continuing HIV/AIDS communication debate: The paper continues by looking at the last Communication for Development Round-table, held in Nicaragua in 2001. This focused explicitly on the theme of HIV/AIDS communication, the success of which is fundamental to meeting the MDG of halting the spread of HIV by 2015. The Round-table welcomed the revitalized energy and funding being devoted to the HIV/AIDS pandemic and issued a declaration designed to capture the main conclusions of the meeting. Round-table participants were both explicit and candid in their assessment that communication strategies had, for many various reasons, failed in preventing the HIV/AIDS pandemic.

16

Importance of Communication

Effective business communication is crucial for the success of individuals as well as organizations. Good communication skills help individuals effectively interact with others in an organization. These skills are important for career development as they boost confidence; ensure clarity of thought and information flow. Good communication is a prerequisite for good managers. It is essential for organizations too. An organization is benefited by the internal and external information gathered and passed on by employees. The management can use such information to gain an edge in business.

Basic Forms of Communication

The basic forms of communication are of two types such as verbal and non-verbal communication. It can be in the form of meetings, speeches or writing, gestures or expressions.

Non-verbal Communication

Non-verbal communication is a primitive form of communication that does not involve the use of words. It rather uses gestures, cues, vocal qualities, spatial relationships etc. to convey a message. It is commonly used to express emotions like respect, love, dislike, unpleasantness, etc.

Non-verbal communication is less structured compared to its verbal counterpart and is most often spontaneous. As it is not planned, it is sometimes considered more reliable than verbal communication, as it reflects the communicator's true feelings. Non-verbal communication enhances the effectiveness of the message as gestures and body language are registered easier and quicker with the audience than verbal communication. Non-verbal communication, when combined with verbal communication, makes a presentation more effective and has greater impact on the audience.

Verbal Communication

However, non-verbal communication has its limitations. Many complex ideas, thoughts or messages have to be communicated sequentially to be meaningful. Verbal communication involves the arrangement of words in a structured and meaningful manner, adhering to the rules of grammar. The message is then conveyed to the audience in either spoken or written form.

Speaking and Writing

Effective verbal communication involves the use of both speech and writing to transmit a message. While oral communication is more effective in reaching a focused target audience, as it involves interaction and additional non-verbal cues to augment the speech, written communication is necessary for reaching a large number of scattered recipients. Depending on the situation and the requirements, businesses use both the spoken as well as written channels for communication.

Listening

Businesses have far not paid much attention to listening as a skill. Equal importance should be given to listening and expression. Oral communication cannot be effective unless the audience is good at listening and most of its content is forgotten after a presentation. Developing good listening skills is essential for grasping the contents of an oral presentation and retaining them.

The Process of Communication

Communication goes through a process, involving the following phases:

- Sender
- Message
- Channel
- Receiver
- Feedback

Barriers to Communication

The process of communication is susceptible to many barriers. These can be categorized into problems caused by the sender, problems in message transmission, problems in reception, and problems in receiver comprehension.

Dealing with Communication Barriers

Though most communication barriers require situation specific handling, a few basic methods for dealing with them are available. These methods such as know your subject, focus on the purpose, know your audience, and be organized.

Summary

- Communication is the process of transmitting messages.
- Communication can be verbal, non-verbal or both. Non-verbal communication involves the use of gestures and facial expressions to convey a message.
- Verbal communication involves the written and spoken forms.
- The process of communication comprises the sender, message, channel, receiver, and feedback.
- There are many barriers to effective communication.
- These barriers can arise at the level of the sender, receiver, in the channel of communication, the medium or at the stage of message comprehension.
- The barriers to effective communication can be overcome

by a thorough knowledge of the subject, by focusing on the purpose, by knowing the audience and by organizing content.

The ability to communicate is the primary factor that distinguishes human beings from animals. And it is the ability to communicate well that distinguishes one individual from another.

Communication is the process of exchanging messages or information between two or more parties. Businesses today are heavily dependent on information to meet organizational needs. Effective communication plays a key role in fulfilling these needs and contributes significantly to organizational success. Despite its importance, business communication has not grown, as it should. Realizing this, both industry and academic sectors have begun training employees and students on business communication and its relevance. It has become all the more evident that business communication is vital for effective functioning of business units.

The fact, is that apart from the basic necessities, one needs to be equipped with habits for good communication skills, as this is what will make them a happy and successful social being.

In order to develop these habits, one needs to first acknowledge the fact that they need to improve communication skills from time to time. They need to take stock of the way they interact and the direction in which their work and personal relations are going. The only constant in life is change, and the more one accepts one's strengths and works towards dealing with their shortcomings, especially in the area of communication skills, the better will be their interactions and the more their social popularity.

The dominating question that comes here is: How to improve communication skills? Well, the answer is simple. One can find plenty of literature on this. There are also experts, who conduct workshops and seminars based on communication skills of men and women. In fact, a large number of companies are bringing in trainers to regularly conduct sessions on the subject, in order to help their work force maintain better interpersonal work relations.

Today, effective communication skills has become a predominant factor even while recruiting employees. While interviewing candidates, most interviewers judge them on the basis of the way they communicate. They believe that skills can be improvised on the job; but ability to communicate well is important, as every employee becomes the representing face of the company. There are trainers, who specialize in delivering custom-made programs on the subject. Through the session they not only facilitate better skills in the department of communications, but also look into the problems that come in the way of being able to convey messages effectively. They discuss these issues with the management and then sought to design programs accordingly. For instance, time mismanagement becomes a cause for stress and frustration, which then hampers the possibility of healthy communications at work. Then in weeks to come the company organizes a program on time management. Thus, a workshop on communication skills helps the management t to deal with the finer employee nuances about which they lack awareness.

Fundamentals of Communication

Communication is the glue that enables people to work together to accomplish results. It is also subject to inevitable breakdowns, and these breakdowns can create chaos, hamper timelines, and generate ill will between people.

We can help your employees learn how to communicate to generate action rather than cause breakdowns. These are skills most of us never really learned, and are simple tools that can make a big difference in how things get done.

Purpose

This set of programs strengthens fundamental communication skills needed to work with others effectively. It is suitable for anyone, but highly recommended for managers and supervisors who must work through and with others on a daily basis.

Structure

A modular program of mix and match topics all designed to help people be as specific and thorough in their communication as possible. These modules are four hours in length which make them easy to deliver to busy people. They are workshop based and provide lots of opportunity to practice the tools.

"The most important thing in communication is to hear what isn't being said."

Peter Drucker

Principles of Speaking and Listening

Effective communication requires *both* a listener and a speaker who not only share words, but also communicate meaning that both can understand. Often people walk away from a conversation thinking they know what was said and find out later that they really did not have the same understanding. This module addresses the critical skills of listening and speaking effectively.

Communicating for Results

Part of building shared understanding is providing the proper context, background, and specific points in a comprehensive way. Skipping over points leads to misunderstandings, breakdowns, and perhaps flared tempers. Communicating for Results teaches how to cover all the bases when communicating.

Generating Commitment

Engaging others in working together to accomplish results is what makes for good teamwork. The bottom line in engagement is commitment. Without commitment, people don't get things done. This class teaches how to generate commitment from others.

Building Agreement

A lot of the communication that occurs in the workplace has to do with completing work on time and to specification. But many people do not know how to make clear, specific requests and assure that work is followed up and completed as agreed. Participants learn about making requests, promises, and fulfilling agreements.

Language of Accountability

Accountability is essential inside organizations. If you can't count on people to do what they say, then nothing works. But there is a way to build accountability that ensures success, and that is taught in the module.

Managing Breakdowns

The problem is not that there are breakdowns in communication. Whenever people are involved, breakdowns will happen. The real challenge is using breakdowns to renew commitment, agreement, and action to move things forward. In this class, participants learn how to manage a breakdown so it promotes movement rather than derailment.

Conflict Management

Many people hate conflict because it often involves intense emotions and fuels problems rather than resolves them. Often the missing ingredient is being able to confront difficulties and find alternative solutions without emotional charge. Conflict Management offers a new way of working with the differences in opinion, disappointment, and frustration we have with one another.

Generating Possibility

Creativity is a very important ingredient to business success. In a fast moving, competitive market environment, organizations must come up with new ideas for products and services all the time. Unfortunately, groups of people often kill the creative spirit rather than foster possibility. This class helps people create a space of possibility in their conversations.

Bibliography

Andrew F.: *Online Communication: Linking Technology, Identity, & Culture*, Mahwah, NJ: Lawrence Erlbaum Associates, 2005.

Bugeja, J.: *Living Ethics: Developing Values in Mass Communication*, Boston, Allyn and Bacon, 1996.

Carey, W.: *Public Opinion and the Communication of Consent*, New York: Guilford Publications, 1995.

Crowley, David. J. : *Communication in History*, Boston, Allyn and Bacon, 2003.

Daniel Wackman: *Handbook of Communication Science*, Newbury Park, CA: Sage, 1987.

David Sloan: *Historical Methods in Communication*, Hillsdale, NJ: Lawrence Erlbaum, 1989.

Denton, Craig: *Graphics for Visual Communication*, Dubuque, William C. Brown, 1996.

Earl R.: *Writing for Mass Communication*, White Plains, NY: Longman, 1996.

James, W.: *Public Opinion and the Communication of Consent*, New York: Guilford Publications, 1995.

Paul Heyer: *Communication in History*, Boston, Allyn and Bacon, 2003.

Sherman, Barry: *Telecommunications Management*, New York, McGraw Hill, 1995.

Warner, Charles: *Media Management Review*, Mahwah, Lawrence Erlbaum Associates, 1997.

Index

□□□